环球雅思学校

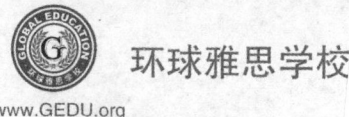

www.GEDU.org

MW01613292

剑桥雅思

真题核心词汇

选自剑桥雅思真题系列 1—8

IELTS

李宁◎编著

升级版

吉林出版集团有限责任公司

图书在版编目(CIP)数据

剑桥雅思真题核心词汇 / 李宁编著.--长春: 吉林出版集团有限责任公司, 2011.8
ISBN 978-7-5463-6661-6

Ⅰ.①剑… Ⅱ.①李… Ⅲ.①IELTS—词汇—自学参考资料 Ⅳ.①H313

中国版本图书馆CIP 数据核字(2011)第153722 号

剑桥雅思真题核心词汇

编　　著：李　宁
特约策划：北京环球卓尔英才文化传播有限公司
责任编辑：于　鑫　孙昌斌
特约编辑：王慧玉　吕颜辉
封面设计：大象无形设计策划有限公司
开　　本：787mm × 1092mm　1/32
字　　数：233千字
印　　张：13.75
版　　次：2011年8月第1版
印　　次：2011年8月第1次印刷

出　　版：吉林出版集团有限责任公司
发　　行：吉林出版集团外语教育有限公司
地　　址：长春市泰来街1825号
邮　　编：130011
电　　话：总编办：0431-86012683
发行部：0431-86012675 0431-86012826（Fax）
网　　址：www.360hours.com
印　　刷：北京启恒印刷有限公司

ISBN 978-7-5463-6661-6　　定价：39.80元（内附MP3光盘）

版权所有　侵权必究　举报电话 0431-86012683

环球雅思图书编委会核心小组

总 策 划　张永琪　张晓东

执行策划　刘海华　王慧玉

图书编辑　吕颜辉　李晟月　宋美丽

编　　委　环球雅思教学研究中心GTRC

（按姓氏笔画排列，括号内为该委员所在职的环球雅思学校所在地）

【听力】尹小音（上海）　王后娇（深圳）　方　程（上海）　王　燕（北京）
卢峭梅（北京）　刘丹妮（北京）　孙维娟（天津）　刘源源（长沙）
吴　艳（北京）　李　琛（贵州）　陈婷婷（北京）　林　刚（成都）
赵　雪（北京）　徐　丹（上海）　徐　佩（上海）　黄　天（北京）
鲁成英（北京）　曾丽娟（上海）　谭　刚（成都）

【阅读】王业兵（广州）　邓　忠（成都）　王亮亮（深圳）　王　强（北京）
王　辉（西安）　祁连山（北京）　西　震（北京）　余　波（北京）
张　岳（北京）　李　峥（上海）　李荣华（广州）　杨　琳（上海）
杨焯然（上海）　李婷婷（北京）　张　腾（广州）　李瀚帆（广州）
施正南（广州）　赵曙明（广州）　贾丽娟（北京）　聂清燕（天津）
高　静（北京）　黄欣如（广州）　董长根（上海）

【写作】王建军（北京）　安　帆（成都）　刘　伟（天津）　朱润萍（大连）
齐　辙（北京）　杨　凡（北京）　杨　涛（北京）　李　鹏（北京）
张　嵩（北京）　季春桦（上海）　洪　伟（西安）　俞伟国（上海）
钟　钰（广州）　慎小嶷（北京）　赖劲松（广州）

【口语】牛书杰（重庆）　王　陆（北京）　王洪川（北京）　吕本清（天津）
刘　薇（北京）　李一萌（北京）　李　宁（上海）　何佳韦（广州）
陈　湃（北京）　高　洁（广州）　戴维吉（长沙）　David（美国）
Karl（英国）　Lyn（澳大利亚）　Martin（新西兰）

序 言

雅思词汇一直是广大考生在备考雅思时最感迷茫的一块。备考雅思该储备多少词汇，哪些词汇又是参加雅思考试最需要掌握的呢？这也是我从事雅思培训行业近十年间时常思考的问题。

对雅思词汇的有效记忆，特别是对剑桥雅思真题核心词汇的掌握和认知，对于考生来说是任重而道远的。如何在有限的复习时间内取得最佳的单词记忆效果？如何在最短的时间内掌握高频复现率词汇？是雅思教学的重要课题之一。

对词汇感觉生疏是雅思考生阅读中的拦路虎。此拦路虎会导致考生在考场中经常出现一种大脑短路现象。很多单词看着眼熟，但就是反应不出它的正确释义，或是听到这个单词却无法正确拼写，这会非常影响考生的阅读速度，进而影响整场考试的心情。

那么，怎么记才能效率最高、效果最好？本书很好地解决了这一问题，这也正是我推荐此书的理由。

李宁老师以他十余年的雅思教学经验来整理编辑此书，提取考试真题之精华，解析考试中遇到的生词和难句。他一直以学术的视角去分析雅思考试的规律和解题技巧。在环球雅思各个校区经常能看到他阳光、健康、亲和的身影，尤其是他刻苦钻研、爱岗敬业的精神令人深受感动。他对于中国学生在词汇记忆方面的弊端和困扰了如指掌，经过了多年的总结和不断提炼，才完成了此书的编写。

祝愿更多的学生在李老师这本著作的指导下日行千里，能够真正做到在优美的词汇串联旋律篇章中完成记忆和理解。

上海环球雅思学校校长

2011年7月

前　言

中国雅思二十二岁了。

二十二年——对于中国的莘莘学子来说是任重而道远的，雅思学习的热潮和井喷现象更是一波高于一波。雅思听、说、读、写四项考查能力中，词汇不仅是根基也是考试的突破口。从听力的场景词汇和机经词汇到阅读的高频词汇、口语的常用词汇以及写作的核心逻辑主线词汇，词汇的意义在于它是一切的铺垫。随着“剑桥雅思真题系列1-8”在国内相继问世，通过研读“剑桥雅思真题”系列来备考的考生也越来越多，现在几乎人手一套。写《剑桥雅思真题核心词汇》的想法就此产生，每每看见学生在那边拼命啃字典查找词汇，笔者在想：是不是应该编写一本适合于考生的针对剑桥雅思的真题词汇集来助考生一臂之力？

本书的编写力求专业性、实用性和真实性。阅读本书后，希望大家有这样一种感觉——整个“剑桥雅思真题系列1-8”学习中的精华一览无余，所有经典词汇尽收眼底。在编写《剑桥雅思真题核心词汇》的过程中，笔者大量收集了雅思考试的原形真题，从雅思考试真题入手（学术类和培训类），解释批注学术背景重点词汇和生活场景词汇，真正体现一个“真”字。

雅思考生必须遵循英语词汇学学习的特点，有指导性、有针对性地学习雅思高频词汇，以取得最佳备考效果。把词汇学习从单纯记忆词汇的层面提高到从文章中去学习词汇、短语，从雅思真题中去学习雅思高频词汇，从文章上下文的意境中去猜测和学习英语词汇，其终极目标是协助考生掌握足够的词汇量、拓展词汇库，有效地将其运用于雅思的书面考试和口头考试中。

语言学习包括学习语音、语法、词汇三大语言要素。词汇学习对每个英语学习者都至关重要。威尔金斯韦（1971）曾经说过："没有语法，表达甚微；没有词汇，表达为零。"一个语言学者无论发音如何标准，语法如何精确，词汇量的不足或者知之甚少，将直接影响说话者的语言交际效果。所以学好词汇、运用词汇、理解词汇的关键是输入足够的词汇，形成一个有机联系的词汇库。本教材的特点和创新在于从大量鲜活生动的真题例句中精选词汇，通过详尽的解释和批注，以及对词性的转变模式一一加以列举，加强考生熟练驾驭和运用词汇的能力。提供给考生的例句也是尽量详尽，避免词汇解释的单一性，从多元角度解释词汇，展示词汇在不同意境下具有的相同或者深层次的解释和释义。雅思考生在学习词汇的同时应兼顾学习英语词汇的标准。即：

——择词的准确性：基本意思Denotation 和引申意思Connotation。

Do not write or speak so that your words may be understood, but write or speak so that your words must be understood.

——择词的鲜明度：莎士比亚的名言—Brevity is the soul of wit.

——择词的生动感：有美感Gracefulness。

教书育人，授人以鱼，不如授人以渔。希望"授人以渔"的过程中，考生是享受的，是受益匪浅的。希望本书的出版能为广大雅思考生带来福音。在编写的过程中，我要特别感谢上海环球雅思中心的领导和同仁一直以来对我孜孜不倦的教导和培养，以及他们对本书做出的重要指导性意见和建议。同时我也要感谢一直陪伴我成长的恩师张海燕教授、张璐教授、都莲英老师、苏文通、Professor Malcolm Drummond等对我的悉心教育和培养。此书也是集体智慧的结晶，我深切感谢我的同事、年轻的雅思教师董琛、赵朝永、刘佩茹、杨贵华、李华平、乐健、刘家豪、杜宪政、沈俊杰老师。出于对材料的权威性和实用性的把握，老师们在编写过程中在内容的准确性和实用性上花了很大的工夫，力求精准把握雅思词汇考试纲要，笔者在此深表谢意！最后感谢我挚爱的家人，衷心感谢他们多年来对我的支持和鼓励！

若本书存在纰漏，还望读者批评、指教。

2011年7月

目录

第一章 雅思真题词汇分类详解

第二章 剑七、剑八词汇精选

第三章 雅思词汇分类拓展

第四章 雅思重点词汇辨析

第一章　雅思真题词汇分类详解

一　自然景观类

What we're seeing is natural capriciousness and the consequence of human activity.

我们所看到的是大自然的变幻莫测和一些人类活动所导致的恶果。

capriciousness [kə'prɪʃəsnɪs] *n.* 任性；善变

释 a sudden and usually foolish desire to have or do something, or a sudden and foolish change of mind or behaviour

拓 *n.* caprice; *a.* capricious; *ad.* capriciously

例 Hitler's capriciousness helped him a lot in waging the war.

希特勒的反复无常对他发动战争起到很大作用。

---

consequence ['kɒnsɪkwəns] *n.* 结果，后果

释 an often bad or inconvenient result of a particular action or situation

拓 *a.* consequent; *ad.* consequently

用 of little / no consequence

例 I'm quite willing to accept the consequences. 我完全愿意承担后果。

Worse, below it was a not-very-firm glacial deposit hundreds of meters thick.

更糟的是，这下面有几百米的不坚固冰层。

glacial ['gleɪʃl] *a.* 冰的，冰川(期)的

释 relating to ice and glaciers, or formed by glaciers

拓 *n.* glacier

例 The scientists were surprised by the glacial scenery of South Pole. 科学家们被南极的冰川景象震惊了。

---

deposit [dɪ'pɒzɪt] *n.* 堆积物；*vt.* 付定金

释 a natural layer of sand, rock, or other material; to pay a sum of money as the first part of a larger payment

拓 *n.* depositor

用 deposit of; deposit in; deposit with

例 He deposited a small amount of money toward the purchase of the car. 他为买这辆汽车先付了少量订金。

These fracture zones, where the collisions occur, are where earthquakes happen.

这些冲撞产生的断裂带就是地震发生的区域。

fracture ['fræktʃə] *n.* 断裂；骨折

释 a crack or broken part in a bone or other hard substance

拓 *a.* fracturable

例 He got a fracture in his left knee. 他左腿膝盖骨折了。

---

collision [kə'lɪʒən] *n.* 碰撞

释 a violent impact of moving objects

用 collision with; collision between

例 A bus was involved in a collision with a truck. 一辆公共汽车和卡车相撞了。

---

earthquake ['ɜːθkweɪk] *n.* 地震

释 a sudden violent movement of the Earth's surface, sometimes causing great damage

例 Wenchuan earthquake was one of the worst catastrophes of the century. 汶川地震是本世纪最大的灾难之一。

Cavernous weathering of granite on the island of Paros is, common along many coastlines.

帕罗斯岛洞穴花岗岩风化的现象，在许多沿海地区也出现了。

weather ['weðə] *vt.& vi.* （使）风化

释 to change, or make something change, colour or shape because of the effect of the sun, rain or wind

例 The stone has weathered to sand. 石头风化成了沙子。

---

coastline ['kəʊst,laɪn] *n.* 海岸线

释 the land on the edge of the coast, especially the shape of this land as seen from the air

例 The erosion of the coastline by the sea was ignored by people.
人们忽视了海水对海岸线的冲刷。

This approach has made considerable sense in an island with sites to spare because of its particular geology and its history of quarrying.

这种方法已经清楚地解释了为什么有人来观看这个岛屿的景象，是因为它的特殊地质现象和它被发现的历史。

approach [ə'prəʊtʃ] *n.* 途径，方法

释 ideas or actions intended to deal with a problem or situation

拓 *a.* approachable

例 The college has decided to adopt a different approach to discipline.
学院决定采取另外一种方式解决纪律问题。

---

considerable [kən'sɪdərəbl] *a.* 相当的，可观的；重要的

释 great in amount, size, importance, etc.

拓 *ad.* considerably; *vt. & vi.* consider; *prep./conj.* considering;

a. considerate; *n.* consideration

例 That building wasted a considerable amount of time and money.

那个建筑耗费了相当多的时间和资金。

---

quarry ['kwɒri] *vt.* 挖出

释 to dig out stone, etc.

用 quarry for sth.; quarry sth. from / out of sth.

例 The area is being quarried for limestone. 这个地方正在开采石灰石。

A seabed consisted of 29 meters of soft alluvial silt and mud deposits.

29米长的软冲积泥沙和泥浆堆积组成了海床。

consist [kən'sɪst] *vi.* 组成，构成

释 to be made of or formed from something

拓 *n.* consistency; *a.* consistent; *ad.* consistently

用 consist of sth.

例 A university consists of teachers, administrators and students.

大学由教师、行政人员和学生组成。

---

alluvial [ə'luːvɪəl] *a.* 冲积的，淤积的

释 consisting of earth and sand that has been left by rivers, floods, etc.

例 Alluvial plains can be found in this country here and there.

冲积平原在这个国家到处可见。

Between them, these two outcrops of hard, weathered granite make up a quarter of the new island's surface area.

在它们之间，这两个坚硬、风化了的花岗岩的露头覆盖了新岛屿表面地区的四分之一。

outcrop ['aʊtkrɒp] *n.* (矿脉等)露出，露头

释 a large rock or group of rocks that sticks out of the ground

例 Practically every rock outcrop shows numberless joints. 实际上，所有岩石的露头都显示出许许多多的节理。

---

granite ['grænɪt] *n.* 花岗石，花岗岩

释 a very hard, grey, pink and black rock, which is used for building

例 The valley ended in a perpendicular rim of granite. 山谷的尽头是花岗石的断崖。

The eruption was so fierce that dust thrown into the stratosphere darkened the skies, canceling the following summer holiday in Europe.

火山喷发异常猛烈，以至于火山灰喷射到平流层中，天空变得阴沉、模糊，即将到来的欧洲暑期度假也随之被取消了。

stratosphere ['strætəʊsfɪə] *n.* 同温层，平流层

释 the atmospheric layer between the troposphere and the mesosphere

例 Reactions between oxygen and ultraviolet radiation from the sun create a layer of ozone throughout Earth's stratosphere(upper atmosphere). 氧气与太阳产生的紫外线辐射发生反应，产生了臭氧层，它遍布在地球的平流层(上部大气圈)。

二 气候现象类

Europe is simultaneously baking and freezing, and will continue to do so as a result of global warming, alarmists asserted in global media reports in November 2005.

在2005年11月的全球媒体报道中，有忧虑者称欧洲的气候将伴随全球变暖而不断变化，忽热忽冷。

simultaneously [ˌsɪməlˈteɪnɪəsli] *ad.* 同时发生地

释 at the same instant

拓 *a.* simultaneous

例 The game will be broadcast simultaneously on TV. 比赛将在电视中直播。

---

baking [ˈbeɪkɪŋ] *a.* 烘烤的；灼热的

释 roast; extremely hot

例 Tom is eager to buy a baking machine. 汤姆想买一个烘烤机。

---

global warming 全球气候变暖

释 a general increase in world temperatures caused by increased amounts of carbon dioxide around the Earth

例 The risk is that global warming will make hurricanes more common. 这种风险是全球变暖将会导致飓风频频发生。

---

alarmist [əˈlɑːmɪst] *n.* 危言耸听者，大惊小怪者，忧虑者；*a.* 骇人的

释 people who worry about dangers that do not really exist; causing unnecessary fear and anxiety

例 Man who worries about death is an alarmist. 担心死亡的人是杞人忧天。

---

assert [əˈsɜːt] *vt.* 宣称，断言

释 to state firmly that something is true

用 assert that

例 They asserted that the boy was innocent. 他们断言那男孩是无辜的。

Gentler but more persistent bad weather — the downpours of the summer monsoon — is also being taken into account.

长期阴郁闷热的恶劣天气，如夏季季风带来的倾盆大雨，也被考虑进来了。

persistent [pə'sɪstənt] *a.* 持续的

释 continuing to exist or happen，especially for longer than is usual or desirable

拓 *n.* persistence; *ad.* persistently

例 21st century is a time of high and persistent unemployment.

21世纪是一个持续高失业率的时期。

---

downpour ['daʊnpɔːr] *n.* 倾盆大雨

释 a lot of rain that falls in a short time

例 The old house was destroyed by a heavy downpour. 一场大雨冲毁了那座老房子。

---

monsoon [ˌmɒn'suːn] *n.* 季风

释 a wind in Southern Asia that blows from the south-west in summer, bringing rain, and the north-east in winter

例 Heavy rains occur during a summer monsoon. 暴雨出现在夏季季风期。

This odd climatic phenomenon was accused of wrecking tourism, causing allergies, melting the ski-slopes and causing 22 deaths.

这种异常的天气破坏了旅游业，导致很多人过敏、滑雪道融化及22人死亡。

climatic [klaɪ'mætɪk] *a.* 气候上的

释 connected with the weather of a particular area

拓 *n.* climate / climatology; *ad.* climatically

例 Nowadays climatic changes are often in an odd way. 现今气候变化无常。

---

phenomenon [fɪ'nɒmɪnən] *n.* 现象

释 something that happens or exists in society, science, or nature, especially something that is studied because it is difficult to understand.

例 The employment problem tends to be a city phenomenon. 就业问题常常是一个城市现象。

---

accuse [ə'kjuːz] *vt.* 控告

释 to say that sb. believe someone is guilty of a crime or of doing something bad

拓 *n.* accusation

用 accuse of

例 He accused her of stealing his mobilephone. 他控告她偷了他的手机。

---

wreck [rek] *vt.* 破坏

释 to completely spoil something; to damage or destroy something

拓 *a.* wrecked; *n.* wreckage

例 It was her husband's drink that wrecked their marriage. 她丈夫嗜酒，导致了他们婚姻的破裂。

---

allergy ['ælədʒi] *n.* 过敏症

释 a medical condition in which you become ill or react badly when you have eaten or touched a particular substance

拓 *a.* allergic

用 allergy to

例 Tom has an allergy to cats and pollen. 汤姆对猫和花粉过敏。

The knock-on effects are likely to include more warming, cloudier skies, increased precipitation and higher sea levels.

一系列连续的影响可能包括气候变暖，天空多云，降水增加和海平面不断升高。

precipitation [prɪˌsɪpɪ'teɪʃən] *n.* 降雨量；坠落，沉淀，凝结

释 the quantity of rain, snow, etc falling to the earth at a specific place within a specified period of time; a chemical process in which solid material is separated from a liquid

拓 *a. / vt. / n.* precipitate; *ad.* precipitately

例 There will be precipitation on northern hills tonight. 今夜北部山区有降雪。

For example, the dull weather of winter drastically cuts down the amount of sunlight that is experienced, which strong affects some people.

比如，冬天阳光的稀缺会严重影响人们的生活。

drastically ['dræstɪkəli] *ad.* 大大地；激烈地；彻底地

释 especially of actions severe and sudden or having very noticeable effects

拓 *a.* drastic

例 Chinese luxury goods like silks, teas and porcelains were in great demand and transformed their way of life drastically. 中国的奢侈品，例如丝绸、茶和瓷器大受欢迎，也大大地改变了他们的生活方式。

三 环境保护类

But by the time the sediment has come to rest in the fields and lagoons it is laden with municipal, industrial and agricultural waste.

但是当沉淀物到达田地和泻湖中时，已经载满了城市垃圾和工农业废品。

sediment ['sedɪmənt] *n.* 沉淀物

释 the solid material that settles at the bottom of a liquid

拓 *a.* sedimentary

例 White sediment was left when the water dried. 水抽干后，留下白色的沉淀物。

---

lagoon [lə'guːn] *n.* 泻湖，咸水湖

释 a lake of salt water that is partly separated from the sea by rocks, sand, or coral

例 This area isolates a restricted lagoon environment. 这地区隔离起来，形成封闭的泻湖环境。

---

laden ['leɪdn] *a.* 装满的，负载的

释 heavily loaded with something, or containing a lot of something

用 fully laden; laden with

例 His voice was soft, yet laden with threat. 他的声音柔和，但语气充满恐吓。

---

municipal [mjuː'nɪsɪpəl] *a.* 市政的，市的

释 relating to or belonging to a town, city or district that has its own local government

拓 *ad.* municipally; *n.* municipality

例 The city is planning to build a municipal library. 该市正计划建一座市立图书馆。

Developing countries in Asia could face an "unprecedented" water crisis within a decade due to mismanagement of water resources.

由于水资源管理不善，十年内，亚洲的发展中国家将面临“史无前例的”水危机。

unprecedented [ʌn'presɪdentɪd] *a.* 空前的，史无前例的

释 never having happened before, or never having happened so much

拓 *ad.* unprecedentedly

用 unprecedented in

例 China's tertiary industry is developing at an unprecedented rate. 中国的第三产业正以空前的速度发展。

---

crisis ['kraɪsɪs] *n.* 危机，危急关头

释 a situation that has reached an extremely difficult or dangerous point

拓 *n.* crises (*pl.*)

例 He suffered enormous loss in the financial crisis. 他在经济危机时遭受了巨大损失。

---

decade ['dekeɪd] *n.* 十年

释 a period of ten years

例 Just now he told me the greatest scientific achievement of the decade. 他刚才给我讲了这十年来最伟大的科学成就。

---

due to 因为，由于

释 because of something

例 Her successes were largely due to good luck. 她的成功主要靠运气。

---

mismanagement [ˌmɪs'mænɪdʒmənt] *n.* 管理不善

释 If someone mismanages something they are in charge of, they deal with or manage it badly.

拓 *vt.* mismanage

例 This has mainly been caused by the mismanagement of the world's resources. 这主要是由对世界资源管理不善而引发的。

The factory and town which might cause disturbance are located out of the way, about 15 kilometers from the area most densely populated by birds.

可能造成干扰的工厂和城镇位于路段以外，离稠密的鸟类栖息地约15公里。

densely ['densli] *ad.* **密集地，浓厚地**

释 thickly; in a concentrated manner

拓 *a.* dense; *n.* density

例 America is one of the most densely populated cities in the world. 美国是世界上城市人口密集度最高的地方之一。

The second question concerned is the geographical location of rainforests.

涉及的第二个问题是热带雨林的地理位置。

geographical [dʒɪə'græfɪkəl] *a.* **地理（学）的**

释 relating to the place in an area, country, etc. where something or someone is

拓 *n.* geography; *ad.* geographically

例 The professor will give a lecture of geographical features.
教授将要做一个关于地理特征的讲座。

Considerable uncertainty exists, however, about the enhanced greenhouse effect.

然而，关于已经好转的温室效应还存在很多不确定性因素。

enhance [ɪn'hɑːns] *vt.* **提高，加强，增加**

释 to improve something

拓 *n.* enhancement

例 She made many efforts to enhance his reputation. 她做了许多努力来提高他的声誉。

In Mexico City, vehicle pollution is a major health hazard.

在墨西哥城，车辆造成的污染是健康的主要危害。

hazard ['hæzəd] *n.* 危险，危害； *vt.* 冒……的危险

释 something that may be dangerous, or cause accidents or problems; to risk something or put it in danger

拓 *a.* hazardous

用 hazard to / for; the hazards of sth.

例 Polluted water sources are a hazard to human beings. 污染的水源对人类有危害。

Ironically, one major casualty of that extreme position has been the environment itself.

具有讽刺意味的是，这一危险处境的最大受害者是环境本身。

ironically [aɪ'rɒnɪkli] *ad.* 说反话地，讽刺地

释 showing that you really mean the opposite of what you are saying

拓 *a.* ironic; *n.* irony

例 Ironically, most people came to watch the match on the day it poured with rain. 说来颇具讽刺，很多人前来看比赛，老天爷却偏偏下起瓢泼大雨。

---

casualty ['kæʒuəlti] *n.* 伤亡者，伤亡人数；急救室

释 a person who is killed or injured in a war or in an accident; the part of a hospital where people who need urgent treatment are taken

用 英国英语 casualty = 美国英语 emergency room（急诊室）

例 Heavy casualties in the war were reported. 据报道，战斗中伤亡惨重。

Development of the most destructive kind has continued apace over vast areas.

最具破坏性的开发在大范围内继续迅速扩大。

destructive [dɪs'trʌktɪv] *a.* 破坏性的

释 causing damage to people or things

拓 *ad.* destructively; *n.* destructiveness / destruction

例 The destructive force of the storm is huge. 暴风雨的破坏力巨大。

---

apace [ə'peɪs] *ad.* 快速地，急速地

释 with rapid movements; quickly

例 Ill news runs apace. 坏事传千里。

In some cases this response also embraced the misconception that rainforest destruction would reduce atmospheric oxygen, making the atmosphere incompatible with human life on Earth.

在某些情况下，这种反应也含有误解，即对热带雨林的破坏将减少大气中的氧气，使大气不适合人类在地球上生存。

embrace [ɪm'breɪs] *vt.* 包含；拥抱

释 to include as part of something broader; to put your arms around someone

例 This book embraces many subjects. 这本书包括许多话题。

---

misconception [ˌmɪskən'sepʃən] *n.* 误解；错误想法

释 an idea which is wrong or untrue, but which people believe because they do not understand the subject properly

拓 *a.* misconceived; *vi.* misconceive

用 misconception that; misconception about sth.

例 There is a popular misconception that too much exercise is bad for your health. 人们普遍认为太多的运动有害健康，这是错误的观点。

atmospheric [ˌætməsˈferɪk] *a.* 大气的

释 relating to the Earth's atmosphere

拓 *ad.* atmospherically

例 Atmospheric movement is the precondition of rainfall. 大气运动是形成降雨的先决条件。

---

incompatible [ˌɪnkəmˈpætəbl] *a.* 不相容的，不能并存的

释 incapable of association or harmonious coexistence

拓 *ad.* incompatibly; *n.* incompatibility

用 incompatible with

例 I don't know why they ever got married. They're totally incompatible. 我不知道他们为什么结婚，他们一点儿都合不来。

There emerged an awareness in Western societies that resources for the provision of fossil fuel energy were finite and exhaustible.

西方社会出现这样一种意识，即矿物燃料能源是有限的、可耗尽的。

provision [prəˈvɪʒən] *n.* 供应；食物和饮料

释 the act of supplying sb. with sth.; supplies of food and drink

用 provision of；provision for

例 They are making provision for their refugees. 他们正为难民筹备物资。

---

exhaustible [ɪgˈzɔːstəbl] *a.* 可被用尽的

释 capable of being used up

拓 *vt.* & *n.* exhaust; *a.* exhaustive; *ad.* exhaustively

例 It is clear that many of the earth's resources are exhaustible.

很明显地球上的许多资源是有限的。

A solution emerged was uniquely well adapted to cope with the pollution.

一个特别适合处理污染问题的方案出台了。

unique [juːˈniːk] *a.* 独一无二的；独特的，稀罕的

释 being the only one of its kind; unusual and special

拓 *ad.* uniquely; *n.* uniqueness

用 unique to

例 It is a unique life-style, a unique and distinctive place to live. 这是一种非同凡响的生活方式，是一个超群脱俗的居住之处。

Chemical fertilizers and pesticides may contaminate water resources.

化肥和农药可能会污染水资源。

pesticide [ˈpestɪsaɪd] *n.* 杀虫剂，农药

释 a chemical used to kill pests (such as rodents or insects)

例 He needs a pesticide that will kill corn borers. 他需要一种能消灭玉米螟虫的杀虫剂。

---

contaminate [kənˈtæmɪneɪt] *vt.* 弄脏，污染

释 to make a place or substance dirty or harmful by putting something such as chemicals or poison in it

拓 *a.* contaminated; *n.* contamination

例 Drinking water supplies are believed to have been contaminated. 人们认为饮用水已被污染。

Recycling paper is beneficial in that it saves some of the energy, labor and capital.

再生纸有利于节省资源、劳力和资金。

recycle [ˌriːˈsaɪkl] *vt.* 使再循环，再利用

释 to put used objects or materials through a special process so that they can be used again

拓 *n.* recycling; *a.* recyclable / recycled

例 We should take all our papers to be recycled. 我们要重新利用所有的纸张。

---

beneficial [ˌbenɪˈfɪʃəl] *a.* 有益的，有利的

释 having a helpful or good effect, or something intended to help

拓 *ad.* beneficially; *n.* & *vt.* & *vi.* benefit

用 beneficial for / to

例 The drug has a beneficial effect on the immune system. 该药对免疫系统有益。

Simple changes could improve the rate substantially, though it is unrealistic to make very high levels of water-use efficiency in many developing countries.

尽管在发展中国家做到高度合理、有效地利用水资源是不现实的，但简单的改进可以充分地提高这个比率。

efficiency [ɪˈfɪʃənsi] *n.* 效率

释 the quality of doing something well and effectively, without wasting time, money, or energy

拓 *a.* efficient; *ad.* efficiently

用 efficiency of

例 We prefer workers who work with high efficiency. 我们更喜欢工作效率高的人。

Some people complain of the air being "heavy" and of feeling irritable.

有人抱怨空气"沉重"而且出现过敏反应。

irritable ['ɪrɪtəbl] *a.* **易怒的，急躁的；过敏的**

释 getting annoyed quickly or easily; abnormally sensitive to stimulus

拓 *vt.* irritate; *n.* irritability / irritation; *ad.* irritably

例 Tom used to be an irritable man. 汤姆以前是个急躁的人。

CFC emissions have been substantially reduced in recent years.

近年来，CFC的排污量已大量减少。

substantially [səb'stænʃəli] *ad.* **相当多地，大大地**

释 very much or a lot

拓 *n.* / *a.* substantial

例 The sheep population has increased substantially in recent years. 最近几年，绵羊的数目增长得特别快。

Although new incinerators are now much cleaner than earlier ones, people are scared of exposure to dangerous chemicals.
people are scared of exposure to dangerous chemicals.

虽然新的焚烧炉比以往干净多了，人们还是害怕危险的化学物质漏出。

incinerator [ɪn'sɪnəreɪtə] *n.* **焚烧装置，焚烧炉**

释 a machine designed to burn waste in high temperature

例 That leaf was almost certainly torn up and sent to the incinerator. 几乎可以肯定这一页后来被撕下来并扔进了焚烧炉中。

---

scared [skeəd] *a.* **害怕的**

释 frightened of something, or nervous about something

拓 *vt.* & *vi.* scare; *a.* scary

用 scared of (doing) sth.; scared to do sth.

例 I've always been scared of cats. 我一直都很怕猫。

exposure [ɪks'pəʊʒə] *n.* 暴露，揭露，曝光

释 when someone is in a situation where they are not protected from something dangerous or unpleasant; the action of showing the truth about someone or something, especially when it is bad

拓 *vt.* expose

用 exposure to; exposure of

例 The survivors were weak from exposure and lack of flood.

幸存者由于风餐露宿和缺乏食物而变得很虚弱。

Modern mines and significant resources are spent on rehabilitating mined land.

现代矿山和重要的资源都用在恢复开采区的工作上。

rehabilitate [ˌriːhə'bɪlɪteɪt] *vt.* & *vi.* （使）恢复原状，（使）复权，恢复名誉

释 to return someone or something to a good or healthy condition, state or way of living

拓 *n.* rehabilitation

例 After 10 years in official disgrace, he's been rehabilitated.

蒙受10年官方的耻辱之后，他现在又恢复了原来的名誉。

The need to achieve sustainable development of energy resources, the way in which the resource is extracted, transported and used is critical.

实现能源的可持续发展，能源的提取、运输及使用方式至关重要。

sustainable [sə'steɪnəbl] *a.* 合理利用的，可持续的

释 able to continue without causing damage to the environment

拓 *vt.* sustain; *n.* sustainability

例 The government should do more to promote sustainable economy. 政府应该做更多的工作去促进经济可持续发展。

Most falling foul of strict building regulations, have been forced to dismantle their individualistic homes and return to more conventional lifestyles.

严把居住环境关，拆除违章建筑，还百姓一个正常的生活环境。

foul [faʊl] *a.* 肮脏的；难闻的；卑鄙的；*n.* 犯规

释 dirty and smelling bad; very evil or cruel; an action that is against the rules of the game

拓 *ad.* foully; *n.* foulness ; *vi.* foul

用 in a foul mood / temper

例 It was foul of him to betray such a kind girl. 背叛这样一个善良的女孩，他可真是卑鄙。

---

dismantle [dɪs'mæntl] *vt.* 拆除；取消

释 to take a machine or piece of equipment apart so that it is in separate pieces; to end an organization or system gradually

例 Jim dismantled the computer in three minutes. 吉姆用3分钟时间就把电脑拆卸了。

---

conventional [kən'venʃ ənl] *a.* 常见的；传统的，常规的

释 traditional and ordinary

拓 *n.* conventionality / convention；*ad.* conventionally

例 We had a conventional opening ceremony. 我们举行了一个传统的开业典礼。

For example, one graphic illustration to which children might readily relate is the estimate that rainforests are being destroyed at a rate equivalent to one thousand football fields every forty minutes.

例如，孩子们或许很快就会看到这样一个生动的例证，据估计，热带雨林正在以每40分钟就有一千个足球场那么大的面积被破坏。

graphic ['græfɪk] *a.* 生动的；图表的

释 vivid; a graphic account or description of an event is very clear and gives a lot of details, especially unpleasant ones

拓 *ad.* graphically; *n.* graphicness

例 The graphic arts include lithography and calligraphy. 平面造型艺术包括平版印刷术和书法。

---

equivalent [ɪ'kwɪvələnt] *a.* 等价的；相等的；*n.* 相等物

释 having the same amount, value, purpose, qualities; thing that is equivalent

拓 *n.* equivalence

用 equivalent to

例 There is no English equivalent for "bon voyage", so we have adopted the French expression. (bon voyage表示一路顺风。) 英语中没有关于"bon voyage"的相应表达，所以我们采用了法语的表达法。

The apparent simplicity of Indian ways of life has been judged an evolutionary processing, adaptation to forest ecology.

印度人明显的简朴生活方式被视为一种适应森林环境的进化过程。

apparent [ə'pærənt] *a.* 明显的，表面上的

释 easy to see or understand

拓 *ad.* apparently; *n.* apparentness

用 apparent from sth. that; apparent to sb. that

例 It soon became apparent to everyone that she couldn't dance.
很快大家都明白她不会跳舞。

---

evolutionary [ˌiːvəˈluːʃnəri] *a.* 发展的，渐进的

释 connected with evolution; connected with gradual development and change

拓 *n.* evolution / evolutionism

例 Darwin's theory of evolution is widely accepted. 达尔文的进化论已经被广泛接受。

---

adaptation [ˌædæpˈteɪʃən] *n.* 适应；改编，改编本

释 the process of changing sth. to suit a new situation; a film or movie, book or play that is based on a particular piece of work but that has been changed for a new situation

拓 *a.* adaptable / adaptational

用 adaptation to; adapation of

例 A screen adaptation of Shakespeare's *The Merchant of Venice* is popular in China. 莎士比亚《威尼斯商人》的电影改编版在中国大受欢迎。

The indigenous Amazonian Indians are necessary to the well-being of the forest.

亚马逊河流域的印第安土著人对维护森林的良好状态起着至关重要的作用。

indigenous [ɪnˈdɪdʒɪnəs] *a.* 固有的；土产的；土著的

释 naturally existing in a place or country rather than arriving from another place

用 indigenous to

例 There are many indigenous cultures which existed in Australia.
有许多土著文化留存在澳洲。

well-being ['wel'biːɪŋ] *n.* 康乐，安宁，幸福

释 the state of feeling healthy and happy

例 People doing yoga exercise benefit from an increased feeling of well-being. 练瑜伽会使人越来越身心愉悦。

As sea levels rise, countries in low-lying coastal areas will be hit by seawater penetration of ground water.

随着海平面的上升，沿海低洼处国家的地下水就会受到海水渗透的影响。

low-lying ['ləʊˌlaɪɪŋ] *a.* 地势低洼的

释 at, near or below the level of the sea

例 The areas of low-lying land have been flooded. 地势低的地区已被洪水淹没。

---

penetration [ˌpenɪ'treɪʃən] *n.* 渗透，浸透，侵入

释 a movement into or through something or someone

拓 *vt.* & *vi.* penetrate; *a.* penetrative

例 Sunscreens can help reduce the penetration of ultraviolet rays into the skin. 防晒霜能帮助减少紫外线侵入皮肤。

They live in precarious balance with one of the toughest environments on earth.

他们居住在一个世界上环境恶劣的地方，同大自然艰难地维持着平衡。

precarious [prɪ'keərɪəs] *a.* 不确定的；危险的

释 in a dangerous state because not safe or firmly fixed

拓 *n.* precariousness; *ad.* precariously

例 His health remained precarious. 他的健康状况还不稳定。

tough [tʌf] *a.* 坚硬的；艰苦的，棘手的，严厉的

释 strong; not easily broken or weakened or defeated; having or causing difficulties or problems

拓 *n.* toughness; *vt.& vi.* toughen; *ad.* toughly

例 These dolls are made from tough plastic. 这些娃娃都是硬塑料制成的。

The broad socio-ecological view of health was endorsed at the first International Conference of Health Promotion held in 1986.

1986年首届世界健康促进大会确定了广义的社会生态学观点。

endorse [ɪn'dɔːs] *vt.* 支持，赞同

释 to express formal support or approval for someone or something

拓 *n.* endorsement

用 endorse a proposal / an idea / a candidate

例 I definitely endorse everything the President has said. 我支持总统的一切言论。

These regions are fragile (i.e. highly vulnerable to abnormal pressures) not just in terms of their ecology, but also in terms of the culture of their inhabitants.

这些地区是比较脆弱的（也就是说，很容易受到非正常压力的干扰），不仅仅表现在生态环境，而且还表现在地区居民的文化方面。

fragile ['frædʒɪl] *a.* 易碎的；脆弱的

释 easily damaged, broken or harmed

拓 *n.* fragility

例 This glass is beautiful, but looks very fragile. 这杯子很漂亮，但是看起来很容易碎掉。

abnormal [æb'nɔːməl] *a.* 反常的，不正常的，不规则的

释 very different from usual in a way that seems strange, worrying, wrong, or dangerous

拓 *n.* abnormality; *ad.* abnormally

例 It is abnormal for a man to walk in his sleep. 梦游是不正常的。

The greenhouse effect is a natural phenomenon involving the increase in global surface temperature due to the presence of greenhouse gases-water-vapor, carbon dioxide, troposphere ozone, methane and nitrous oxide.

温室效应是一种自然现象，例如全球表面温度的上升是由于温室气体的影响，比如水蒸气、二氧化碳、对流层臭氧、甲烷和一氧化二氮。

greenhouse ['griːnhaʊs] *n.* 温室

释 a building with a roof and sides made of glass, used for growing plants that need warmth and protection

例 They planted many beautiful flowers in their greenhouse. 他们在温室里种了很多好看的花。

---

presence ['prezəns] *n.* 出席，在场

释 the fact of being in a particular place

拓 *a.* present

用 in presence; in the presence of sb.

例 She was so quiet that her presence was hardly noticed. 她那么安静，几乎没有人注意到她的存在。

---

troposphere ['trɒpəsfɪə] *n.* 对流层

释 the lowest atmospheric layer, between the surface of the earth and about 6-10 kilometers above the surface

例 The balance must be made up by heat transported through the troposphere. 必须通过对流层的热传输来建立平衡。

---

nitrous ['naɪtrəs] *a.* 氮的

释 coming from, relating to or containing nitrogen

In the Sahara in Africa, where two-thirds of the sparse population live in permanent settlements, many of the oasis that provide natural supplies of water have been enlarged by human industry.

在非洲撒哈拉地区，有三分之二的稀疏人口永久居住在那里，很多能够提供天然水源的绿洲都被人类工业扩大了。

sparse [spɑːs] *a.* 稀少的，稀疏的

释 small in numbers or amount, often scattered over a large area

拓 *ad.* sparsely; *n.* sparseness / sparsity

例 The television coverage of this event was rather sparse. 电视上对这件事报道很少。

---

oasis [əʊ'eɪsɪs] *n.* 绿洲

释 a place in a desert where water and plants are found

例 The small town was an oasis of prosperity in a desert of poverty. 这个小镇是贫穷沙漠中的一块繁荣的"绿洲"。

However, they are the most vulnerable to the acute effects of heavily polluted stagnant air.

然而，他们最容易受到重度空气污染的影响。

stagnant ['stægnənt] *a.* 不流动的；不景气的

释 not flowing or moving, and smelling unpleasant; not growing or developing

拓 *n.* stagnation / stagnancy

例 Due to low investment, our industrial output remained stagnant. 由于投资少，我们的工业产量一直停滞不前。

The role of government in environmental management is difficult but inescapable.

政府在环境管理方面做的事情是比较难的，但同时也是非做不可的。

inescapable [ˌɪnɪsˈkeɪpəbl] *a.* 无法逃脱的，不可避免的

释 impossible to avoid or ignore

拓 *ad.* inescapably

例 The inescapable conclusion is that he was murdered by someone in his own house. 必然会得出这样的结论：他是在自己家里被人谋杀的。

To protect it, the new coastline is being bolstered with a formidable twelve kilometers of sea defenses.

为了保护它，新的海岸线上筑起了12公里的坚固防线。

bolster [ˈbəulstə] *vt.* 支持

释 to support or improve something or make it stronger

例 The soldiers bolstered their morale by singing. 士兵们唱歌来鼓舞士气。

---

formidable [ˈfɔːmɪdəbəl] *a.* 强有力的；令人畏惧的；难以应付的

释 very powerful or impressive, and often frightening; difficult to deal with

拓 *ad.* formidably

例 A younger counter staff helps to eradicate the formidable image. 起用年轻的柜台职员有助于消除令人生畏的形象。

Often dams are built to protect the area from soil erosion and to serve as permanent sources of water.

兴建水坝往往是为了防止该地区的水土流失，并提供永久的水源。

erosion [ɪ'rəʊʒən] *n.* 腐蚀，侵蚀

释 the gradual destruction and removal of rock or soil through processes of nature, as by streams and winds

拓 *vt.* erode; *a.* erosional; *ad.* erosionally

例 Soil erosion by rain and wind is a serious problem here.
雨和风对土壤的侵蚀在这儿是个严重问题。

Noise is controlled by modifying equipment and by using insulation and sound enclosures around machinery.

通过改造设备及在机器周围采用绝缘及隔音措施，噪音得到了控制。

insulation [ˌɪnsju'leɪʃən] *n.* 隔离；孤立；绝缘

释 when you insulate something, or when something is insulated; material which is used to insulate something

拓 *vt.* insulate; *a.* insulated / insulating; *n.* insulator

用 insulation from

例 The animal's thick fur provides very good insulation against the cold weather. 动物厚厚的皮毛是抵御严寒的最好武器。

---

enclosure [ɪn'kləʊʒə] *n.* 围墙；围绕

释 an area surrounded by a wall of fence

拓 *vt.* enclose; *a.* enclosed

用 enclosure of

例 The enclosure of public land meant that ordinary people couldn't use it. 公共土地的圈围意味着普通人将不能使用它。

Until now, Britain has opted for burying most of its rubbish.

至今，英国都是使用掩埋的方法来处理大部分垃圾。

bury ['beri] *vt.* 埋葬

释 to put a dead body into the ground, or to put sth. into a hole in the ground and cover it

用 be buried under sth.; bury sth. in

例 Tribes returned to a particular place to bury their dead. 部落的人返回到特定地点埋葬死者。

---

rubbish ['rʌbɪʃ] *n.* 垃圾，废物

释 waste material or unwanted or worthless things

拓 *a.* rubbishy

例 He picked up the rubbish with distaste. 他厌恶地捡起垃圾。

At the same time, sand was dredged from the waters and piled on top of the layer of stiff clay that the massive dredging had laid bare.

与此同时，人们从水中捞取沙子，堆积在坚硬的黏土的最高层，大量的捞取物都毫无遮掩地堆在那里。

dredge [dredʒ] *n.* 挖泥机；*vt.* & *vi.*疏浚；捞取

释 a machine for removing earth; to remove unwanted things from the bottom of a river, lake, etc. using a sucking or other devices

拓 *n.* dredger

用 dredge up / away / out; dredge for

例 To dredge the moon out from the bottom of the water—effort in vain. 水底捞月——徒劳无功。

stiff [stɪf] *a.* 坚硬的；严厉的；呆板的

释 firm or hard, not easily bent or moved; not friendly or relaxed

用 stiff with

例 His rather stiff manner puts kids off. 他那相当生硬的态度使孩子们都不敢来。

Because the tropical forest has been depicted as ecologically unfit for large-scale human occupation, some environmentalists have opposed development of any kind.

由于热带森林地区被描述成在生态上不适合大规模的人类居住，一些环保主义者反对发展任何一种开发形式。

tropical ['trɒpɪkəl] *a.* 热带的

释 coming from or existing in the hottest parts of the world

例 This kind of plant lives in the tropical rainforest climate. 这类植物在热带雨林气候下生存。

---

ecological [ˌekə'lɒdʒɪkəl] *a.* 生态的；生态学的

释 relating to ecology or the environment; the relationships between the air, land, water, animals, plants, etc., usually of a particular area，or the scientific study of this

拓 *ad.* ecologically; *n.* ecologist / ecology

例 The destruction of the tropical monsoon forests is an ecological disaster that threatens the future. 热带季风林的破坏是生态的灾难，威胁着人类的未来。

Restaurant owners and patrons should abandon the use of disposable chopsticks for the good of their health and the environment.

餐馆老板和顾客为了自身健康和环境保护应放弃使用一次性筷子。

abandon [ə'bændən] *vt.* 放弃，遗弃；沉溺

释 to leave someone, especially someone you are responsible for; to give oneself over unrestrainedly

拓 *a.* abandoned; *n.* abandonment

例 Those who abandon themselves to despair can not succeed.
那些自暴自弃的人是无法成功的。

---

disposable [dɪ'spəʊzəbəl] *a.* 一次性使用的

释 intended to be used once or for a short time and then thrown away

拓 *vt. & vi.* dispose

例 The couple bought a dozen of disposable diaper. 这对夫妇买了很多一次性尿布。

The intensity of farming in the rich world should decline, and the use of chemical inputs will diminish.

在富裕国家，应当减少过度耕种及化学物品的使用。

intensity [ɪn'tensɪti] *n.* 激烈，强烈，剧烈

释 the quality of being felt very strongly or having a strong effect

例 The poem showed great intensity of feeling. 这首诗表现出强烈的激情。

The Indians, whose presence is in fact crucial to the survival of the forest, have suffered the most.

对保护森林起到决定性作用的印第安人遭受了最大的苦难。

crucial [ˈkruːʃəl] *a.* 关键的，决定性的

释 extremely important, because everything depends on it

拓 *ad.* crucially

用 crucial to; crucial in / to doing sth.

例 Negotiations are under way at a crucial stage. 谈判正处于一个关键的阶段。

---

survival [səˈvaɪvəl] *n.* 生存，幸存

释 the state of continuing to live or exist, often despite difficulty or danger

拓 *vt. & vi.* survive

用 survival of

例 A lot of companies have to fight for survival in the economic depression. 许多公司在经济萧条中为了生存而挣扎。

Hearing specialist have long believed that prolonged exposure to excessively loud noise degrades hearing and so industrial standards are based on people's average exposure to sound energy.

听力专家认为长时间遭受噪音污染会导致听力下降，所以工业标准是根据人们听觉的承受力来制定的。

prolong [prəˈlɒŋ] *vt.* 延长，拖延

释 to deliberately make something such as a feeling or activity last longer

拓 *a.* prolonged; *n.* prolongation

例 We were having such a good time here, so we decided to prolong our stay by another couple of weeks. 我们在这儿玩得很愉快，所以决定再玩几个星期。

excessively [ɪk'sesɪvli] *ad.* 过分地；极度地

释 much more than reasonable or necessary

拓 *a.* excessive

例 We have heard Doctor John admire that film excessively. 我们曾听到约翰博士极度赞扬过那部电影。

---

degrade [dɪ'greɪd] *vt.* 降低

释 to lower in grade, rank, or status

拓 *a.* degrading; *ad.* degradingly; *n.* degrader

用 degrade yourself by doing sth.

例 How can you degrade yourself by writing such trite words?
你怎么能写这些陈词滥调来降低自己的身份?

Defendants of mining point out that, environmentally, local mining has two important factors in its favor.

采矿方被告指出，地方采矿在两个重要方面均对环境是有利的。

defendant [dɪ'fendənt] *n.* 被告

释 a person in a law case who is accused of having done something illegal

拓 *vt.& vi.* defend; *n.* defender

例 The attack on this defendant, by the district attorney seemed too unfair. 区检察官对这位被告的攻击似乎太不公正了。

四 动植物类

The accuracy with which dolphins leap high to take small fish out of a trainer's hand provides anecdotal evidence.

海豚高高跃起接过教练手中的小鱼的精确性为此提供了有趣的证据。

accuracy ['ækjurəsi] *n.* 准确（性），精确度

释 faithful measurement or representation of the truth, correctness, precision

拓 *a.* accurate; *ad.* accurately

例 They questioned the accuracy of the information in the contract. 他们质疑合同中信息的准确性。

---

anecdotal [ˌænɪkˈdəʊtl] *a.* 逸事的，趣闻的

释 based on anecdotes and possibly not true or accurate

拓 *n.* anecdote

例 Their research was based largely on anecdotal evidence. 他们的研究主要以趣闻为基础。

Last year, evolution was the breakthrough of the year, we found it full of new developments in understanding how new species originate.

去年是进化研究取得重要突破的一年，我们对于新物种起源的了解不断取得新的进展。

breakthrough ['breɪkˌθruː] *n.* 突破，突破性

释 an important discovery or event that helps to improve a situation or provide an answer to a problem

用 breakthrough in

例 The department of surgery have made a great breakthrough in the kidney transplantation. 外科在肾移植方面取得了重大突破。

species ['spiːʃiːz] *n.* 物种，种类

释 a group / set of animal or plants whose members are similar and can breed together to produce young animals or plants

用 species of

例 Contamination poses a threat to the continued existence of this species. 污染对这个物种的生存构成了威胁。

---

originate [ə'rɪdʒɪneɪt] *vi.* 开始，源于；*vt.* 发明；引起

释 to come from a particular place or start in a particular situation; to creat sth. new

拓 *n.* originator / origination

用 originate from; originate in; originate with

例 The disease is thought to have originated in the tropics. 这种疾病据说起源于热带地区。

Pupils' responses indicate some misconceptions in basic scientific knowledge of rainforests' ecosystems such as their ideas about rainforests as habitats for animals, plants and humans and the relationship between climatic change and destruction of rainforest.

小学生的反应表明了对雨林生态系统的基础科学知识存在某些误解，比如，他们对于雨林作为动植物和人类栖息地的看法，以及他们对气候变化与雨林破坏之间关系的理解。

ecosystem ['ekəʊˌsɪstəm] *n.* 生态系统

释 all the animals and plants in a particular area, and the way in which they are related to each other and to their environment

例 It is a basic national policy of China to protect forests, plant trees, and improve the ecosystem. 保护森林、植树造林、改善生态系统是中国的一项基本国策。

---

rainforest ['reɪnfɒrɪst] *n.* （热带）雨林

释 a tropical forest with tall trees that are very close together, growing in an area where it rains a lot

例 In answer to the final question about the importance of rainforest conservation, the majority of children simply said that we need rainforests to survive. 在回答最后一个关于保护热带雨林的重要性问题时，大多数孩子简单地回答我们需要雨林生存。

---

habitat ['hæbɪtæt] *n.* (植物的)产地，（动物的）栖息地

释 the natural surroundings in which an animal or plant usually lives

例 The place is the habitat for giant panda. 这里是大熊猫的栖息地。

---

destruction [dɪs'trʌkʃən] *n.* 破坏，毁灭

释 the act of destroying something; the process of being destroyed

拓 *a.* destructive; *ad.* destructively; *n.* destructiveness; *vi.* destruct

用 destruction of

例 The flood caused serious destruction to the town. 洪水严重毁坏了这个城镇。

Just in case some are still lively, bees can be pacified with a few puffs of smoke blown into each hive's narrow entrance.

如果有些蜜蜂还是很活跃，那么从狭窄的蜂房口吹进几口烟，就能使它们平静下来。

pacify ['pæsɪfaɪ] *vt.* 使……平静，安慰

释 to make someone calm, quiet, and satisfied after they have been angry or upset

用 pacify with

例 Jim allowed himself to be pacified with this arrangement. 吉姆作出妥协接受了这一安排。

---

puff [pʌf] *vt.* 喷，吹

释 to move in a particular direction, sending out little clouds of steam or smoke

用 puff at; puff on; puff away

例 Don't puff smoke into my face! 别往我脸上吐烟！

---

hive [haɪv] *n.* 蜂房，蜂箱（= beehive）

释 a small box where bees are kept, or the bees that live in this box; a structure where bees live, especially a beehive, or the group of bees living there

例 A hive cannot exist without a queen. 蜂房不可无蜂王。

The NAVHDAGA (North American Versatile Hunting Dog Association) is a legally recognized nonprofit organization dedicated to preserving, improving and promoting versatile hunting dogs by sponsoring training and testing programs throughout North America.

北美多功能猎犬协会是一家合法承认的非盈利性机构，该机构通过提倡训练和检测课程来致力于维护、改进和推动北美多功能猎犬事业的发展。

versatile ['vɜːsətaɪl] *a.* 多才多艺的，多方面的

释 able to change easily from one activity to another or able to be used for many different purposes

拓 *n.* versatility / versatileness; *ad.* versatilely

例 Text editor is a program that enables a user to modify and copy programs and text files in a versatile manner. 文本编辑程序是指能让用户以多种方式来修改并拷贝程序和文本文件。

---

sponsor ['spɒnsə] *vt.* 发起，赞助；*n.* 保证人，赞助者

释 to support a person, organization or activity by giving money, encouragement or other help; a person who gives support

用 sponsor of

例 The senator announced that he would sponsor the health care plan.这位参议员宣布他将发起这一保健计划。

A modern hard-core sociobiology might even go so far as to claim that this aggressive instinct evolved as an advantageous trait.

现代社会生物学核心人士甚至可能会宣称，这种攻击性本能演化成为一种优势特性。

hard-core ['hɑːdkɔː] *a.* 核心的

释 a small group of people within a larger group, who strongly believe in the group's principles and usually have a lot of power in it

例 The hard-core in the party make all the decisions. 这个党的核心成员决定一切。

---

sociobiology [ˌsəʊsɪəʊˌbaɪ'ɒlədʒi] *n.* 社会生物学

释 the branch of biology that conducts comparative studies of the social organization of animals(including human beings) with regard to its evolutionary history

---

aggressive [ə'gresɪv] *a.* 侵犯的；攻击性的；有进取心的

释 behaving in an angry and violent way towards another person; behaving in very determined and forceful way in order to succeed

拓 *n.* aggressiveness / aggression; *ad.* aggressively

例 A successful businessman must be aggressive. 一个成功的商人必须有进取心。

---

trait [treɪt] *n.* **特征，特性，品质**

释 a particular characteristic that can produce a particular type of behaviour

例 Jim's two most pleasing traits are generosity and energy.
吉姆最讨人喜欢的两个特征是豪爽和充满活力。

Throughout its time as a larva, approximately 15 months, the glow-worm emits a green light.

在近15个月内的幼虫期内，这种发光虫发出绿色的光。

larva ['lɑːvə] *n.* **幼虫**

释 a form of an insect or an animal such as a frog that is not yet completely developed

拓 *a.* larval

例 I think this worm is a larva of a butterfly. 我觉得这虫子是蝴蝶的幼虫。

Rats produce ultrasonic squeaks to prevent their scuffles turning nasty.

老鼠在吱吱叫时发出超声波，从而避免其斗争得越来越凶残。

ultrasonic [ˌʌltrə'sɒnɪk] *a.* **（声波）超声的**

释 higher than humans can hear

例 Ultrasonic signals echo off floors and walls, creating ambiguity in the distance readings. 地板和墙壁会反射超声波信号，造成距离读数的不明确。

squeak ['skwi:k] *n.* 吱吱声，短促的尖叫声

释 a short, high cry or sound, that is not usually very loud

拓 *a.* squeaky

例 Shirley gave a little squeak of surprise. 雪莉轻轻地惊叫了一声。

---

scuffle ['skʌfəl] *n.* 混战；*vi.* 扭打

释 a short and sudden fight, especially one involving a small number of people; to fight or struggle in a confused way

例 Five pickets were injured in the scuffle. 在混战中有五名纠察队员受伤。

Without genetic variability a species lacks the capacity to evolve and cannot adapt to changes in its environment.

没有遗传变异性，物种就会缺少进化和适应环境变化的能力。

genetic [dʒɪ'netɪk] *a.* 遗传的，起源的

释 connected with genes, relating to or determined by the origin, development, or casual antecedents of something

拓 *ad.* genetically; *n.* gene / genetics / geneticist

例 It's very difficult to treat genetic diseases. 遗传性疾病治疗起来很困难。

---

variability [ˌveərɪə'bɪlɪti] *n.* 易变，变化性，变异性

释 the fact of sth. being likely to vary

拓 *a.* variable

例 There is considerable variability in the size of individual polar bears. 北极熊的个体大小差异很大。

Once the beetle larvae have finished pupation, the residue is a first-rate source of fertilizer.

甲虫幼虫化蛹后留下的残渣是极好的肥料。

pupation [pjuːˈpeɪʃn] *n.* [昆]化蛹

释 the act of becoming a pupa

拓 *n.* pupa; *a.* pupal

例 The firefly passed through the stages of being an egg, being a larva, molting and pupation, etc. 萤火虫一生历经卵、幼虫、蜕皮、化蛹等过程。

---

residue [ˈrezɪˌdjuː] *n.* 残渣，剩余

释 the part that is left after the main part has gone or been taken away, or substance that remains after a chemical process such as evaporation

派 *a.* residual

例 Residues of pesticides can build up in the soil. 残余的杀虫剂会在土壤中积淀起来。

In the first type, a returning scout scampered in circles, alternating to right and left, stopping occasionally to regurgitate food samples to the excited bees chasing after her.

第一种是，返回侦察后就地绕圈，左右交替进行，偶尔停下吐出食物给追逐她的蜜蜂。

scout [skaʊt] *n.* 侦察员；*vt.* & *vi.* 侦察，搜索

释 a person employed to watch for something to happen; to explore often with the goal of finding something or somebody

派 *n.* scouter

用 scout around / round

例 They stopped scout in the mountainous area. 他们停止了在那个山区的侦察活动。

scamper [ˈskæmpə] *vi.* 奔跑，快跑

释 to run with quick short steps, like a child or small animal

用 scamper about

例 The children were scampering around the garden. 孩子们在花园里嬉戏奔跑。

---

regurgitate [rɪˈgɜːdʒɪteɪt] *vt.* & *vi.* （使）涌回；（使）反胃

释 to bring food that you have already swallowed back into your mouth; to become thrown

拓 *n.* regurgitation

例 Some birds and animals regurgitate food to feed their young.
一些鸟类和动物吐出食物喂养自己的孩子。

A few decades later, the same pterosaur, or winged reptile, was adopted to describe the growing list of similar fossils.

几十年后，人们用同一种翼龙，或者叫带翼爬行动物，来描述新发现的类似化石。

winged [wɪŋd] *a.* 有翼的

释 having wings

例 Dragons are winged beings portrayed in the ancient mythologies.
在古代神话里龙被描绘成有翅膀的生物。

---

reptile [reptaɪl] *n.* 爬行动物

释 an animal that crawls or moves on its belly (as a snake) or on small short legs (as a lizard)

例 Snakes and crocodiles are both reptiles. 蛇和鳄鱼都是爬行动物。

Beekeepers can carry their hives for farmers who need bees to pollinate their crops.

养蜂人把蜂箱带到需要给庄稼授粉的农民那里。

pollinate ['pɒlɪˌneɪt] *vt.* 给……授粉

释 to give a flower or plant pollen so that it can produce seeds

拓 *n.* pollination / pollen

例 Wild bees will naturally then pollinate human crops. 野生蜜蜂随之将很自然地帮助人类农作物授粉。

Sociobiology is concerned with elucidating the biological basis of all behavior.

社会生物学关注的是如何阐明所有行为的生物基础。

elucidate [ɪ'luːsɪdeɪt] *vt.* 阐明，说明

释 to explain something that is difficult to understand by providing more information

拓 *n.* elucidation *a.* elucidatory

例 The notes help to elucidate the most difficult parts of the text. 这些注释有助于弄清文中最难懂的部分。

Bamboos are perennial grasses that remain in a vegetative state for many years and then suddenly flower.

竹子是一种四季常有的植物，会在成熟多年后突然开花。

perennial [pə'renɪəl] *a.* 四季不断的，长期的；反复的

释 present at all seasons of the year; continuing or existing for a long time, or happening again and again

拓 *ad.* perennially

例 Lack of resources has been a perennial problem. 资源的缺乏是个长期的问题。

If the ant relied on some form of dry adhesion, its feet would pop abruptly on the surface which is wet.

如果蚂蚁依赖某种形式的干燥粘合力的话，那么当物体的表面潮湿时，蚂蚁是站不住的。

adhesion [əd'hi:ʒən] *n.* 粘附（力），黏着

释 the ability to stick or become attached to sth.

拓 *vi.* adhere; *a.* adhesive

例 The glue has good adhesion. 这种胶水粘合力很强。

---

abruptly [ə'brʌptli] *ad.* 突然地，意外地

释 quickly and without warning

拓 *a.* abrupt; *n.* abruptness

例 Abruptly Eric realized he was sober and very weary. 艾瑞克蓦然感到自己酒意全无，浑身疲惫不堪。

The beetles immediately disappear beneath the tunneling.

甲壳虫立即消失于地下通道中。

beneath [bɪ'ni:θ] *prep.* 在……之下；向……下面

释 in or to a lower position than something; under something

例 The moon is now beneath the horizon. 月亮此刻落到地平线下面了。

---

tunneling ['tʌnəlɪŋ] *n.* 隧道

释 a hollow conduit or recess

拓 *n. / vt. & vi.* tunnel

例 An important application of this phenomenon is in the operation of the scanning tunneling microscope. 该现象的一个重要应用是操作隧道微观的测定。

If it were not for the dung beetle, chemical fertilizer and dung would be washed by rain into streams.

如果不是因为蜣螂，化学肥料和粪便将会被雨水冲到河里去。

fertilizer ['fɜːtɪlaɪzə] *n.* 肥料

释 a substance added to soil to make plants grow more successfully

拓 *vt.* fertilize; *a.* fertile

例 Sheep dung makes one of the best fertilizers. 羊粪是最好的肥料之一。

Although at least some cetaceans have taste buds, the nerves serving these have degenerated or are rudimentary.

虽然至少有一些鲸类有味蕾，但是味觉神经已慢慢退化或未完全发育。

cetacean [sɪ'teɪʃən] *n.* 鲸类动物；鲸鱼

释 large aquatic carnivorous mammal with fin-like forelimbs no hind limbs, including whales, dolphins, porpoises, etc.

例 The sperm whale is believed to dive deeper than any other cetacean. 人们相信抹香鲸比其他鲸类动物潜得更深。

---

bud [bʌd] *n.* 芽，花蕾；*vt.& vi.* （使）发芽

释 a partially opened flower; to produce buds

例 It was springtime and the fruit trees were in bud. 现在是春天，果树都开花了。

---

degenerate [dɪ'dʒenəreɪt] *vi.* 退化

释 to become worse in quality

拓 *a.* degenerative; *n.* degeneration

用 degenerate into

例 The march degenerated into a riot. 示威游行变成了暴动。

rudimentary [ˌruːdəˈmentəri] *a.* 未成熟的；基本的

释 not highly or fully developed; dealing with only the most basic matters or ideas

拓 *ad.* rudimentarily

例 He has only a rudimentary knowledge of the subject. 他对这一科只有初步的认识。

These temporary hive extensions contain frames of empty comb for the bees to fill with honey.

这些临时蜂巢的扩建包括用来储存蜂蜜的空蜂巢。

temporary [ˈtempərəri] *a.* 暂时的，临时的

释 continuing for only a limited period of time

拓 *ad.* temporarily

例 They just reached a temporary agreement. 他们只是达成一个临时协议。

---

extension [ɪksˈtenʃən] *n.* 延长，扩充

释 the act of making something longer or larger

用 extension of; extension to

例 He asked for an extension of his visa. 他申请延长签证的有效期。

Dung beetles are sheltered from predators such as birds and foxes.

蜣螂躲避鸟类和狐狸等掠食者的攻击。

shelter [ˈʃeltə] *vt.& vi.* 躲避；保护

释 to protect yourself, or another person or thing, from bad weather, danger or attack

拓 *a.* sheltered

用 shelter from; shelter for

例 We sheltered under a tree until the shower passed. 我们在树下躲雨，直到雨过天晴。

---

predator ['predətə] *n.* 食肉动物

释 an animal that kills and eats other animal

例 Lions, tigers and other predators are very dangerous. 狮子、老虎和其他食肉动物都很危险。

Some plants reach maximal photosynthesis at one-quarter full sunlight, and others, like sugarcane, never reach a maximum.

有些植物在1／4充分光照时，达到光合作用的最大值，其他植物比如甘蔗的光合作用就永远不会到达最高点。

photosynthesis [ˌfəutəu'sɪnθəsɪs] *n.* 光合作用

释 synthesis of compounds with the aid of radiant energy(especially in plants)

例 In apple trees photosynthesis occurs almost exclusively in the leaves.苹果树的光合作用几乎只发生在叶内。

---

sugarcane ['ʃugəˌkeɪn] *n.* 甘蔗

释 juicy canes whose sap is a source of molasses and commercial sugar; fresh canes are sometimes chewed for the juice

例 Sugarcane is needed to make rum. 甘蔗是制造朗姆酒的必需品。

---

maximum ['mæksɪməm] *n.* 极点，最大；*a.* 最高的，最大极限的

释 being the largest amount or number allowed or possible; the greatest or most complete or best possible

拓 *n.* maxima / maximums (*pl.*); *vt.* &*vi.* maximize

用 maximum of

例 The stereo was turned up to maximum volume. 音响被调到了最大音量。

Most species burrow into the soil and bury dung in tunnels directly.

许多物种都是挖洞然后直接把粪便埋入洞穴。

burrow ['bʌrəʊ] *vt. & vi.* 挖洞

释 to make a hole or passage in the ground

用 burrow into / under / through

例 Mother turtles burrow into the sand to lay their eggs. 乌龟妈妈在沙地里挖洞产卵。

The hives are stacked onto wooden pallets, back-to-back in sets of four.

蜂房堆积在一个木制的平台上，背对背有四层。

stack [stæk] *vt. & vi.* 堆积

释 to make things into a neat pile, or to form a neat pile; to put neat piles of things on something

用 stack up; be stacked with sth.

例 The floor was stacked with DVD boxes. 地板上整齐地堆着DVD盒子。

---

pallet ['pælɪt] *n.* 平台；货盘，托板；简陋小床

释 a flat wooden structure onto which heavy goods are loaded so that they can be moved using a fork-lift truck (= a small vehicle with two strong bars of metal on the front which is used for lifting heavy goods); a narrow bed

例 Alice slept on a pallet in the outside. 爱丽丝在外面睡铺板。

This commitment had now been clearly defined as the World Zoo Conservation Strategy, which based on all unrealistic optimism about the nature of the zoo industry.

承诺已经明确定义为世界动物园保护策略，而这种策略是基于一种对动物园产业不实际的乐观态度。

commitment [kəˈmɪtmənt] *n.* 承诺；奉献，献身

释 a promise to do something or to behave in a particular way; the willingness to work hard

拓 *vt.* commit; *a.* committed

用 commitment to

例 I would like to thank the staff for having shown such commitment. 我想感谢所有员工给出了这样的承诺。

---

optimism [ˈɒptɪmɪzəm] *n.* 乐观，乐观主义

释 the tendency to be hopeful and to emphasize the good part of a situation rather than the bad part; the belief that good things will happen in the future

拓 *n.* optimist; *a.* optimistic; *ad.* optimistically

用 optimism for, optimism about

例 At the airport, she expressed optimism about the talks. 在机场，她对谈判持乐观态度。

A bee's brain is the size of a grass seed, yet in this tiny brain are encoded some of the most complex and amazing behavioral patterns witnessed.

蜜蜂的大脑与一粒小草种子的大小相当，然而据观察，在这个微小的大脑里却有着某些最复杂、惊人的行为模式编码。

encode [ɪnˈkəʊd] *vt.* 把……编码

释 to put a message or other information into a code

例 Many satellite broadcasts are encoded so that they can only be received by people who have paid to see them. 卫星接收器具有编码，只有付费才能观看。

witness ['wɪtnɪs] *n.* 目击者，证人；*vt. & vi.* 目击

释 someone who sees an event and reports what happened; to be a witness

用 witness to; key / principal witness

例 According to witnesses, the robbery was carried on by two young men. 据证人陈述，有两名年轻男子参与抢劫。

What they discovered was experimental proof of the incredible power-to-weight ratio of birds.

他们发现了鸟类难以置信的动力重量比率这一实验证据。

incredible [ɪn'kredəbl] *a.* 难以置信的

释 impossible, or very difficult to believe

拓 *ad.* incredibly

例 The latest missiles can be fired with incredible accuracy. 最新的导弹的准确性无与伦比。

---

ratio ['reɪʃɪəʊ] *n.* 比，比率

释 a relationship between two amounts, represented by a pair of numbers showing how much greater one amount is than the other

用 the ratio of sth. to sth.

例 The ratio of men to women at the meeting was 2:1. 出席会议的男女比例是2:1。

The sperm whale apparently produces a monotonous series of high-energy clicks.

抹香鲸似乎可以发出一种高聚能的单调的滴答声。

apparently [ə'pærəntli] *ad.* 显然地；表面上，似乎

释 according to what you have heard or read; according to the way something appears

拓 *a.* apparent

例 Apparently it's going to rain today. 看样子今天要下雨。

---

monotonous [mə'nɒtənəs] *a.* 单调的

释 never changing and therefore boring

拓 *n.* monotony; *ad.* monotonously

例 New secretaries came and went with monotonous regularity.
秘书不停地更换。

"Unique human" component of language is found in gregarious birds.

人类特有的语言组成特性也能在群居鸟类中找到。

gregarious [gre'geərɪəs] *a.* 社交的，群居的

释 liking to be with other people, or (of animals or birds) living in groups

拓 *ad.* gregariously; *n.* gregariousness

例 Ken is a gregarious, outgoing sort of person. 肯是一个喜欢社交的、随和的人。

This type of bird is very inconspicuous because of its dull feathers.

这种羽毛颜色暗淡的鸟很难被察觉。

inconspicuous [ˌɪnkən'spɪkjuːəs] *a.* 不明显的，难以察觉的

释 not easily or quickly noticed or seen; not attracting attention

拓 *ad.* inconspicuously

例 He spent the whole evening trying to look inconspicuous in some corner. 他整个晚上都试图躲在某个角落里。

The honey produced here is fragrant and sweet and can be sold by the beekeepers.

这里出产的蜂蜜又香又甜，并且可供养蜂人出售。

fragrant ['freɪgrənt] *a.* 芬芳的，馥郁的

释 with a pleasant smell

拓 *n.* fragrance

例 The air in the park was warm and fragrant. 公园里的空气温暖馨香。

In 1873, a remarkable pterosaur specimen came to light that confirmed Cuvier's deduction.

1873年，一件非常有特点的翼龙标本被发现，这证实了Cuvier的推理。

remarkable [rɪ'mɑːkəbl] *a.* 显著的，异常的，非凡的

释 unusual or special and therefore surprising and worth mentioning

拓 *ad.* remarkably; *n.* / *vt.* & *vi.* remark

例 Meeting you here in Paris is a remarkable coincidence. 真是太巧了，能在巴黎遇见你。

---

specimen ['spesɪmən] *n.* 样本，标本

释 something shown or examined as an example

例 He is still a fine specimen of hard work. 他一直都是努力工作的典范。

---

deduction [dɪ'dʌkʃən] *n.* 扣除；推论，推理，演绎

释 an amount of percentage deducted; reasoning from the general to the particular

拓 *vt.* deduct; *a.* deductible / deductive

用 deduction from; deduction that

例 The deduction that he was dead was wrong. 关于他已经死亡的推论是错误的。

Arboreal marsupials may not recover to prelogging densities for over a century.

树栖有袋类动物的数量在一个世纪内也不会恢复到砍伐前的密度了。

arboreal [ɑːˈbɔːrɪəl] *a.* 树木的；树栖的

释 relating to trees; living in trees

例 Human vision like that of other primates has evolved in an arboreal environment. 人类的视觉和其他灵长目动物一样，是在丛林环境中进化出来的。

---

marsupial [mɑːˈsuːpɪəl] *n.* 袋类动物

释 any Australian animal that carries its young in a pocket of skin on the mother's stomach

例 The koala is a nocturnal, tree dwelling marsupial mammal. 考拉属喜夜间生活的，居于树上的有袋类哺乳动物。

---

density [ˈdensɪti] *n.* 密集，密度

释 the quality of being dense; the degree to which sth. is dense

拓 *a.* dense

例 The area had a population density of five people per square mile. 该地区的人口密度为每平方英里五人。

To observers, as well as to influential natural scientists and regional planners, the luxuriant forests of Amazonian seem unconquerable.

对于观察员和有影响力的自然科学家及区域规划者来说，郁郁葱葱的亚马逊森林似乎是不可战胜的。

influential [ˌɪnflʊˈenʃl] *a.* 有权势的，有影响的

释 connected with the power to have an effect on people or things, or a person or thing that is able to do this

拓 *n.* / *vt.* influence

用 influential in doing sth.

例 Our newspaper is an influential media in this city. 我们的报纸在本市的媒体中有很大影响力。

---

luxuriant [lʌgˈʒʊərɪənt] *a.* 繁茂的，丰富的；肥沃的

释 growing thickly, strongly and well; pleasantly dense or full

拓 *n.* luxuriance; *ad.* luxuriantly

用 luxuriant in sth.

例 Luxuriant forests covered the hills. 山上长满茂密的树木。

---

unconquerable [ʌnˈkɒŋkərəbl] *a.* 不可征服的，不能克服的

释 not capable of being conquered or vanquished or overcome

拓 *ad.* unconquerably

例 There is nothing unconquerable under the sun. 世上没有不可征服的东西。

Behavioral ecologist looked at their predatory behavior when they reached adulthood.

行为生态学家观察过它们到成年时候的捕食行为。

predatory [ˈpredətri] *a.* 掠夺的，捕食生物的

释 of animal living by killing and eating other animals

拓 *n.* predator

例 The domesticated cat retains its predatory instincts. 家猫依然保持着捕食动物的天性。

---

adulthood [əˈdʌlthʊd] *n.* 成年

释 the part of someone's life when they are an adult

拓 *a.* / *n.* adult

例 People in China legally reach adulthood at 18. 在中国，法定成年年龄是18岁。

Without further expansion they could save around 2,000 species of endangered land vertebrates.

如果没有进一步扩张，他们可拯救约2000种濒危陆地脊椎动物。

vertebrate ['vɜːtɪbreɪt] *n.* 脊椎动物

释 an animal that has a spine

例 A dog is a vertebrate animal. 狗是脊椎动物。

Four smelling chemicals are often used to irritate the bees and drive them down into the hive's bottom boxes.

四种有气味的化学品通常被用于激怒蜜蜂并把它们驱赶到蜂箱的底端。

irritate ['ɪrɪteɪt] *vt.* 激怒，使发怒

释 to make angry or annoyed

拓 *ad.* irritated / irritating; *n.* irritant / irritation

例 Don't irritate her, she's on a short fuse today. 别惹她，她今天动不动就发火。

The optimum time for playing would depend on when it was most advantageous for the young of a particular species to do so.

对于一个特定的物种来说，最适合玩耍的时间取决于什么时候玩耍对它们中的幼虫有利。

advantageous [ˌædvən'teɪdʒəs] *a.* 有利的

释 giving benefits or helping to make you more successful

拓 *n.* advantage; *ad.* advantageously

用 advantageous to

例 This is advantageous to our nation. 这对我们民族有利。

The loss of genetic diversity associated with reductions in population size will contribute to the likelihood of extinction.

基因多样性的丧失加上物种数量的减少，将可能导致物种的灭亡。

contribute [kən'trɪbju:t] *vt. & vi.* **贡献，有助于，捐助**

释 to give something, especially money, in order to provide or achieve something together with other people

拓 *n.* contributor / contribution; *a.* contributory

用 contribute to sth.

例 He offered to contribute to the Red Cross. 他主动提出向红十字会捐款。

The dominant idea, raised by 64% of the pupils, was that rainforests provide animals with habitats.

占优势地位的观点是由64%的学生提出来的，他们认为雨林为动物提供了栖息地。

dominant ['dɒmɪnənt] *a.* **占优势的；(基因)显性的**

释 more important, strong or noticeable than anything else of the same type; of a gene which always produces a particular characteristic in a person, plant or animal

拓 *vt. & vi.* dominate; *n.* dominance / domination; *a.* dominating

例 The dominant influence in her life was her father. 一生中对她影响最大的是她的父亲。

Breeding in most organisms occurs during a part of the year only, and so a reliable cue is needed to trigger breeding behavior.

大部分有机体的繁殖发生在每年的特定时间，因此要刺激它们的繁殖行为，就需要一个可靠的信号。

organism [ˈɔːgənɪzəm] *n.* 生物体；机体

释 a single living plant, animal, virus, etc.; a system made up of parts that are dependent on each other

例 Factories and cities are more complex organisms. 工厂和城市是更为复杂的机体组织。

Before the breeding season begins, food reserves must be built up to support the energy cost of reproduction, and to provide for young birds both when they are in the nest and after fledgling.

在繁殖季节开始之前，必须储备食物，以补充繁殖所需能量，并为刚出生的以及还在成长期的雏鸟提供食物。

reserve [rɪˈzɜːv] *n.* 预备品；贮存；*vt.* 保留；预订

释 something kept back or saved for future use or a special purpose; to keep something for someone or something

拓 *n.* reservation; *a.* reserved; *n.* reservoir

例 These seats are reserved for special guests. 这些座位是为特别嘉宾准备的。

---

reproduction [ˌriːprəˈdʌkʃən] *n.* 再现，复制；生殖

释 a copy of a work of art, picture, music, etc.; the process of producing babies or young animals and plants

拓 *vt. & vi.* reproduce; *a.* reproductive

例 The trees will propagate themselves by the reproduction of their seed. 这些树将通过种子的再生而自行繁衍。

fledgling ['fledʒlɪŋ] *n.* 刚会飞的幼鸟；*a.* 初出茅庐的，毫无经验的

释 a young bird that has just learnt to fly; describing a person, organization, or system that is new or without experience

例 He is a fledgling writer. 他是个初出茅庐的作家。

In time they multiply and within three or four years benefits to the pasture are obvious.

他们及时培育繁殖，在三四年里，对牧场的益处是显而易见的。

multiply ['mʌltɪplaɪ] *vt. & vi.* 繁殖；乘，增加

释 to breed; to do a calculation in which you add a number to itself a particular number of times

用 multiply sth. by sth.

例 When animals have more food, they generally multiply faster. 当动物有更多的食物时，它们一般繁殖更快。

---

pasture ['pɑːstʃə] *n.* 牧场

释 a land or field that is covered with grass and is used for cattle, sheep, etc. to feed on

例 Primitive forests have given place to tillage and pasture. 原始森林已被耕地和牧场所取代。

The digested dung in these burrows is an excellent food supply for the earthworms.

那些洞里面的消化后的粪是蚯蚓的最佳食品。

excellent ['eksələnt] *a.* 极好的；优秀的

释 extremely good or of very high quality

拓 *ad.* excellently; *n.* excellence

例 She is an excellent athlete and her movements are perfectly coordinated. 她是个优秀的运动员，她所有的动作都非常协调。

But one intervention works incredibly well in a broad range of animals, increasing longevity and prolonging good health.

但是有一种干预可以显著作用于大量动物物种，有延长寿命和维护健康的功效。

intervention [ˌɪntəˈvenʃən] *n.* 插入，介入，干预

释 the act of becoming involved in an argument, fight, or other difficult situations in order to change what happens

拓 *vi.* intervene

例 His intervention brought their quarrel to a climax. 他的干预使他们的争吵达到了最激烈的程度。

---

longevity [lɒnˈdʒevɪti] *n.* 长寿

释 the amount of time that someone or something lives

例 The Chinese cuisine culture claimed that garlic promoted longevity. 中国烹饪文化认为大蒜有助于人类长寿。

There are plenty of anecdotes describing how glowworms have been used as emergency bicycle lamps.

有很多的奇闻轶事是描述萤火虫是如何被用来当做紧急自行车灯的。

anecdote [ˈænɪkdəʊt] *n.* 轶事，奇闻

释 a short often amusing story, especially about something someone has done

拓 *a.* anecdotal

例 She told one or two amusing anecdotes about her years in UK. 她讲了一两件在英国的趣事。

emergency [ɪ'mɜːdʒənsi] *n.* 紧急情况，突发事件

释 an unexpected and dangerous situation that must be dealt with immediately

用 in an emergency

例 The demonstration grew worse and the government declared a state of emergency. 游行恶化，政府宣布进入紧急状态。

五 科学技术类

The techniques were successfully deciphering disorder related genes, which could be applied to a larger project.

该技术成功破译无序基因，可以应用于较大的项目。

decipher [dɪ'saɪfə] *vt.* 译解；辨认（潦草字迹）

释 to convert code into ordinary language; to find the meaning of something that is difficult to read or understand

拓 *n.* decipherment

例 Researchers are gradually deciphering the genetic structure found in the cells of organisms. 研究者正渐渐破译存于有机体细胞内的基因结构。

---

apply [ə'plaɪ] *vt.* 使用，应用，运用

释 to bring or put into use or operation

拓 *n.* application / applicant

用 apply to; apply for

例 Scientific discoveries are often applied to industrial processes. 科学发明通常都应用于工业生产过程。

When an LGVs batteries run low, it will take itself off line and go to the nearest battery maintenance point for replacement batteries.

当激光引导无人搬运车的电池电量太低时，它会自动卸下电池并去最近的电池维护点替换电池。

battery ['bætəri] *n.* 电池

释 a device that produces electricity to provide power for radios, cars, etc.

例 My car battery has run down. 我汽车上的电池用完了。

---

maintenance ['meɪntɪnəns] *n.* 维护，保持，维修

释 the act of keeing something in good condition by checking or repairing it regularly

拓 *vt.* maintain

例 He had to work hard for the maintenance of his family. 他为了养家不得不去拼命工作。

---

replacement [rɪ'pleɪsmənt] *n.* 代替，更换

释 the act of replacing one thing with another

拓 *vt.* replace; *a.* replaceable

用 replacement for

例 We need a replacement for the secretary who left. 我们需要一个人代替已离职的秘书。

The children of the newly-literate mothers were also better nourished than those of women who could not read.

这些刚刚脱盲的妈妈要比那些文盲妈妈更懂得如何培养他们的孩子。

literate ['lɪtərɪt] *a.* 有读写能力的；受过教育的

释 able to read and write; having knowledge of a particular subject, or a particular type of knowledge

拓 *n.* literature; *a.* literary; *ad.* literarily

例 Every literate person should read this book. 凡是有文化的人都应读一读此书。

---

nourish [ˈnʌrɪʃ] *vt.* 滋养，养育；培养

释 to provide people or living things with food in order to make them grow and keep them healthy; to allow a feeling, an idea, etc. to develop or grow stronger

拓 *n.* nourishment; *a.* nourishing

例 We need good food to nourish the starving infants. 我们需要营养食品滋养这些挨饿的婴儿。

It celebrated scientific and engineering achievements by openly parading the sophisticated techniques used in construction.

为了庆祝科学和工程上的成就，他们公开展示了应用于建设中的尖端技术。

parade [pəˈreɪd] *vt. & vi.* 游行；展示

释 to walk somewhere in a formal group of people, in order to celebrate or protest about something; to show somebody/ something in public so that people can see them / it

例 The victorious team will parade through the city tomorrow morning. 明天上午获胜队将在城内举行庆祝游行。

---

sophisticated [səˈfɪstɪkeɪtɪd] *a.* 久经世故的；尖端的

释 having a good understanding of the way people behave and / or a good knowledge of culture and fashion; clever and complicated in the way that it works or is presented

拓 *n.* sophistication

例 Managerial economics is becoming a sophisticated art. 管理经济

学正成为一门高深的艺术。

There are interesting parallels with the study of deviance.

这和变异研究有很多有趣的相似之处。

parallel ['pærəlel] *n.* 相似(之处)

释 something that is very similar to something else, or a similarity between two things

用 in parallel

例 I'm trying to see if there are any obvious parallels between the two cases. 我试着寻找两个案件中是否有明显的相似之处。

---

deviance ['diːvɪəns] *n.* 异常，偏差

释 a state or condition markedly different from the norm

拓 *a.* / *n.* deviant

例 Social deviance will cause serious results. 社会异常会造成严重后果。

And a casual experiment conducted by a bacteriologist may hold the key.

一位细菌学家不经意做的一个试验可能抓住了关键。

bacteriologist [bækˌtɪərɪə'ɒlədʒɪst] *n.* 细菌学家

释 a biologist who studies bacteria and other very small living things, especially those which cause disease

拓 *n.* bacteriology; *a.* bacteriological

例 Louis Pasteur, French chemist and bacteriologist, was born at Dole. 法国化学家、细菌学家路易斯·巴斯德生于多尔。

The invention of the container crane made it possible to load and unload containers without capsizing the ship.

该集装箱起重机的发明使人们在装卸集装箱时不倾覆船。

capsize [kæp'saɪz] *vt. & vi.* 弄翻，倾覆

释 to cause a boat or ship to turn upside down accidentally while on water

例 The boat capsized in heavy seas. 船在大海中倾覆了。

A rocket motor's pullers are minute, high-speed particles produced by burning propellants in a suitable chamber.

火箭发动机的动力是火箭推进系统在瞬间产生的高速微粒。

particle ['pɑːtɪkl] *n.* 粒子

释 a very small piece of something

例 Electrons and protons are atomic particles. 电子和质子是原子粒子。

---

propellant [prə'pelənt] *n.* 推进物，推进燃料

释 an explosive for firing a bullet

拓 *vt.* propel; *n.* propeller

例 There is a mass of solid propellant. 这儿有大量的固体推进剂。

These provide more ultraviolet and blue green light than ordinary fluorescent and tungsten lights.

这些比普通日光灯及钨灯发出更多的紫外线和蓝绿光。

ultraviolet [ˌʌltrə'vaɪəlɪt] *a.* 紫外线的

释 ultraviolet light cannot be seen by people, but is responsible for making your skin darker when you are in the sun

例 They use ultraviolet lamp to kill pests. 他们用紫外线灯杀害虫。

---

fluorescent [fluːə'resənt] *a.* 荧光的；*n.* 日光灯

释 very bright and easy to see, even in the dark; a light contains a tube filled with gas, which shines with a bright light

拓 *n.* fluorescence

例 He bought me a fluorescent pink T-shirt as a birthday gift.

他给我买了一件粉色荧光T恤衫作为生日礼物。

---

tungsten ['tʌŋstən] *n.* 钨

释 It's a hard metal that is used to make steel and in the thin wires in eletric light bulbs.

例 The wire inside an electric lamp is not made of copper. It is made of tungsten. 电灯里面的细丝不是铜丝而是钨丝。

An underground dweller himself, Carpenter has never paid a heating bill, thanks to solar panels and natural insulation.

卡彭特住在地下室，由于有太阳能电池板和自然的隔热性，他从来不用支付取暖费用。

heating ['hiːtɪŋ] *n.* 加热，供暖，暖气装置

释 the process of supplying heat to a room or building; a system used to do this

例 The heating system in this block doesn't work well. 本区的供暖系统不是很好。

---

solar panel ['səʊlə'pænəl] *n.* 太阳能电池板

释 electrical device consisting of a large array of connected solar cells.

例 There are signs that a solar panel appears unable to pivot easily. 有迹象表明一块太阳能电池板的转轴出现问题。

The invention of rockets is linked inextricably with the invention of "black powder".

火箭的发明与“黑火药”的问世密不可分。

invention [ɪn'venʃən] *n.* 发明

释 the act of inventing something

拓 *n.* inventiveness; *a.* inventive; *ad.* inventively

例 Necessity is the mother of invention. 需要是发明之母。

---

inextricably [ɪn'ekstrɪkəbəli] *ad.* 分不开地

释 in an inextricable manner

拓 *a.* inextricable

例 From ten feet apart they were locked into one another, solidly, intimately, and inextricably. 他们的目光穿越十英尺的距离紧紧拴在一起，那么牢固、亲密、难解难分。

Through new legislation, we have improved enforcement and innovative technology.

通过新立法，我们提高了执行能力，并增强了科技创新能力。

legislation [ˌledʒɪs'leɪʃən] *n.* 立法，法律，法规

释 a law or set of laws

拓 *vt. & vi.* legislate; *a.*legislative

用 legislation on; legislation to do sth.; introduce / bring in legislation

例 The government will introduce legislation to restrict the sale of drugs. 政府将制定法规限制毒品的出售。

---

enforcement [ɪn'fɔːsmənt] *n.* 执行，强制

释 when people are made to obey a rule, law, etc.

拓 *vt.* enforce; *a.* enforceable; *n.* enforceability

例 The police are responsible for the enforcement of the law. 警察负责执法。

innovative ['ɪnəʊveɪtɪv] *a.* 革新的，创新的

释 introducing or using new ideas, ways of doing something

拓 *vt.* & *vi.* innovate; *n.* innovation

例 Applied linguistic is an innovative approach to language teaching. 应用语言学是一种新型语言教学法。

Some observations are held to be relevant and some irrelevant, so that one methodology is chosen and others discarded.

有些观察相关，有些不相关，因此选择了一种方法，而丢弃了其他的。

observation [ˌɒbzə'veɪʃən] *n.* 观察

释 the process of watching something or someone carefully for a period of time

拓 *a.* observable; *ad.* observably

用 observation on; observation about; observation of

例 Bloomfield's approach to linguistics was based on observation of the language.布龙菲尔德的语言学研究方法以对语言的观察为基础。

---

methodology [ˌmeθə'dɒlədʒi] *n.* 方法学，方法论

释 the set of methods and principles that you use when studying a particular subject or doing a particular kind of work

拓 *a.* methodological; *ad.* methodologically

用 methodology for (doing) sth.

例 We've been developing a new methodology for assessing new computer. 我们一直在开发新的方法来评估新电脑。

---

discard [dɪs'kɑːd] *vt.* 丢弃，扔掉

释 to get rid of something

例 Such die-hards will be discarded by history. 这种顽固分子会被历史抛弃。

Researchers have proposed several explanations for why interruption of glucose processing.

研究者就为何终止葡萄糖处理实验给出了几种解释。

propose [prə'pəʊz] *vt. & vi.* 提议

释 to suggest something as a plan or course of action

拓 *n.* proposal; *a.* proposed

用 propose that; propose doing sth.; propose to do sth.

例 Let me propose a toast to your health. 我提议为你的健康干杯！

---

glucose ['gluːkəʊs] *n.* 葡萄糖

释 a monosaccharide sugar that has several forms; an important source of physiological energy

例 I gave him an extra dose of glucose to pep him up. 我给他多注射了一剂葡萄糖以增强他的活力。

The images come to constitute a closed self-perpetuating system of illusions.

那些图像可以组成各种幻象的封闭的无限系统。

perpetuate [pə'petʃueɪt] *vt.* 使永存，使不朽

释 to cause to continue or prevail

拓 *n.* perpetuation; *a.* perpetual

例 They decided to perpetuate the memory of their leader by erecting a statue. 他们决定建一座雕像，永远纪念他们的领袖。

---

illusion [ɪ'luːʒən] *n.* 幻觉，错觉；错误的信仰（或观念）

释 an idea or opinion that is wrong, especially about yourself

拓 *a.* illusional

用 illusion of; illusion that

例 I thought I saw a ghost but it was just an illusion. 我以为我看见鬼了，其实只是一种幻觉。

The secret of the versatility of glass lies in its interior structure.

玻璃的多功能性在于它的内部结构。

interior [ɪnˈtɪərɪə] *a.* **内部的**

释 the inside part of something

用 interior of

例 The interior of the building is luxurious and magnificent. 大楼内部装饰得富丽堂皇。

A series of acquisitions might represent decade's fieldwork documenting technique.

一系列的收获也许能展现十年来的田野调查文件制作技巧。

acquisition [ˌækwɪˈzɪʃən] *n.* **获得，所获之物**

释 the act of contracting or assuming or acquiring possession of something

拓 *vt.* acquire; *n.* acquirer; *a.* acquisitive

例 He is a valuable acquisition to our firm. 他是我们公司新来的得力雇员。

---

document [ˈdɒkjumənt] *n.* **文件，文档；** *vt.* **记载，用文件等证明**

释 a piece of paper that provides information (especially information of an official nature); to record the details of sth.

拓 *n.* documentation; *a.* documentary

例 This document carries the royal seal on the back. 这份文件背后盖有王室印章。

The prime objective of the benchmark process was to compare a range of service delivery processes.

基准测试程序的首要目标是对比一系列递送服务的过程。

benchmark ['bentʃmɑːk] *n.* 基准；衡量标准；标杆

释 something that is used as a standard by which other things can be judged or measured

用 benchmark for

例 The benchmark in rational decision-making is needed in an emerging economy. 新兴经济中理智决策的标准是必需的。

---

delivery [dɪ'lɪvəri] *n.* 递送；交付

释 the act of bringing goods, letters etc. to a particular person or place, or the things that are brought

拓 *vt.* deliver

用 delivery of; on delivery (when sth. is delivered)

例 He guarantees prompt delivery of goods. 他保证立即交货。

It's system of signs that enables us to categorize phenomena that are essentially ambiguous.

这是一个使我们能够对非常模糊的现象进行分类的符号系统。

categorize ['kætəgəraɪz] *vt.* 分类

释 to put people or things into groups according to the type of people or things they are

拓 *n.* categorization / category

用 categorize sth. / sb. as sth.

例 We categorize information and retain just enough to be useful in any area. 我们对信息进行分类，仅在任一领域中留下够用的信息。

essentially [ɪ'senʃəli] *ad.* 本质上，本来

释 used when stating the most basic facts about something = basically

拓 *n.* / *a.* essential

用 essential for / to; it is essential (that); it is essential to do sth.

例 Smoking rates have remained essentially unchanged. 吸烟率基本保持不变。

This involved adding chemicals, such as caustic soda or other alkalis, soaps and detergents, water-hardening agents and bleaching agents.

这包括一些化学添加剂，如苛性钠，或者其他像肥皂、清洁剂、水淬剂和漂白剂之类的碱金属。

caustic ['kɔːstɪk] *a.* 腐蚀性的；刻薄的

释 a caustic substance can burn through things by chemical action; marked by incisive sarcasm

拓 *ad.* caustically

用 caustic comments / remark

例 The caustic verbal attack within the story is very funny. 故事中讽刺刻薄的言语攻击非常有趣。

---

alkali ['ælkəlaɪ] *n.* 碱金属

释 a substance that forms a chemical salt when combined with an acid

例 This kind of soil contains much alkali. 这种土壤含丰富的碱金属。

---

detergent [dɪ'tɜːdʒənt] *n.* 清洁剂

释 a liquid or powder used for washing clothes, dishes, etc.

例 I've tried this new detergent with excellent results.我试用了这种新型清洁剂，效果特好。

bleach [bliːtʃ] *n.* 漂白剂；*vt. & vi.* 变白，漂白

释 a chemical used to make things pale or white, or to kill germs; to make whiter or lighter

例 Her yellow dress was bleached white by the sun. 她的黄裙子被太阳晒得褪成了白色。

---

agent [ˈeɪdʒənt] *n.* [化]剂

释 a chemical that has a particular effect or is used for a particular purpose

例 What he really needs now is a powerful cleaning agent. 他现在真正需要的是强力清洗剂。

The centrifugal force of a rotating object decreases when it slows down.

旋转物体的离心力在减速时降低。

centrifugal [ˌsenˈtrɪfjuːgəl] *a.* 离心的

释 tending to move away from a center

例 The civil war reinforced the centrifugal tendencies within the economy. 内战加剧了经济领域离心倾向。

Glass ceramics served as the nose cones of missiles.

导弹的前部通常由玻璃陶瓷制成。

ceramics [sɪˈræmɪks] *n.* 陶瓷

释 a pot or other object made of clay that has been made permanently hard by heat

例 Generally speaking, ceramics products can be classified into two categories: practical and artistic. 一般来说，陶瓷产品可以分为两类，即实用品和艺术品。

missile ['mɪsaɪl] *n.* 导弹

释 a weapon that is sent through the air and that exploded when it hits the thing that it is aimed at

例 The huge ship was sunk by a homing missile. 这只巨大的军舰被一枚自动寻航的导弹击中。

Sixteen American states now use fingerprint verification systems.

美国目前有16个州在使用指纹识别系统。

verification [ˌverɪfɪ'keɪʃən] *n.* 确认，查证

释 the act of checking something that is true or accurate

拓 *vt.* verify; *a.* verifiable

例 Verification of the product can be carried out in the process in order to identify variation. 产品的验证可在运行过程中进行，以便识别变异。

A large background is benevolent and useful to society — the pursuit of scientific truth.

追求科学真理的大前提是我们的试验方法是仁慈的，并且要对社会有益。

benevolent [bɪ'nevələnt] *a.* 仁慈的，乐善好施的

释 kind, helpful and generous

拓 *ad.* benevolently; *n.* benevolence

例 The old woman had a benevolent feeling towards all cats. 那个老太太对所有的猫都怀有仁慈之心。

---

pursuit [pə'sju:t] *n.* 追求，追赶

释 the act of looking for or trying to find something

拓 *vt.* pursue

用 pursuit of; in (the) pursuit of sth.

例 The pursuit of liberty and happiness is our basic right. 对自由和幸福的追求是我们的基本权利。

The robots are churning out the latest edition every morning.

该机器人每天早晨大量炮制最新的版本。

churn out 大量炮制，粗制滥造

释 to produce large amounts of something quickly, usually something of low quality

例 Some pulp writers churn out two or three short stories a day.
有些低俗的作家一天可以炮制出两三篇短篇小说。

Carelessness of our system of numeration leads to the conviction.

我们计数系统的疏忽导致了判罪。

numeration [ˌnjuːməˈreɪʃən] *n.* **计数，计算**

释 a system of counting or the process of counting

例 There are radical differences between binary and decimal numeration. 二进位和十进位计算有着本质的区别。

---

conviction [kənˈvɪkʃən] *n.* **定罪；坚信**

释 the state of being found or proved guilty; a very strong belief or opinion

拓 *vt. /n. / a.* convict

用 deep / strong conviction; conviction that; conviction for

例 As it was her first conviction for stealing, she was given a less severe sentence. 考虑到她是第一次偷盗，所以对她从轻处罚。

Popper said that the scientific method was hypothetic-deductive.

波普尔认为科学的方法是运用假定推论。

hypothetic [ˌhaɪpəʊˈθetɪk] *a.* 假设的，假定的

释 based on situations or ideas which are possible and imagined rather than real and true

派 *n.* hypothesis; *vt.* & *vi.* hypothesize; *a.* hypothetical

例 A hypothetic reason is the first step to truth. 假设的推理是迈向真理的第一步。

---

deductive [dɪˈdʌktɪv] *a.* 推论的，演绎的

释 using knowledge about things that are generally true in order to think about and understand particular situations or problems

派 *vt.* deduce; *n.* deduction

例 Deductive reasoning is a good method in study. 演绎推理是学习的一个好方法。

Through combustion and gasification techniques which are now at pilot and demonstration stages, we could finish the task.

燃烧和气化技术目前尚处于试验和示范阶段，通过利用它们，我们能够完成这一任务。

combustion [kəmˈbʌstʃən] *n.* 燃烧；氧化

释 the process of burning; chemical activity which uses oxygen to produce light and heat

派 *a.* combustible

例 The combustion in the jungle generated great damage. 丛林火灾造成了巨大的损失。

demonstration [ˌdemənˈstreɪʃən] *n.* 论证；示范，实证

释 the act of showing or making evident; an act of explaining and showing how to do something or how something works

拓 *vt.* & *vi.* demonstrate; *a.* demonstrative; *n.* demonstrator

用 demonstration of

例 His new book is a demonstration of his patriotism. 他的新书是他的爱国精神的证明。

If required, the reel can be loaded directly onto the press.

如果需要的话，卷筒可以直接压在印刷机上面。

directly [dɪˈrektli] *ad.* 直接地；正好

释 in a direct line or manner; exactly in a particular position

拓 *a.* direct

用 directly to / from; directly in front of / behind / under

例 The girl was sitting directly opposite Tom. 女孩就坐在汤姆的正对面。

You can download your results to disk, but bring your own formatted floppy disk or CD-ROM.

你可以把下载的资料放在磁盘里面，但是请带上自己的格式化磁盘或者只读存储光盘。

format [ˈfɔːmæt] *vt.* 使格式化，设计；安排；*n.* 版试，设计

释 to divide a disk into marked sectors so that it may store data; to arrange text in a particular way on a page or a screen; the general arrangement, plan, design, etc.

例 The disk must be formatted for the computer being used. 磁盘必须格式化后才能在计算机上使用。

Puffs of compressed air then shape the glass.

接下来，压缩空气的喷压力使玻璃成型。

compress [kəm'pres] *vt.* 压缩，压榨

释 to press something or make it smaller so that it takes up less space, or to become smaller

拓 *n.* compression; *a.* compressible

用 compress sth. into sth.

例 Snow falling on the sideway is compressed into ice. 降落在人行道上的雪被压成了冰。

And the pulses would travel over glass fibers, not copper wire.

脉冲是通过玻璃纤维传播而不是通过铜线传播的。

pulse [pʌls] *n.* 脉冲，脉波，脉搏；有节奏的跳动

释 the regular beat that can be felt, for example at your wrist, as your heart pumps blood around your body; a strong regular beat in music

例 Her breathing was shallow and her pulse was weak. 她的呼吸缓慢并且脉搏微弱。

---

fiber ['faɪbə] *n.* 纤维

释 the parts of plants that you eat but cannot digest

例 Nylon is a man-made fiber. 尼龙是人造纤维。

---

copper ['kɒpə] *n.* 铜

释 a soft reddish-brown metal that allows electricity and heat to pass through it easily, and is used to make electrical wires, water pipes etc.

例 These commodities include oil, soybeans and metals like copper. 这些商品包括石油、大豆和金属，比如铜。

The reflective surface of aluminum can easily be decorated.

铝的反射面很容易被装饰。

reflective [rɪ'flektɪv] *a.* 反射的；反映的

释 a reflective surface reflects light; showing that something is true about a situation

拓 *vt.* & *vi.* reflect; *n.* reflection

例 TV is reflective of all social problems. 电视是反映社会各方面问题的一个媒介。

---

aluminum [ə'ljuːmɪnəm] *n.* 铝

释 a light metallic element which is silver in color and used especially for making cooking equipment and aircraft parts

例 These cooking utensils are made of aluminum. 这些炊具是铝制的。

---

decorate ['dekəreɪt] *vt.* 装饰；装修

释 to paint the inside of a room, put special, paper on the walls etc.; to make something look more attractive by putting something pretty on it

拓 *n.* decoration; *a.* decorative

用 decorate sth. with sth.; decorate sb. for sth.

例 They plan to spend the weekend decorating. 他们准备周末装修房子。

Turning the thermostat control and the steam button to maximum, hold the iron in a vertical position close to the fabric.

打开恒温控制器，把蒸气阀开到最大，把熨斗放到与织物垂直水平处。

thermostat ['θɜːməˌstæt] *n.* 恒温器

释 an instrument used for keeping a room or a machine at a particular temperature

例 Again Joey went to the thermostat, and again it showed no change.
乔伊再次去查看恒温器，而同样没有任何变化。

---

vertical ['vɜːtɪkəl] *a.* 垂直的；正上方的

释 going straight up or down from a level surface or from top to bottom in a picture, etc.; having a structure in which there are top, middle, and bottom levels

拓 *ad.* vertically

例 The cliff was almost vertical. 那悬崖几乎是笔直的。

The color of metallic gold when it is dispersed very finely in water.

当它在水中充分溶解之后，颜色是金色。

metallic [mɪ'tælɪk] *a.* 金属的

释 like metal in color, appearance, or taste

拓 *n.* / *vt.* metal

例 He bought a metallic blue jacket. 他买了一件金属蓝色的夹克。

---

disperse [dɪs'pɜːs] *vt. & vi.* (使)分散；散布；驱散

释 to drive off or scatter in different directions

例 The strong wind dispersed the cloud from the sky. 大风吹散了天上的云。

Distance therefore poses no obstacle to the globalization of the disk-drive industry.

因此距离不再阻碍磁盘驱动器的全球化过程。

pose [pəuz] *vt. & vi.* 造成，形成，引起；假装

释 to exist in a way that may cause a problem, danger, difficulty; to pretend to be

用 pose for somebody / something

例 Pollution poses a threat to the continued existence of this animals. 污染对这种动物的继续生存造成了威胁。

---

obstacle [ˈɒbstəkl] *n.* 障碍

释 something that makes it difficult to achieve something

用 obstacle to

例 Racial discrimination still has to overcome many obstacles to gain equality. 要想摆脱种族歧视获得平等，必须要克服很多的障碍。

---

globalization [ˌgləʊbəlaɪˈzeɪʃən] *n.* 全球化

释 the process of making something such as a business operate in a lot of different countries all around the world, or the result of this

例 This is the age of economic globalization. 这是经济全球化的时代。

Could such a "caloric restriction mimetic" enable people to stay healthy longer, postponing age-related disorders such as diabetes, arteriosclerosis, heart disease and cancer?

这样的“卡路里限制模拟实验”可以让人们保持长久的健康，延缓与年龄有关的疾病，如糖尿病、动脉硬化、心脏病和癌症吗?

postpone [ˌpəustˈpəʊn] *vt.* 推迟，延期

释 to change the date or time of a planned event or action to a later one

拓 *n.* postponement

用 postpone doing something

例 The opening party was postponed until 9 o'clock. 开业宴请晚会推迟到9点举行。

---

disorder [dɪsˈɔːdə] *n.* 不适，疾病

释 a mental or physical illness which prevents part of your body from working properly

用 a disorder of the liver / brain / digestive system, a mental / psychiatric disorder, in disorder

例 He is suffering from severe mental disorder. 他患有严重的精神病。

---

diabetes [ˌdaɪəˈbiːtɪz] *n.* 糖尿病

释 a medical condition, caused by a lack of insulin, which makes the patient produce a lot of urine and feel very thirsty

例 Now a large study has linked it to diabetes and heart disease.
现在一个大型研究将其与糖尿病、心脏病联系起来。

---

arteriosclerosis [ɑːˈtɪərɪəʊskɪəˈrəʊsɪs] *n.* 动脉硬化

释 a disease in which your arteries become hard, which makes it difficult for the blood to flow rehabilitate

例 Arteriosclerosis affects an increasingly broad segment of the older population. 患动脉硬化的老年人越来越多。

They found that minute crystals of nickel sulphide trapped inside the glass had almost certainly caused the failure.

他们发现放在玻璃内的晶体镍硫化物几乎已经不存在了。

sulphide [ˈsʌlfɪd] *n.* 硫化物

释 a mixture of sulphur with another substance

例 In chemistry class, the teacher introduced the chemical components of sulphide. 老师在化学课上介绍了硫化物的化学成分。

---

trap [træp] *vt. & vi.* 使受限制；设圈套

释 to prevent something such as water, dirt, heat etc. from escaping or spreading; to catch in

用 be / feel trapped in; trap somebody into (doing) something

例 Ten miners were trapped underground. 10个矿工被困在地下。

This button activates a jet of cold water which allows you to iron out any unintentional creases.

此按钮激活了冷水喷射，可以让你烫平任何无意间产生的褶皱。

unintentional [ˌʌnɪnˈtenʃənəl] *a.* 非故意的，无心的

释 not done or made or performed with purpose or intent

拓 *ad.* unintentionally

例 It's an unintentional mistake. 这是一个无心之错。

---

crease [kriːs] *n.* 褶痕，皱痕

释 a line on a piece of cloth, paper, etc. where it has been folded, crushed, or pressed

例 I found my new dress full of crease. 我发现我的新连衣裙全皱了。

This looseness in molecular structure gives the material what engineers call tremendous "formability" which allows technicians to tailor glass to whatever need.

这种分子结构松散的特性使材料具有工程师们所说的巨大的"成形性能"，它使技术人员可以随意地裁制玻璃。

looseness [ˈluːsnɪs] *n.* 松弛；散漫

释 not firmly fastened in place; freedom from restraint

拓 *ad.* loosely; *vt.* & *vi.* loosen

例 Such looseness throws discredit on the whole work. 这样松懈使整体工作受到怀疑。

---

molecular [məˈlekjələ] *a.* 分子的

释 relating to or consisting of molecules

拓 *n.* molecule

例 Molecular biology is the compulsory course for postgraduates.

分子生物学是研究生的必修课。

---

tremendous [trɪˈmendəs] *a.* 巨大的，惊人的

释 very big, fast, powerful

拓 *ad.* tremendously

例 We got a tremendous surprise when he arrived. 他的到来使我们大吃一惊。

New developments now allow snapshots of all sorts of reasoning and problem-solving activities.

新的发展进程允许了解各种推理论证和解决问题的实际活动。

snapshot [ˈsnæpʃɒt] *n.* 快照；简要了解

释 a photograph is taken quickly and often not very skillfully; a brief summary

例 The text book gives us a snapshot of the UK culture. 本书向我们展示了英国文化的面面观。

Thanks to technological advances such as lightweight components, manufactured goods themselves have tended to become lighter.

由于技术的进步，比如轻型零件的产生，使得生产出来的商品越来越轻便。

component [kəmˈpəʊnənt] *n.* 元件，组件，成分

释 one of several parts that together make up a whole machine, systcm , etc.

用 component of

例 The factory supplies components for cars. 这家工厂为汽车提供零部件。

tend [tend] *vt.& vi.* 倾向，易于；照料

释 to be likely to behave in a particular way or have a particular characteristic; to care for

用 tend to do sth.; tend to sb. / sth.; tend upwards / downwards

例 People tend to need less sleep as they get older. 人们岁数大了往往就不需要那么多睡眠了。

Japan's largest maker of cash dispensers is developing new machine that incorporate iris scanners.

日本最大的自动售货机制造商正在研制带有虹膜扫描仪的新机型。

dispenser [dɪ'spensə] *n.* 自动售货机

释 a machine which provides particular amount of a product or substance when you press a button or put money into it

例 After buying a cup of coffee from the dispenser, I came back to gaze over the lovely campus. 从自动售货处买了一杯咖啡后，我返回去欣赏这可爱的校园景色。

---

incorporate [ɪn'kɔːpəreɪt] *vt. & vi.* 包含；合并

释 to include something as part of a group, system, plan, etc.

拓 incorporate sth. into / in / within sth.

例 We've incorporated many environmentally-friendly features into the design of the building. 我们在大楼的设计上融入了许多环保的特性。

---

iris ['aɪrɪs] *n.* 虹膜；彩虹女神；蝴蝶花

释 the round colored paint that surrounds the pupils of your eyes; a rainbow on a rainbowlike appearance; a type of plant with sword-shaped leaves and showy flowers

With lights flashing and warning horns honking, the robots give them their correct name, the laser guided vehicles.

机器人根据灯光闪烁和警笛鸣响给出了他们正确的名字——激光向导车。

honk [hɔːŋk] *n.* 汽车喇叭声；雁叫声；*vt.* 鸣(汽车喇叭)

释 the harsh sound of a car horn; the cry of a wild goose; to cause a car horn to make such a sound

例 Several drivers honked their horns. 几位司机按响了喇叭。

---

laser ['leɪzə] *n.* 激光器，激光

释 a piece of equipment that produces a powerful narrow beam of light that can be used in medical operations, to cut metals, or to make patterns of light for entertainment

例 My boss asked me to buy a laser printer. 老板让我买一台激光打印机。

This is a challenge, keeping twenty boisterous pupils in the class.

在一个班里看管20个闹哄哄的孩子是一种挑战。

boisterous ['bɔɪstərəs] *a.* 喧闹的，欢闹的

释 noisy and full of life and energy

拓 *ad.* boisterously

例 Their class was loud and boisterous. 他们班非常吵闹。

The cars of a roller coaster reach their maximum kinetic energy when at the bottom of their path.

当过山车到达铁轨底部的时候，是最具冲击力的。

kinetic [kɪ'netɪk] *a.* 运动的；动力的

释 relating to the motion of material bodies and the forces associated there with

例 Kinetic energy is the energy arising from motion. 动能是物体运动得到的能量。

---

bottom ['bɒtəm] *n.* 底部，下端

释 the lowest part of something

用 at the bottom of sth.

例 Extra information will be found at the bottom of the screen. 额外的信息在屏幕下方可以找到。

If a pamphlet is on microfilm, its microfilm number is noted on the library's catalogue.

假如小册子被制成微缩胶卷，微缩编码就会被记录在图书馆的目录中。

catalogue ['kætəlɒg] *n.* 目录，总目

释 a complete list of things that you can look at, buy, or use, for example in a library or at an art show

例 The catalogue is under revision. 目录正在修订之中。

Radioactive decay is the process in which an unstable atomic nucleus loses energy by emitting radiation in the form of particles.

放射衰变是不稳定的原子核通过放射粒子射线失去能量的过程。

radioactive [ˌreɪdɪəʊ'æktɪv] *a.* 放射性的

释 containing or producing radioaction

拓 *n.* radioactivity

例 The radioactive material is stored in a special radiation-proof container. 放射性材料被存储在防辐射的特殊容器内。

atomic nucleus [əˌtɒmɪkˈnjuːklɪəs] *n.* 原子核

---

emit [ɪˈmɪt] *vt.* 放射

释 to give off

拓 *n.* emission

例 The cheese was emitting a strong smell. 奶酪散发出强烈的气味。

---

radiation [ˌreɪdɪˈeɪʃən] *n.* 辐射

释 a form of energy that comes from a nuclear reaction and that can be very dangerous to health

例 An accident happened at the power station, resulting in large amounts of radiation being released. 电厂发生故障，导致大量辐射泄漏。

These were scanned under a modified microfiche reader for signs of nickel sulphide crystals.

为了找到硫化镍晶体的踪迹，这些被放在改良的微缩胶片阅读器下扫描。

modify [ˈmɒdɪfaɪ] *vt.* 改变，改善

释 to change something such as a plan, opinion, law or way of behaviour slightly, usually to improve it or make it more acceptable

拓 *n.* modification / modifier

例 Instead of simply punishing them, the teacher encourages students to modify their behavior. 老师鼓励学生改善自己的行为，以此来代替简单的惩罚。

---

microfiche [ˈmaɪkrəʊfiːʃ] *n.* 微缩胶片

释 a small rectangular sheet of film on which information is photographed in a reduced size

But the database does allow lexicographers to search for a word and find out how frequently it is used—something that could only be guessed at intuitively before.

但是数据库帮助辞典编纂者搜索一个词并且知道它所使用的频率，而这些在过去只能凭借我们的直觉去猜测。

frequently ['friːkwəntli] *ad.* 经常地，频繁地

释 many times at short intervals

拓 *a.* frequent; *n.* frequency

例 His speech was frequently interrupted by applause. 他的演说不时被掌声打断。

---

intuitively [ˌɪntju(ː)ɪtɪvli] *ad.* 直觉地，直观地

释 in an intuitive manner

拓 *n.* intuition

例 She seemed to know intuitively how to do it. 她似乎凭直觉就知道如何去做。

The "altitude tent" is developed by AIS to replicate the effect of altitude training at sea level.

AIS发明的海拔帐篷是为了模仿和感受在海平面上接受海拔训练的影响。

altitude ['æltɪtjuːd] *n.* 高度，海拔

释 height above sea level

拓 at an altitude of

例 The plane flew at an altitude of 20, 000 feet. 飞机在两万英尺的高度飞行。

---

replicate ['replɪkeɪt] *vt.* 复制；模写

释 to make or do something again in exactly the same way

拓 *n.* replication

例 There is a need for further research to replicate these findings.

为了更深入的研究，复制这些发现物是有必要的。

To increase the arrow's stability is to move the centre of gravity.

要增加箭的稳定性只要通过移动其重心即可。

stability [stəˈbɪlɪti] *n.* 稳定性

释 the quality of being stable

拓 *vt.* & *vi.* stabilize; *n.* stabilizer

例 Political stability is essential to economic prosperity. 政治稳定对经济繁荣是必要的。

---

gravity [ˈgrævɪti] *n.* 地心引力，重力

释 the force which attracts objects towards one another, especially the force that makes things fall to the ground

拓 *a.* gravitational

例 The stone rolled down the hill by gravity. 石头在重力作用下向山下滚去。

It was moved to and fro by steam blowing out from small exhaust ports at either end.

蒸汽从两端的小排气口喷出，使其来回移动。

to and fro *ad.* 来来回回地

释 backwards and forwards

例 Trucks and cars were shuttling to and fro on the expressways.

高速公路上卡车和汽车正来回穿梭。

---

steam [stiːm] *n.* 蒸汽

释 the hot gas that is produced when water boils

拓 *a.* steamy; steaming; *n.* steamer

例 Who invented the steam engine? 谁发明了蒸汽机?

---

exhaust [ɪg'zɔːst] *n.* 排气；排气装置；出口；*vt. & vi.* 使……精疲力尽

释 device through which waste gases come out; to make someone extremely tired

拓 *a.* exhausted; exhausting; exhaustive; *n.* exhaustion; *ad.* exhaustively

例 My father is completely exhausted. 我父亲精疲力竭了。

Before the eyes of the stunned, thrilled audience, photographs came to and moved across a flat screen.

图像快速穿过了平面屏，观众既震惊又激动。

stun [stʌn] *vt.* 使……震惊

释 to surprise or shock somebody so much that they cannot think clearly or speak

例 The listener sat in stunned silence in a most horrible state. 听者鸦雀无声处在极度恐怖的状态。

---

thrilled [θrɪld] *a.* 极为激动的

释 very excited, and pleased

拓 *n. / vt. & vi.* thrill

用 be thrilled to see / hear / learn sth.; thrilled(that…); thrilled about

例 I was thrilled to hear your wonderful news. 听到你的好消息我非常兴奋。

The vision is objectified or captured through photographs, postcards, films and so on.

这些景象通过照片、明信片和胶片等形式被捕捉到并呈现出来。

objectify [əb'dʒektɪfaɪ] *vt.* 使客观化；使具体化（体现）

释 to make external or objective, or give reality to; to make impersonal or present as an object

例 Experiments in chemicals objectify the principles. 化学实验使这些原理具体化。

六 太空探索与研究类

It will take longer to accomplish than the lunar missions.

这将花费比登月任务更长的时间才能完成。

accomplish [ə'kɒmplɪʃ] *vt.* 完成

释 to finish something successfully

拓 *n.* accomplishment; *a.* accomplished

例 The first part of the plan has been safely accomplished. 计划的第一部分已安全完成。

---

lunar ['luːnə] *a.* 月亮的

释 connected with the moon

例 The astronauts piloted their craft down to the lunar surface. 宇航员驾驶宇宙飞船在月球表面降落。

He set himself the astonishing task of "reviewing the heavens", in other words, pointing his telescope to every accessible part of the sky and recording what he saw.

他给自己安排了一项惊人的任务——观测天空，换句话说，他把望远镜对准所有天空中可以看到的部分，并且记录下所观测的东西。

telescope ['telɪskəʊp] *n.* 望远镜

释 a piece of equipment shaped like a tube, used for making distant objects look larger and closer

例 Details on the moon's surface can only be seen through a telescope. 月球表面的详细情况只有通过望远镜才能看见。

The concept of rocket, or rather the mechanism behind the idea of propelling an object into the air, has been around for well over two thousand years.

火箭的概念，甚至是把机械装置类的物体发射到空中的这种观念，已经存在2000多年了。

mechanism ['mekənɪzəm] *n.* 机械装置；机构，机制

释 a way of doing something which is planned or part of a system

拓 *n.* mechanic; *a.* mechanical; *ad.* mechanically; *vt.* & *vi.* mechanize

例 The cellphone has a delicate mechanism. 这个手机的装配很精致。

---

propel [prə'pel] *vt.* 推进；驱使

释 to push or move something somewhere, often with a lot of force; to force somebody to move in a particular direction or to get into a particular situation

拓 *n.* propeller, propulsion

例 His addiction to hemp propelled him towards a life of crime.
他的毒瘾使他走上了犯罪的道路。

Its diameter compares unfavorably with that of Jupiter and Saturn.

它的直径没有木星和土星的直径长。

diameter [daɪˈæmɪtə] *n.* 直径

释 a straight line from one side of a circle to the other side, passing through the centre of the circle, or the length of this line

例 The diameter of the circle is about 20 cms. 这个圆圈的直径大约是20厘米。

---

unfavorably [ˌʌnˈfeɪvərəbli] *ad.* 不利地，相反地，反对地

释 unfavorable conditions, situations, etc. are not good; if someone's reaction or attitude to something is unfavourable, they do not like it

拓 *a.* unfavorable

例 Careless spelling mistakes in a letter can impress someone unfavorably. 书信中粗心的拼写错误会给人留下不好的印象。

Comets are only normally visible in the immediate vicinity of the sun.

一般情况下，彗星只有在靠近太阳时才能被看见。

vicinity [vɪˈsɪnɪti] *n.* 邻近，附近

释 in the area around a particular place; close to a particular amount or measurement

用 in the vicinity of sth.

例 There is no senior school in the vicinity. 这附近没有高中。

This point is the opposite part of the Earth's orbit.

这点是与地球轨道相反的部分。

opposite [ˈɒpəzɪt] *a.* 相对的，相反的，对面的

释 completely different

拓 *vt.* & *vi.* oppose; *a.* opposed; *n.* opposition

用 be opposite to

例 They have opposite views on the question. 在这个问题上他们持相反的观点。

---

orbit [ˈɔːbɪt] *n.* 轨道，常轨

释 the curved path through which objects in space move around a planet or star

拓 *a.* orbital

例 How many spacecrafts are orbiting the moon? 有多少航天器绕月球轨道飞行？

Not only did it solve a problem that had intrigued man for ages, but, more importantly, it literally opened the door to exploration of the universe.

它不但解决了困惑人们已久的问题，更加重要的是它真正打开了探索宇宙奥秘的大门。

intrigue [ɪnˈtriːg] *vt.* & *vi.* 激起……的兴趣

释 to make somebody very interested and want to know more about something

拓 *a.* intriguing; *ad.* intriguingly

用 intrigued by / with; intrigued to know

例 Some of the members had been intriguing to get the secretary dismissed. 有些人一直密谋想让老板把秘书辞掉。

---

literally [ˈlɪtərəli] *ad.* 逐字地；按照字面上地；真正地

释 according to the most basic or original meaning of a word or expression; used to emphasize the truth of sth. that may seem surprising

拓 *a.* literal

例 Idioms usually cannot be translated literally into another language.
成语一般不能照字面译成另一种语言。

---

exploration [ˌekspləˈreɪʃən] *n.* 探险；测勘，探测

释 the act of travelling through a place in order to find out about it or find something such as oil or gold in it

拓 *vt. & vi.* explore; *n.* explorer; *a.* exploratory

用 exploration into; exploration of

例 The exploration for new sources of energy is vital for the future. 发掘新能源对未来至关重要。

---

universe [ˈjuːnɪvɜːs] *n.* 宇宙

释 the whole of space and everything in it, including the earth, the planets and the stars

用 in the universe

例 The Earth is only one of the numerous planets in the universe.
地球只是宇宙中众多星球中的一个。

The reviewer of the heavens had stumbled across an unprecedented prize.
天象观察员意外得了一个前所未有的大奖。

stumble [ˈstʌmbl] *vi.* 使绊倒；偶然碰见，碰巧发现

释 to hit your foot against something or put your foot down awkwardly while you are walking or running, so that you almost fall; to discover sth./sb. unexpectedly

用 stumble over / on; stumble across

例 In his hurry he stumbled and spilled the milk all over the table.
因为着急他绊倒了，把牛奶撒得满桌都是。

七 人类行为研究类

The heartbeat quickly gets back to normal levels, brain activity accelerates to daytime heights.

心跳很快回到了正常水平，脑部活动加快到与白天的情况持平。

accelerate [əkˈseləreɪt] *vt. & vi.* 加速，快速增加

释 to happen faster or earlier than expected

拓 *n.* acceleration / accelerator

例 Inflation continues to accelerate. 通货膨胀不断加速。

How can we possibly account for this vast discrepancy between what calm, rational, knowledgeable people predict in the comfort of their study and what pressured, flustered, but cooperative 'teacher' actually do in the laboratory real life?

我们怎么解释这个巨大的差距，在压力之下，实验室中的被试教师行为慌乱但却表现得异常配合，完全不像那些冷静、理性而又博学的研究者们所预言的那样。

account [əˈkaʊnt] *vi.* 解释，说明

释 to give reasons for; to explain sth.

拓 *n.* accountancy / accountant / accountability; *a.* accountable

例 She could not account for her absence from classes. 她说不出缺课的原因。

---

discrepancy [dɪsˈkrepənsi] *n.* 区别，差异

释 a difference between two or more things that ought to be the same

拓 *a.* discrepant; *ad.* discrepantly

用 discrepancy in sth.; discrepancy between… and…

例 There is a discrepancy between what he promised and what he did. 他的所言和所行之间有差异。

---

fluster ['flʌstə] *vt.* 慌张，混乱

释 to make sb. nervous and / or confused, esp. by giving them a lot to do or by making them hurry

拓 *a.* flustered

例 He was late for school, looking flustered. 他上学迟到了，看起来特别着急。

For those women who learnt to read through the campaign, the infant mortality rate was 84 per thousand.

发生在那些通过此次运动学会识字的妇女中的婴儿死亡率为千分之八十四。

campaign [kæm'peɪn] *n.* 战役，运动，活动

释 a series of actions intended to achieve a particular result relating to politics or business, or a social improvement

拓 *n.* campaigner

用 campaign against / for

例 The terrorists have intensified their explosion campaign.
恐怖分子增加了炸弹爆炸活动。

---

infant mortality rate 婴儿死亡率

---

infant ['ɪnfənt] *n.* 婴儿，幼儿

释 a baby or a very young child

拓 *n.* infancy

例 We must take measures to reduce infant mortality. 我们必须采取措施降低婴儿死亡率。

mortality [mɔːˈtælɪti] *n.* 死亡数目，死亡率

释 the number of deaths within a particular society and within a particular period of time

例 The mortality resulted from an epidemic. 这次大批人死亡是由一种传染病引起的。

A few years ago, it was one of the most fascinating and disturbing experiments in behavioral psychology.

几年前，它还是行为心理学中最有趣、最令人不安的实验之一。

disturbing [dɪˈstɜːbɪŋ] *a.* 烦扰的

释 making you feel worried or upset

拓 *vt.* disturb; *n.* disturbance; *ad.* disturbingly; *a.* disturbed

例 He has had some disturbing experience. 他有过一些使他很不安的经历。

Even among identical twins who have the exact genes, one in six pairs will differ in their handedness.

即使是基因几乎相同的双胞胎，每六对中就有一对在左右手的使用习惯上是不同的。

identical [aɪˈdentɪkəl] *a.* 相同的，同一的

释 exactly the same, or very similar

拓 *n.* identity; *ad.* identically

用 identical to; identical with

例 They're wearing identical clothes. 他们穿着完全相同的衣服。

---

differ [ˈdɪfə] *vi.* 不一致，不同

释 to be not like something or someone else, either physically or in another way

拓 *n.* difference; *a.* different; *ad.* differently

用 differ from sb. / sth.; differ with sb.; differ about / on sth.

例 The brothers differ widely in their tastes. 他们兄弟的爱好大相径庭。

His scans showed that at the beginning of a joke the listeners' prefrontal cortex lit up.

他的扫描结果证明，观众一听到笑话时，他们的大脑皮层会活跃起来。

scan [skæn] *n.* 扫描；浏览

释 a medical test in which a machine produces a picture of the inside of a person's body on a computer screen after taking x-rays; the act of looking quickly through something written or printed, usually in order to find something

拓 *n.* scanner

例 I gave the book a quick scan, and decided not to buy it . 我迅速浏览了一下这本书，然后决定不买了。

---

prefrontal ['priː'frʌntl] *a.* 前额的

释 anterior to a frontal stucture

---

cortex ['kɔːˌteks] *n.* 外皮（树皮）；[解] 皮质，皮层

释 the outer layer, especially of the brain and other organs

例 It makes up more than half the thickness of the cortex. 它们组成超过一半厚度的皮质。

They may not understand it to the required level — bearing in mind the regional and social variation which permeates speech and which can cause major problems.

考虑到语言中所渗透的区域性和社会性变异以及它们所能引发的重大问题，可知他们的理解没有达到所需求的标准。

variation [ˌveərɪˈeɪʃən] *n.* 变化，变异

释 a difference between similar things, or a change from the usual amount or form of something

拓 *a.* variational

用 variation of / in / among / between

例 White bread is really just a variation of French bread. 白面包是法国面包的一种变异。

---

permeate [ˈpɜːmɪeɪt] *vt.& vi.* 弥漫，渗透，普及

释 if liquid, gas, etc. permeates something, it enters it and spreads through every part of it

拓 *a.* permeable; *n.* permeation / permeability

用 permeate through / into / among

例 The smell of her perfume permeated the room. 房间里弥漫着她的香水味。

Teresa found a connection between self-esteem and stress in people over 70.

特里萨发现了年龄在70岁以上的人自尊和压力之间的联系。

self-esteem [ˌselfɪˈstiːm] *n.* 自尊，自负

释 belief and confidence in your own ability and value

例 Self-esteem and self-control is a kind of responsibilities to yourself. 自爱自控是对自己负责的一种表现。

The cellular damage increases vulnerability to infirmity as grow older.

随着年龄的增长，细胞损伤使我们更容易变虚弱。

cellular ['seljələ] *a.* 细胞的

释 consisting of or relating to the cells of plants or animals

例 The classification of organisms is based on cellular structure and function. 生物体分类学建立在细胞结构和功能的基础之上。

---

vulnerability [ˌvʌlnərəbɪləti] *n.* 易受伤，易受责难

释 the state of being vulnerable or exposed

拓 *a.* vulnerable

例 The parts are marked by a tension between the character's strength and intelligence and her emotional vulnerability. 角色的特点是她的勇气和智慧与感情上的脆弱之间的冲突。

---

infirmity [ɪn'fɜːməti] *n.* 虚弱

释 the state of being weak in health or body(especially from old age)

例 The old man was suffering from age and infirmity. 那个人受年老体弱之苦。

The features of all individuals must be descended from their parents.

所有个体的特征都是从他们的父母那儿遗传来的。

descend [dɪ'send] *vt. & vi.* 降，传

释 to come or go down from a higher to a lower level

拓 *n.* descent

用 descend from

例 You can take the lift up but have to descend on foot. 他可以搭电梯上去，但要自己走下来。

Most left-handers have left hemisphere dominance but also some capacity in the right hemisphere.

大部分左撇子不仅大脑左半球占优势，而且右半球也比较发达。

hemisphere ['hemɪˌsfɪə] *n.* 大脑半球；半球

释 either of the lateral halves of the cerebrum

例 The Western Hemisphere refers to North and South America.

西半球是指南北美洲。

---

dominance ['dɒmənəns] *n.* 优势，支配，统治

释 superior development of one side of the body

拓 *a.* dominant; *ad.* dominantly

用 dominance of; dominance over

例 He acclaimed his dominance over this job. 他宣布了自己对这项工作的主导权。

---

capacity [kə'pæsɪti] *n.* 能力；容量，容积

释 the ability to understand or to do someting; the number of things or people that a container or space can hold

例 She has a great capacity for learning language. 她学习语言的能力很强。

The psychological laboratory has a strong claim to legitimacy and evokes trust and confidence in those who perform there.

心理实验室是符合法律的，能激起在那里治疗的人的信任和信心。

legitimacy [lə'dʒɪtəməsi] *n.* 合法，正当

释 lawfulness by virtue; of being authorized or in accordance with law

拓 *a.* legitimate; *ad.* legitimately; *vt.* legitimize

例 The government expressed serious doubts about the legitimacy of military action. 政府对军事行动的合法性表示非常担忧。

---

evoke [ɪ'vəʊk] *vt.* 唤起，引起

释 to make someone remember something or feel an emotion

拓 *n.* evocation; *a.* evocative; *ad.* evocatively

例 I like songs which can evoke old memories. 我喜欢怀旧的歌曲。

It has become clear that blind people can appreciate the use of outlines and perspectives to describe the arrangement of objects.

现在已经很清楚，盲人能利用轮廓和透视法来描述物体的排列。

perspective [pə'spektɪv] *n.* 远景；透视

释 the technique of representing three-dimentional objects and depth relationships on a two-dimentional surface

用 perspective on; from someone's perspective

例 Children often draw without perspective. 小孩子画画常常不管透视法。

---

arrangement [ə'reɪndʒmənt] *n.* 排列，布置；安排

释 the condition, manner, or result of being arranged

拓 *vt.* & *vi.* arrange

用 arrangement for; an arrangement to do sth.

例 The arrangement of the ornaments in our new house took a long time. 布置新家的装饰品花了很长时间。

Girls were shown to be more sympathetic and expressed views which seem to place an intrinsic value on.

女孩更具同情心，她们在发表意见时，更注重事物的内在价值。

intrinsic [ɪn'trɪnsɪk] *a.* 固有的，内在的

释 of or relating to the essential nature of a thing

拓 *ad.* intrinsically

用 intrinsic to

例 The intrinsic value of a coin is the value of metal it is made of.
一枚硬币的固有价值就是造这枚硬币的金属的价值。

High levels of serotonin in certain areas of the nervous system make people more active and reactive and, possibly, more aggressive.

存在于神经系统某些区域的高水平的羟色胺会使人更积极主动，可能更加上进。

serotonin [ˌserə'təʊnɪn] *n.* 含于血液中的复合胺；羟色胺

释 a chemical in the body that helps carry messages from the brain and is believed to make you feel happy

Clark Hull devised a test of children that was explicitly based on Clark Hull's principles.

克拉克·赫尔为孩子设计了一个测试，该测试很明确是以克拉克·赫尔理论为基础的。

devise [dɪ'vaɪz] *vt.* 设计；想出

释 to plan or invent a new way of doing something

例 She devised a method for promotion. 她想出了一个促销的办法。

---

explicitly [ɪk'splɪsɪtli] *ad.* 明确地

释 in a way that is very clear and direct

拓 *n.* explicitness; *a.* explicit

例 The report states explicitly that the system was to blame. 报告明确指出问题出在制度上。

The new world will largely depend on human creativity, and creativity flourishes where people come together face-to-face.

新世界需要人类的创造力，而只有当人们紧密团结起来时，创造力才会充分发挥出来。

flourish ['flʌrɪʃ] *vi.* 兴旺发达；茂盛，繁荣；挥动

释 to develop well and be successful; to grow well and be very healthy; to wave something in your hand in order to make people notice it

拓 *a.* flourishing

例 According to the new policies, small businesses are flourishing. 由于新政策的实施，小型企业逐渐发展起来了。

The psychiatrists felt that "most subjects would not go beyond 150 vols" and they further anticipated that only four percent would go up to 300 volts.

精神病医师认为大多数受试者不会超过150伏，他们还进一步预测，只有4%的受试者会使用高300伏的电压。

psychiatrist [saɪ'kaɪətrɪst] *n.* 精神病医师，精神病学家

释 a doctor who studies and treats mental illnesses

拓 *n.* psychiatry

---

anticipate [æn'tɪsɪpeɪt] *vt.* 预期，期待

释 to expect that something will happen and be ready for it; to think about something that is going to happen, especially something pleasant; to do something before someone else

拓 *n.* anticipation

用 anticipate doing sth.; anticipate that

例 I didn't anticipate having to do the washing myself! 我没想到要自己洗衣服。

Role ambiguity results when there is some uncertainty in the minds.

角色模糊源自头脑中对角色的不确定。

uncertainty [ʌn'sɜːtnti] *n.* 不确定，犹豫，无把握

释 the state of being uncertain

拓 *a.* uncertain; *ad.* uncertainly

用 uncertainty about / as to; uncertainty of

例 There is considerable uncertainty about the company's future. 这家公司的前景相当渺茫。

The fact indicates that left-handers have a more bilateral speech function.

事实表明左撇子具有较强的双语能力。

bilateral [baɪ'lætərəl] *a.* 双边的；(身体)双侧的，对称的

释 involving both of two parts or sides of the body or brain

拓 *ad.* bilaterally

例 The two countries signed a bilateral agreement to promote trade prosperity. 两国签署了双边协议，以促进贸易繁荣。

Humans, however, search for images by their cognitive, deep meaning content.

然而，人类通过一种深度认知去寻找影像。

cognitive ['kɒgnɪtɪv] *a.* 认知的，认识的，有认识力的

释 related to the process of knowing, understanding, and learning something

拓 *n.* cognition

例 Cognitive psychology is a very important subject. 认知心理学是一门非常重要的学科。

Gloomy weather can cause depression, but sunshine appears to raise the spirits.

阴沉天气导致压抑，但阳光能使人精神焕发。

gloomy ['gluːmi] *a.* 阴沉的，忧闷的

释 making you feel that things will not improve; sad because you think the situation will not improve; dark, especially in a way that makes you feel sad

例 Lucy is always in that gloomy mood. 露西总是一副闷闷不乐的样子。

While children who persistently bully are more likely to grow up to be real violent, and convicted of anti-social offences.

从小一直欺负别人的人长大后可能变成真正的暴徒，并做出一些反社会的行为。

persistently [pə'sɪstəntli] *ad.* 固执地，坚持地

释 refusing to give up or let go; preserving obstinately

拓 *vt.* & *vi.* persist; *n.* persistence; *a.* persistent

例 China has persistently exercised great restraint in the development of nuclear weapons. 中国在发展核武器问题上一贯持十分保守的态度。

---

violent ['vaɪələnt] *a.* 暴力的

释 involving actions that are intended to injure or kill people, by hitting them, shooting them, etc.

拓 *n.* violence; *ad.* violently

例 Violent movies are potential triggers for juvenile delinquency.
暴力影片可能引发青少年犯罪。

---

convict [kən'vɪkt] *vt.* 宣告……有罪，使……认罪

释 to prove or officially announce that someone is guilty of crime after a trial in a law court

拓 *n.* conviction; *a.* convicted

用 convict sb. of sth.

例 He was convicted of shoplifting. 他被指控在商场盗窃。

Parents might be at risk of transmitting a single-gene defect to any children that they conceive.

在怀孕时，父母有可能遗传给孩子单基因缺陷症。

gene [dʒiːn] *n.* 基因

释 a part of a cell in a living thing that controls what it looks like, how it grows, and how it develops; people get their genes from their parents

拓 *a.* genetic; *ad.* genetically

例 Genes are transmitted from one generation to another. 基因代代相传。

---

conceive [kən'siːv] *vt. & vi.* 怀孕；构思

释 to cause a baby to begin to form; to form or develop an idea in the mind

用 conceive of

例 Deer usually conceive in November. 鹿通常在十一月份怀胎。

She started gradually moving the feeding dish further and further away and noticed as he did so.

她慢慢往远处移动喂食的盘子，并且注意到人也在移动。

gradually ['grædʒʊəli] *ad.* 逐渐地

释 slowly, over a long period of time

拓 *a.* gradual

例 Gradually, he lost his confidence. 他渐渐地失去了信心。

Those who felt in control of their lives pumped out lower levels of stress hormones such as cortical.

那些可以控制自己生活的人释放出低浓度的压力激素，比如大脑皮质激素。

pump [pʌmp] *vt. & vi.* 抽水，涌出，涌现

释 to make liquid or gas move in a particular direction, using a pump; to come out quickly

用 pump sth. into sth.

例 Bleeding blood pumped from the wound. 伤口在喷血。

Physical anthropology, or biological anthropology as it is also called, concerns the study of human biology.

体质人类学是研究人类生物学的学科，也叫生物人类学。

anthropology [ˌænθrə'pɒlədʒi] *n.* 人类学

释 the scientific study of people, their societies

拓 *n.* anthropologist; *a.* anthropological

例 British-born American anthropologist — Ashley Montagu — whose books, such as *The Natural Superiority of Women*(1953), helped popularize anthropology. 英裔美国人类学家蒙塔古·阿什利的著作，如《女性的自然优越性》(1953)，促进了人类学的普及。

biological [ˌbaɪəˈlɒdʒɪkəl] *a.* 生物学的；生物的

释 relating to the natural processes performed by living things

拓 *ad.* biologically; *n.* biology / biologist

例 The school has a large biological laboratory. 这所学校有一个很大的生物实验室。

The least intelligent are most vulnerable, but tests show that even intelligent children are being affected.

智商低的孩子是最容易受到伤害的，但是实验表明，即使聪明的孩子也会受到影响。

vulnerable [ˈvʌlnərəbl] *a.* 易受伤害的

释 weak and easily hurt physically or emotionally

拓 *ad.* vulnerably; *n.* vulnerability

用 be vulnerable to sth.

例 Tourists are more vulnerable to attack, because they do not know which areas are dangerous. 游客更加容易受到攻击，因为他们不知道哪里危险。

---

affect [əˈfekt] *vt.* 影响

释 to have an influence on someone or something, or to cause them to change

拓 *a.* affecting

例 It is said that the rhythm of tides is affected by the moon.
据说，潮汐的涨落受月亮的影响。

Most people consider almond honey too bitter to eat.

好多人认为杏仁蜜太苦很难吃。

almond [ˈɑːmənd] *n.* 杏仁

释 a flat pale nut with brown skin that tastes sweet, or the tree that produces these nuts

---

bitter [ˈbɪtə] *a.* 苦的，痛苦的

释 having a sharp, pungent taste; not sweet; feeling angry, jealous, and upset because you think you have been treated unfairly

拓 *n.* bitterness

用 bitter about; a bitter disappointment

例 They learned a bitter lesson. 他们接受了惨痛的教训。

Older children seem to acquire the ability to appreciate value and evaluate conflicting views.

年纪大一点儿的儿童似乎有能力欣赏价值观和评价互相矛盾的观点。

appreciate [əˈpriːʃɪeɪt] *vt.* 欣赏；领会，充分意识

释 to recognize or understand that something is valuable, important or as described

拓 *n.* appreciation; *a.* appreciative / appreciable; *ad.* appreciatively

用 appreciate doing sth.; appreciate that

例 I don't think he appreciates how much time I spent preparing this meal. 他没有意识到我为准备这顿晚饭花费了多长时间。

---

evaluate [ɪˈvæljueɪt] *vt.* 评估，评价

释 to judge or calculate the quality, importance, amount or value of something

拓 *a.* evaluative; *n.* evaluation

例 Let's evaluate the proof. 让我们评估一下这份证据的价值。

A baby receives the genetic inheritance from its parents.

孩子从父母那里得到基因遗传。

inheritance [ɪnˈherɪtəns] *n.* 遗传；遗产

释 something from the past or from your family that affects the way you behave, look, etc; money or objects that someone gives other people when they die

拓 *vt.* & *vi.* inherit; *n.* inheritor

用 inheritance of sth. from sb.

例 The inheritance of her good looks is from her mother. 她的美貌来自母亲的遗传。

Human beings started to show a preference for developing a new language.

人类开始显示对学习一门新语言的偏爱。

preference [ˈprefərəns] *n.* 较喜欢的东西，偏爱

释 a thing that is liked better or best

拓 *vt.* prefer; *a.* preferable

用 in preference to sth.

例 A window seat is my preference. 我喜欢靠窗座位。

A representative sample of language, compiled for the purpose of linguistic analysis, is known as a corpus.

为了分析语言学，把一些有代表性的语言汇编在一起，称之为语料库。

representative [ˌreprɪˈzentətɪv] *n.* 代表，典型；*a.* 代表性的，代议制的；典型的

释 someone who speaks or does something officially for another person or group of people; being an example of what other members of the same group or type are like

拓 *vt.* represent; *n.* representation; *a.* representational

用 representative of

例 This case is representative of the attitudes of the police. 这个事例典型地反映了警方的态度。

He noted that this distinctive asymmetry in the human population is itself systematic.

他指出，这种人口独特的不对称性是自成体系的。

asymmetry [eɪ'sɪmətri] *n.* 不对称

释 with two halves, sides or parts which are not exactly the same in shape and size; without symmetry

拓 *a.* asymmetric; *ad.* asymmetrically

例 Information asymmetry is the source of consumer loan credit risks. 信息不对称是消费信贷信用风险产生的根源。

---

systematic [ˌsɪstə'mætɪk] *a.* 有系统的，分类的，体系的

释 using a fixed and organized plan

例 This problem cries out for a long-term, open-minded, systematic search. 这个问题十分需要长期的、不带偏见的、系统的探索研究。

He points out that play often involves complex assessments of playmates, ideas of reciprocity and the use of specialized signals and rules.

他指出游戏通常涉及对游戏伙伴的复杂评估、互助的观念以及对特有标志和规则的使用。

complex ['kɒmpleks] *a.* 复杂的；*n.* 复合体

释 made of many different things or parts that are connected; difficult to understand

拓 *n.* complexion / complexity

例 There is a complex procedure in Chinese handicraft. 中国手工艺的流程复杂。

---

reciprocity [ˌresɪˈprɒsəti] *n.* 互惠，互助，互换

释 a situation in which two people, countries, etc. provide the same help or advantages to each other

拓 *vt. & vi.* reciprocate; *a.* reciprocal

例 Nations should accord to the principle of reciprocity in trade. 国家间要遵守贸易互惠的原则。

---

specialize [ˈspeʃəlaɪz] *vi.* 专门研究

释 to become an expert in a particular area of work, study or business; to spend more time on one area of work, etc. than on others

拓 *n.* specialization / specialist; *a.* specialized

用 specialize in sth.

例 He specialized in English linguistics. 他专攻英语语言学。

The image of green consumerism as associated in the past with the more eccentric members of society has virtually disappeared.

以前人们认为绿色消费都是那些古怪的社会成员的行为，现在人们已经没有这个想法了。

consumerism [kənˈsuːməˌrɪzəm] *n.* 用户至上主义，商品的消费和销售性服务

释 the state of advanced industrial society in which a lot of goods are bought and sold

拓 *vt.* consume; *n.* consumer / consumption; *a.* consuming

例 The founders of Coffee Lox well understood the appeal of consumerism at a friendly level. Coffee Lox的创立者非常理解商品的销售性服务在友好层面上的吸引力。

---

eccentric [ɪkˈsentrɪk] *a.* 古怪的，反常的

释 strange or unusual, sometimes in an amusing way

拓 *n.* eccentricity; *ad.* eccentrically

例 She is so eccentric that she is regarded as a bit of a curiosity. 她非常古怪，算是个奇人。

---

virtually [ˈvɜːtʃʊəli] *ad.* 几乎，实际上

释 almost, or very nearly, so that any slight difference is not important

拓 *a.* virtual

例 Their twins are virtually identical. 他们的两个双胞胎几乎一模一样。

This diversity of number name can also be found in some widely used languages such as Japanese.

数字名字的多样性也可以在许多广泛使用的语言中找到，比如日语。

diversity [daɪˈvɜːsəti] *n.* 差异，多样性

释 a range of many people or things that are very different from each other

拓 *vt.* & *vi.* diversify; *n.* diversification; *a.* diverse

用 diversity of sth

例 There is a wide diversity of opinions on the question of traffic jam. 关于交通堵塞这个问题有好多不同的看法。

The objective of the Human Genome Project is simple to state, but audacious in scope.

人类基因工程的目标很容易阐明，但范围却非常宽泛。

audacious [ɔːˈdeɪʃəs] *a.* 英勇无畏的；大胆的，无礼的，放肆的

释 showing a willingness to take risks or offend people

拓 *ad.* audaciously; *n.* audaciousness / audacity

例 You will succeed in your audacious enterprise. 你英勇豪迈的事业一定会成功的。

A facial expression, for example, can dramatically alter the meaning of what is said.

比如说，面部表情可以使说话人的话语意思发生明显变化。

dramatically [drəˈmætɪkli] *ad.* 显著地；戏剧地；引人注目地

释 in a dramatic manner

拓 *a.* dramatic; *n.* drama

例 Your performance will improve dramatically. 你的业绩将会有显著的提高。

Viewed from this angle, humor is just a form of creative insight, a sudden leap to a new perspective.

从这个角度看，幽默只是创新性洞察力的一种形式，是对新观点的跳跃性思维。

insight [ˈɪnsaɪt] *n.* 洞察力

释 a clear, deep and sometimes sudden understanding of a complicated problem or situation

拓 *a.* insightful

用 insight into

例 Good teachers have insight into children's emotions. 优秀的教师能洞察学生内心的情感。

perspective [pə'spektɪv] *n.* 观点，看法

释 a particular way of considering something

用 get / keep sth. in perspective; put sth. into perspective

例 In heart's perspective the distance looms large. 在心灵的远景里，相隔的距离显得更广阔了。

All corpora always need to be supplemented by data derived from the intuitions of native speakers of the language, through either introspection or experimentation.

所有语料库都需要把通过实验和观察获得的反映讲母语的人的直觉反应的数据补充进来。

corpus ['kɔːpəs] *n.* 全集；汇编；语料（复数为corpora）

释 the collection of a single writer's work or of writing about a particular subject, or a large amount of written and sometimes spoken material collected to show the state of a language

拓 *n.* corpora (*pl.*)

例 This paper aims at analysing a corpus of spoken dialect. 本文旨在分析口语的汇集资料。

---

supplement ['sʌplɪmənt] *vt.* 补充，增补

释 to add something else in order to improve it or complete it

拓 *a.* supplementary

用 supplement to

例 They had to get a job to supplement the family income. 他们不得不找一份工作以贴补家庭收入。

---

intuition [ˌɪntju'ɪʃən] *n.* 直觉

释 the ability to know sth. by using your feelings rather than considering the facts

拓 *a.* intuitive; *ad.* intuitively

用 intuition that

例 Nobody told me where to find him. It was sheer intuition. 没有人告诉我到哪儿去找他。我纯粹是凭感觉找到他的。

---

introspection [ˌɪntrəˈspekʃən] *n.* 内省，反省

释 examination and consideration of your own ideas, thoughts and feelings

例 He thus typified the constant introspection where with he tortured, but could not purify himself. 他就这样不断地自省，其实只是在自我折磨，丝毫得不到自我净化。

One interesting correlation Manton uncovered is that better-educated people are likely to live longer.

Manton发现了一种有趣的关联——受过良好教育的人能活得更长。

correlation [ˌkɒrəˈleɪʃn] *n.* 相互关系，相关，关联

释 a connection between two ideas, facts, etc., especially when one may be the cause of the other

拓 *vt. & vi.* correlate

用 correlation between; correlation with

例 The correlation of social power with wealth is obvious in today's society. 社会权力与财富在当今社会有着明显的相关性。

---

be likely to 可能(可预期的)

例 Smokers who inhale are likely to become addicted to nicotine. 吸烟时把烟吸入肺里的人容易对尼古丁上瘾成性。

I have not been sleeping very well the past three days, keeping having some weird dreams while I slept.

我连续三天没有睡好觉，一直做噩梦。

weird [wɪəd] *a.* **怪异的**

释 very strange and unusual, and difficult to understand or explain

拓 *ad.* weirdly; *n.* weirdness

例 It was a weird old house, full of creaks and groans. 这是一所神秘而可怕的旧宅到处吱嘎吱嘎作响。

But in recent years IQ has had much more credibility and weight.

近年来智商测试的可信度增加了。

credibility [ˌkredəˈbɪlɪti] *n.* **可信性，确实性；可靠**

释 the quality of deserving to be believed and trusted

拓 *a.* credible

用 credibility of

例 The scandal event has damaged his credibility as a leader. 作为一个领导，丑闻事件损害了人们对他的信任。

八　社会问题类

Annual per capita water withdraws in the USA.

美国每年的人均水消耗量在减少。

per capita [pɜːˈkæpɪtə] *n.* **人均**

释 if you state an amount per capita, you mean that amount for each person.

例 Our per capita incomes rose sharply last year. 去年我们的人均收入剧增。

withdraw [wɪð'drɔː] *vt.* & *vi.* 撤回，取回，撤退

释 to take or move out, or to remove

拓 *a.* withdrawable / withdrawn; *n.* withdrawer / withdrawal

用 withdraw from

例 The old coins have been withdrawn from circulation. 旧硬币已经收回不再流通了。

Public fascination partly reflected the seeming symmetry of the whole society.

公共魅力从某种角度来说反映了整个社会表面上的对称性。

fascination [ˌfæsə'neɪʃən] *n.* 魔力，入迷，魅力

释 a very strong attraction, that makes sth. very interesting

拓 *vt.* fascinate; *a.* fascinated / fascinating

用 have a fascination for

例 The fascination of the game lies in trying to guess what your opponent is thinking. 这个游戏的魅力就在于要努力去猜对手在想什么。

---

reflect [rɪ'flekt] *vt.* 反映

释 to show, express or be a sign for something

拓 *n.* reflection; *a.* reflective

用 reflect on / upon sth.; reflect that

例 The statistics reflect a change in people's spending habits. 统计数据显示了人们消费习惯的改变。

---

symmetry ['sɪmɪtri] *n.* 匀称，整齐，对称（性）

释 the quanlity of having parts than match each other, especially in a way that is attractive, or similarity of shape or contents

拓 *a.* symmetrical; *ad.* symmetrically

例 The increasing symmetry between men's and women's jobs can be predicted. 男女工作职位增加的对等均衡性是可以预见的。

Catastrophes such as fire, flood, drought or epidemic may reduce population sizes to a small fraction of their average level.

诸如大火、洪水、旱灾和传染病可能使人口数量大幅减少。

catastrophe [kəˈtæstrəfi] *n.* **大灾难，大祸**

释 an event resulting in great loss and misfortune

拓 *a.* catastrophic

例 The earthquake was a terrible catastrophe. 这次地震是一场可怕的灾难。

---

epidemic [ˌepɪˈdemɪk] *n.* **传染病，流行病**

释 the appearance of a particular disease in a large number of people at the same time

例 The Sanitary Board tries to stamp out the epidemic. 卫生局试图消灭这种流行病。

---

fraction [ˈfrækʃən] *n.* **小部分**

释 a very small amount of something

用 a fraction of

例 She paused for a fraction of a second. 她停顿片刻。

The impetus behind the development of these early plastics was generated by a number of factors.

促使这些早期整形手术发展的动力包含很多因素。

impetus [ˈɪmpɪtəs] *n.* **动力，推动力**

释 a force that moves something along

用 impetus to; impetus for

例 Impetus of a physical object in motion is quite powerful. 运动中物体的冲力非常强大。

It is one manifestation of how work and leisure are organized as separate and regulated spheres of social practice in modern societies.

这从一方面显示了工作和休闲在当代社会生活中是如何被作为独立的和规定好的两个领域组织起来的。

manifestation [ˌmænɪfeˈsteɪʃn] *n.* 显示，证明

释 a very clear sign that a particular situation or feeling exists

拓 *vt. /a.* manifest; *ad.* manifestly

用 manifestation of

例 This riot is only one manifestation of people's discontent. 这骚乱仅仅是人们不满的一种表露而已。

---

sphere [sfɪə] *n.* 范围，领域；球；球体

释 a ball shape; an area of activity, influence or interest

拓 *n.* spheroid; *a.* spherical

例 The sun, earth and moon are spheres. 太阳、地球和月亮都是天体。

A dearth of adequately funded schools and family breakdown and violence are two problems in that country.

资本充裕学校的缺乏与家庭的破裂和暴力是那个国家的两大问题。

adequately [ˈædɪkwətli] *a.* 足够地，充分地，适当地

释 enough in quantity or of a good enough quality for a particular purpose

拓 *n.* adequacy; *a.* adequate

用 adequate for; adequate to do sth.

例 Sleeping rooms and mess rooms shall be adequately ventilated.
卧室和餐室应有良好的通风。

---

violence ['vaɪələns] *n.* 暴力

释 behaviour that is intended to hurt other people physically

拓 *a.* violent; *ad.* violently

用 do violence to sth.

例 Government condemned the act of violence. 政府谴责暴力行为。

The study argues that the type of action needed against passive smoking should be similar to that being taken against illegal drugs and AIDS.

研究表明，对付被动吸烟应采取类似于对付违法药品和艾滋病的措施。

illegal [ɪ'li:gl] *a.* 不合法的，非法的

释 prohibited by law or by official or accepted rules

拓 *ad.* illegally

例 A campaign to stop the illegal sale of cigarettes to children under 16 was implemented by the government. 政府实施了一项针对16岁以下少年的禁烟运动。

After the National Literacy Crusade, the children of the women who remained illiterate were found to be severely malnourished.

全国文化普及运动之后，人们发现，那些母亲仍为文盲的孩子处于极度的营养不良状态。

severely [sɪ'vɪəli] *ad.* 严重地

释 very badly or to a great degree

拓 *a.* severe; *n.* severity

例 Parents shouldn't punish their children so severely. 父母不应该如此严厉地惩罚孩子。

---

malnourished [mælˈnʌrɪʃt] *a.* 营养不良的

释 in bad health because of a lack of food or a lack of the right type of food

拓 *n.* malnutrition

例 UNICEF estimates that around the world 150 million children are malnourished. 联合国儿童基金会预计全世界约有1.5亿的儿童营养不良。

The communities are helping to set the research agenda to reflect their most important concerns.

该社区帮助制定研究议程，以此反映他们最关心的问题。

agenda [əˈdʒendə] *n.* 议事日程

释 a list of problems or subjects that a government, organization, etc. is planning to deal with

用 be high on the agenda / be top of the agenda (= be one of the most important problems to deal with)

例 The government set an agenda for constitutional reform. 政府出台了宪法改革的日程。

---

reflect [rɪˈflekt] *vt.* 反映

释 to show, express or be a sign of something

拓 *n.* reflection

用 be reflected in sth.; reflect what / that

例 That choice reflected your good taste. 那个选择反映了你的高雅品位。

In many cases the glossy brochures, article prints and prescriptions they deliver are primary sources of drug education for healthcare givers.

在很多情况下，彩页宣传册、文章和药方是健康教育者宣传禁毒教育的主要方式。

glossy ['glɒsi] *a.* 光滑的，有光泽的

释 shiny and smooth

拓 *n.* gloss

例 She got glossy black hair. 她有一头乌黑的秀发。

---

brochure ['brəʊʃə] *n.* 小册子

释 a thin book giving information or advertising something

例 The characteristics of the DVD are fully detailed in our brochure.

我们这本小册子详尽地说明了这台DVD的性能。

---

prescription [prɪs'krɪpʃən] *n.* 药方

释 a piece of paper on which a doctor writes what medicine a sick person should have, so that they can get it from a pharmacist; a particular medicine or treatment ordered by a doctor for a sick person

拓 *vt. & vi.* prescribe; *a.* prescribed

用 prescription for

例 Government is trying to cut the price of prescription drugs.

政府在尝试降低处方药的价格。

Yet a green organization opposing such a weakening is seen as altruistic, even if an impartial view of the controls in question might suggest they are doing more harm than good.

然而，绿色组织反对此类削弱被看作是利他主义，即使一个公正的看法也可能意味着他们的做法是弊多于利。

oppose [əˈpəʊz] *vt. & vi.* 反对，以……对抗，抗争

释 to disagree with something or someone, often by speaking or fighting against them

拓 *a.* opposing / opposed; *n.* opposition

用 oppose doing sth.

例 Don't oppose your idea against mine. 不要把你的观点同我的对立起来。

---

altruistic [ˌæltruˈɪstɪk] *a.* 利他主义的，无私的

释 willingness to do things which benefit other people, even if it results in disadvantage for yourself

拓 *n.* altruist / altruism; *ad.* altruistically

例 I doubt whether his motives for donating the money are altruistic — he's probably looking for publicity. 我怀疑他捐钱的动机是否是无私的，他很可能是想引起公众的注意。

---

impartial [ɪmˈpɑːʃəl] *a.* 公平的，不偏不倚的

释 not supporting any of the sides involved in an argument

拓 *vt.* impart; *ad.* impartially; *n.* impartiality

例 He is an impartial judge. 他是一位公正的法官。

What lies behind this explosion in international commerce?

国际商务中心爆炸案的幕后真相是什么？

explosion [ɪksˈpləʊʒən] *n.* 爆炸，爆发

释 when something such as a bomb explodes

拓 *vt. & vi.* explode; *a.* explosive; *ad.* explosively

用 explosion of

例 There was a terrible explosion at the chemical factory. 那家化工厂发生了一起可怕的爆炸事故。

---

commerce ['kɒmɜːs] *n.* 商业，贸易

释 the activities involved in buying and selling things

拓 *n.* commercialization / commercialism; *a.* commercial; *vt.* commercialize; *ad.* commercially

例 Overseas commerce is a major source of their national income.

海外贸易是该国收入的主要来源。

九　人物类

For all its faults and eccentricities his two-volume work is a masterpiece and a landmark in his own words, 'setting the orthography, displaying the analogy, regulating the structures, and ascertaining the significations of English words.'

他的两卷巨著尽管存在错误且行文古怪，用他本人的话说却是一部里程碑式的杰作，它“设定英语词汇的正确拼法，展示类比，规范结构，并探明词义。”

eccentricity [ˌeksen'trɪsɪti] *n.* 古怪，怪癖，古怪的行为

释 strange or unusual behaviour; the state of being eccentric

拓 *a.* eccentric; *ad.* eccentrically

例 Her eccentricity had become legendary long before she died.

早在去世之前，她的古怪脾气就流传开了。

---

masterpiece ['mɑːstəpiːs] *n.* 杰作

释 a work of art such as a painting, film or book which is done or made with great skill, and is often a person's greatest work

用 masterpiece of

例 It is one of the great masterpieces of Chinese art. 它是中国艺术最杰出的作品之一。

---

landmark ['lændmaːk] *n.* 路标，地界标；里程碑

释 something that is easy to recognize, such as a tall tree or a building, and that helps you know where your are; an event, a discovery, an invention, etc. that marks an important stage in something

例 Known as Grimm's Law, it was a landmark in the development of modern philology. 众所周知"格里姆定律"，是当代语言学发展史上的一个里程碑。

---

orthography [ɔː'θɒgrəfi] *n.* 正确拼字，正字法

释 the way in which words are spelled; a method of representing the sounds of a language by written or printed symbols

拓 *a.* orthographic; *ad.* orthographically

例 In dictionaries, words and phrases are listed according to their orthography. 在词典中，单词和短语是按照字母拼写顺序排列的。

---

analogy [ə'nælədʒi] *n.* 相似，类似

释 a comparison between things which have similar features, often used to help explain a principle or an idea

拓 *n.* analogue / analysis; *a.* analogous; *ad.* analogically

用 analogy between / with / to; make / draw an analogy; by analogy with

例 Shakespeare makes an analogy between the citizens of a country and the parts of a person's body. 莎士比亚把一个国家的国民类比为人体的各个部分。

ascertain [ˌæsəˈteɪn] *vt.* 确定，探知，弄清

释 to find out something; to discover; to make certain

拓 *a.* ascertainable

用 ascertain that; ascertain how / whether / what

例 Have you ascertained whether he's coming or not? 你确定他今天来吗？

---

signification [ˌsɪgnɪfɪˈkeɪʃən] *n.* 含义，意义，重要性

释 the message that is intended or expressed or signified

例 I told him that such a proposal could be of no signification , but to entangle us both in great difficulties. 我告诉他这样一个建议没有什么意义，只是使我们两人都陷入很大的困难。

They are backed up by technicians who design instruments to collect date from athletes.

他们有来自技术人员的支持，正是这些技术人员设计出了用于收集运动员数据的仪器。

technician [tekˈnɪʃən] *n.* 技术员，技师

释 a worker trained with special skills, especially in science

拓 *a.* technical; *ad.* technically

例 He is an electrical technician by profession. 他的职业是电工技师。

---

instrument [ˈɪnstrʊmənt] *n.* 乐器，工具；仪器，器械

释 a tool or device used for a particular task, especially for delicate or scientific work

拓 *n.* instrumentalist; *a.* instrumental

例 The dentist picked up several instruments. 牙科医生把一些器械收拾好。

The richer and more important the person, the more careful and elaborate would be his or her burial, and the stronger and safer the tomb in which they would be buried.

越是富有和重要的人，葬礼越是会精心安排，坟墓也更为坚固和安全。

elaborate [ɪ'læbərət] *a.* 精细的，详尽的，精心的；*vi.* 详细地说明，推敲

释 very complicated and detailed; to add more information to or explain something that you have said

拓 *n.* elaboration; *ad.* elaborately

用 elaborate on

例 He elaborated a plan of study. 他仔细制订了学习计划。

She was probably already proved herself to be an exceptional candidate.

她很可能已经证明了自己是一个特殊的候选人。

prove [pruːv] *vt.* 证明

释 to use facts, evidence to show that sth. is true

拓 *n.* proof

用 prove to be; prove that

例 It proved that everything was wrong. 结果证明一切都是错的。

---

exceptional [ɪk'sepʃənl] *a.* 异常的，特别的

释 very unusual

拓 *ad.* exceptionally

例 This weather is exceptional for July. 七月里这样的天气是反常的。

candidate ['kændɪdeɪt] *n.* 候选人，求职者

释 a person who is trying to be elected or is applying for a job

用 candidate for

例 Leo was the strongest candidate for the job. 利奥是应聘这份工作的求职者中最有优势的。

Soon he would revolutionize the study of animal behaviour generally.

不久，他将对动物行为学研究进行一次广泛的改革。

revolutionize [ˌrevə'luːʃənaɪz] *vt.* 使革命化；彻底改革

释 to completely change the way people do something or think about something

拓 *n.* revolution; *a.* revolutionary

例 New technology is going to revolutionize daily life. 新的技术将改变我们的日常生活。

---

behaviour [bɪ'heɪvjə] *n.* 行为，举止

释 the things that a person or animal does

拓 *n.* behavioral; *ad.* behaviorally

用 be on your best behaviour; behaviour of

例 The boss will not tolerate bad behaviour. 老板不容忍这种不良行为。

Lack of clarity in the role of the focal person can cause insecurity, lack of confidence, irritation and even anger among members of his role set.

焦点人物由于缺少透明度，容易感到危险、不自信、易怒，甚至对他的角色群中的成员吆三喝四。

clarity ['klærɪti] *n.* 清楚，透明，明晰

释 the quality of being expressed clearly

拓 *vt. & vi.* clarify; *n.* clarification

例 The contract is lack of clarity in the law. 这份合同缺少法律的明确性。

---

insecurity [ˌɪnsɪˈkjʊərɪti] *n.* 不安全，不牢靠

释 not safe or protected

拓 *a.* insecure; *ad.* insecurely

例 When I was at home alone, I was always having feelings of insecurity. 一个人在家的时候，我总是感觉不安全。

---

irritation [ˌɪrɪˈteɪʃən] *n.* 激怒，恼怒，生气

释 state of being annoyed by sb., esp. by sth. you continuously do or by sth. that continuously happens

拓 *vt.* irritate; *a.* irritating / irritated; *ad.* irritatingly

用 irritation at / with

例 Tom could not hide his irritation that he had not been invited to the Christmas party. 因为未被邀请参加圣诞聚会，汤姆无法掩饰内心的愤怒。

They are a clutch of individualistic homemakers who have burrowed underground in search of tranquility.

她们是一群极具个人主义的家庭主妇，为了寻求宁静的生活一直居住在地下室。

clutch [klʌtʃ] *n.* 一组(小东西)

释 a small group of similar things

用 a clutch of; clutch at

例 He's won a whole clutch of awards. 他获得一大堆奖。

---

individualistic [ˌɪndɪˌvɪdʒuəˈlɪstɪk] *a.* 个人主义的，个人的

释 referring to someone who does things in his own way and has different opinions from most other people

拓 *ad.* individualistically; *n.* individual / individualist

例 She has a highly individualistic approach to learning English.

她有自己学习英语的方法。

---

tranquility [træŋ'kwɪləti] *n.* 宁静

释 state of being pleasantly calm, quiet, and peaceful

拓 *vt.* tranquillize; *ad.* tranquilly; *a.* tranquil

例 The tranquility of the countryside is the dominant reason for his living there. 乡村的寂静是吸引他住在那儿的主要原因。

He disliked to collaborate with other astronomers of his time.

他不喜欢与同时代的其他天文学家合作。

collaborate [kə'læbəreɪt] *vi.* 合作；通敌(勾结)

释 to work together with a person or group in order to achieve something, especially in science or art; to help a country that your country is fighting a war with, especially one that has taken control of your country

拓 *n.* collaboration / collaborator; *a.* collaborative

用 collaborate on; collaborate with

例 The two countries are collaborating on several purchasing projects.

两国正在就几项采购项目进行合作。

---

astronomer [ə'strɒnəmə] *n.* 天文学家

释 a scientist who studies the stars and planets

拓 *n.* astronomy

例 Being an astronomer is my dream. 成为一个天文学家是我的梦想。

Nothing could diminish her enthusiasm for the project.

什么也不能影响她对这项计划的热忱。

diminish [dɪˈmɪnɪʃ] *vt. & vi.* **减少，变小**

释 to become or make something smaller or less; to deliberately make someone or something appear less important or valuable than they really are

例 The medical expenses diminished her savings. 医疗费耗去了她的积蓄。

---

enthusiasm [ɪnˈθjuːzɪæzəm] *n.* **热情，热心**

释 a feeling of energetic interest in a particular subject or activity and an eagerness to be involved in it

拓 *n.* enthusiast; *a.* enthusiastic; *ad.* enthusiastically

用 enthusiasm for

例 Nothing great is ever achieved without enthusiasm. 缺乏热情难成大事。

You can automatically find lowest price, and optimal shopping list maker will assign best shops for your products.

你可以通过最佳购物向导找到你想要商品的最好商店和最低价格。

optimal [ˈɒptɪməl] *a.* **最佳的，最理想的**

释 best; most likely bring success or advantage

拓 *vt.* optimise

例 You'll know all when you see the optimal solution graph. 看到最佳解图后，你就会明白一切。

The problem for biologists, psychologists and anthropologists is to find out two plausible explanations.

对于生物学家、心理学家和人类学家而言，找出两个合乎情理的解释是问题的关键。

biologist [baɪˈɒlədʒɪst] *n.* 生物学家

释 a scientist who studies biology

拓 *n.* biology; *a.* biological; *ad.* biologically

---

anthropologist [ˌænθrəˈpɒlədʒɪst] *n.* 人类学家

释 a person who studies anthropology

拓 *n.* anthropology; *a.* anthropological

---

plausible [ˈplɔːzəbl] *a.* 有道理的，可信的

释 reasonable and likely to be true or successful

拓 *ad.* plausibly; *n.* plausibility

例 Her story certainly sounds plausible. 她的故事听起来合乎情理。

A comedian will present a situation followed by an unexpected interpretation that is also apt.

一个喜剧演员要能在出乎意料的情境中灵活演出。

comedian [kəˈmiːdɪən] *n.* 喜剧演员

释 someone whose job is to tell jokes and make people laugh

拓 *n.* comedy

例 The comedian's act drew a large crowd. 那个喜剧演员的表演吸引了一批观众。

---

interpretation [ˌɪntɜːprɪˈteɪʃən] *n.* 演出，演奏

释 the way in which someone performs a play, a piece of music, etc.

拓 *a.* interpretive

例 His skillful interpretation of this song is wonderful. 他对这首歌曲的演奏很精彩。

---

apt [æpt] *a.* 灵巧的，灵敏的；适当的

释 exactly right for a particular situation or purpose

拓 *ad.* aptly

例 The words are apt and well chosen. 用词适当，并经缜密斟酌。

Early cinema programmes were a mixture of items, combining comic sketches, free-standing narratives, serial episodes or animated film.

早期的电影节目融合了连环画、自由叙述、连续片断或者动画片断。

sketch [sketʃ] *n.* 素描；草图

释 a simple, quickly-made drawing that does not show much details

例 At the conference, he gave a sketch of recent happenings. 在会上，他简述了最近发生的事件。

---

episode ['epɪsəʊd] *n.* 插曲，插话；情节

释 an event or a short period of time during which something specific happens

拓 *a.* episodic

例 One of the funniest episodes in the book occurs in chapter 8. 最有趣的情节之一出现在书中的第8章。

---

animate ['ænɪmeɪt] *vt.* 使……有生气，赋予生命

释 to give life or energy to something

拓 *a.* animated; *n.* animation

例 A smile animated his face. 一丝笑容给他脸上增添了生气。

She was eager to submerge herself in the feminist movement.

她迫切希望投身于女权运动中。

submerge [səbˈmɜːdʒ] *vt. & vi.* 使漫水，潜入水中；使陷入

释 to go below the surface of the sea or a river or lake

拓 *n.* submersion / submergence

例 At the first sign of danger the submarine will submerge. 一有危险迹象，潜艇就会潜入水中。

---

feminist [ˈfemɪnɪst] *n. / a.* 男女平等主义者(的)

释 a person who believes in feminism, often being involved in activities intended to achieve change

例 My point of view is that, a feminist is made, not born. 我认为，女权主义者不是生来如此的，而是环境造成的。

Ptolemy's successors used increasingly unscrupulous techniques to obtain manuscripts.

托勒密的继承者使用更加不道德的方法来获得手稿。

unscrupulous [ʌnˈskruːpjələs] *a.* 肆无忌惮的，无天理的

释 behaving in a way that is dishonest or unfair in order to get what you want

拓 *ad.* unscrupulously

用 be unscrupulous about

例 He is an unscrupulous rogue. No one believes him. 他是一个狡猾之徒，没有人信他。

---

manuscript [ˈmænjuskrɪpt] *n.* 手稿，原稿

释 the original copy of a book or article before it is printed

例 I have read his novel in manuscript. 我已经看过他小说的手稿。

十 农业类

This has led to a serious decline in farm output and a change in the local diet, because there is insufficient labour to maintain terraces and irrigation systems and tend to crops.

这种情况造成了农产品产量的严重下降和当地人口饮食结构的改变，因为没有足够的劳动力维持梯田和浇灌系统以及生产农作物。

decline [dɪ'klaɪn] *n.* 衰退，跌落

释 a decrease in the quality, quantity, or importance of something

用 decline in; decline of; dramatic / rapid / sharp / steep decline; long-term / short-term/ steady gradual decline; in decline

例 But more important is the decline in birth rates when people leave the countryside . 但更重要的原因是，当人们走出农村，生育率便开始下降了。

---

insufficient [ˌɪnsə'fɪʃənt] *a.* 不足的

释 not enough, or not great enough

拓 *ad.* insufficiently; *n.* insufficiency

用 insufficient for

例 The food was insufficient for our needs. 食物不能满足我们的需要。

---

maintain [meɪn'teɪn] *vt.* 保持；维修，保养

释 to make something continue in the same way or at the same standard as before

拓 *n.* maintenance

例 We should maintain a high sense of responsibility. 我们应该保持高度的责任心。

terrace ['terəs] *n.* 梯田

释 one of a series of flat areas of ground that are cut into the side of a hill like steps so that crops can be grown there

拓 *n.* terracing

例 Terraced fields can be seen everywhere in this area. 这一地区到处可见梯田。

---

irrigation [ˌɪrɪ'geɪʃn] *n.* 灌溉

释 the act of supplying land or crops with water

例 Water is channeled through a series of irrigation canals. 把水引入一系列灌溉渠中。

When local resources became depleted, the tribe moved on.

当本地资源耗尽的时候，该部落就会迁移。

deplete [dɪ'pliːt] *vt.* 耗尽，使……枯竭

释 to reduce something in size or amount, especially supplies of energy, money or similar

拓 *n.* depletion; *a.* depleted

用 deplete of

例 Mankind must take care not to deplete the earth of its natural resources. 人类必须注意，切莫耗尽地球上的自然资源。

The farmers needed homes which were permanent dwellings.

农民需要永久性住房。

permanent ['pɜːmənənt] *a.* 永久的，持久的

释 lasting for a long time or for all time in the future; existing all the time

拓 *ad.* permanently; *n.* permanence

例 This car wax gives permanent protection against heavy rain.

这种汽车蜡能长久防止大雨侵蚀。

---

dwell [dwel] *vi.* 居住

释 to live somewhere

拓 *n.* dweller / dwelling

用 dwell in

例 He has dwelt in London for two years. 他在伦敦住了两年。

The remainder is used to irrigate farm crops.

其余的是用来灌溉农作物的。

irrigate ['ɪrɪgeɪt] *vt.* 灌溉

释 to supply land or crops with water

拓 *n.* irrigation

例 In some developed countries, helicopter are used to irrigate crops.

在有些发达国家，人们使用直升机灌溉庄稼。

To feed an increasingly hungry world, farmers need very incentive to use their soil and water effectively and efficiently.

世界饥饿问题日益严重，农民必须更有效地利用土地和水资源。

incentive [ɪn'sentɪv] *n.* 刺激，鼓励，动机

释 something that encourages you to work harder, start a new activity

用 create / give sb. an incentive; incentive to do sth.

例 The child has no incentive to study harder because he lost his confidence. 这孩子没有努力学习的动力，因为他丧失自信了。

effectively [ɪ'fektɪvli] *ad.* 有效地

释 in a way that is successful and achieves what you want

拓 *n.* effectiveness / effect; *a.* effective

例 They attempted to make the system work more effectively. 他们试图使该系统工作得更有效。

---

efficiently [ɪ'fɪʃntli] *ad.* 有效地

释 if someone or something is efficient, they work well without wasting time, money, or energy

拓 *n.* efficiency; *a.* efficient

例 The manager said it was an efficiently organized event. 经理说这是一场组织效率极高的活动。

For maximum dung burial in spring, summer and autumn, farmers require a variety of species with overlapping periods of activity.

农民在春夏秋季节中需要不断使用各种手段尽可能地处理好粪肥。

burial ['berɪəl] *n.* 埋葬

释 the act or ceremony of burying a dead body into a grave

拓 *vt.* bury

用 burial of

例 He possesses a common burial place. 他有一块普通墓地。

---

overlap [ˌəuvə'læp] *vt. & vi.* 重叠，重复

释 if two or more things overlap, the second one starts before the first one has finished, or part of one thing covers part of another thing

用 overlap with

例 History and politics overlap and should be studied together. 历史与政治有相同之处，应该一起来研究。

European peasants would insert a wooden drill in a round hole and rotate it briskly between their palms.

欧洲的农民把一个木钻插在一个洞里面，在手心之间使他们快速旋转。

drill [drɪl] *n.* 钻孔机，钻子

释 a tool with a sharp point and curving edges for making holes in hard materials

例 He wrote a book on electrician's drill. 他写了一本关于电工钻的书。

---

rotate [rəʊ'teɪt] *vi.* （使）旋转

释 to turn with a circular movement around a central point or to make something do this

拓 *n.* rotation

例 The Earth rotates on its axis once every 24 hours. 地球每24小时绕轴心转一周。

---

briskly ['brɪskli] *ad.* 活泼地，精神勃勃地

释 in a brisk manner

拓 *n.* briskness

例 After examination, he went out of the classroom briskly. 考试结束，他轻松愉快地走出了教室。

---

palm [pɑːm] *n.* 手掌

释 the inside surface of your hand，in which you hold things

例 She held the English book in the palm of her hand. 她手里拿着那本英语书。

The usual way to reclaim land is to pile sand rock on to the seabed.

把沙石堆积到河床上是开垦土地的通常做法。

reclaim [rɪ'kleɪm] *vt.* 开垦

释 to make land, such as desert or flooded areas, suitable for farming or building

拓 *n.* reclaimation

用 reclaim from

例 This land will be reclaimed for a new train station. 这土地上要新建一座火车站。

---

seabed ['siːbed] *n.* 海底，海床

释 the bottom of a sea or ocean

例 Earth movements in the past elevated great area of the seabed.

过去的地球运动使海底大片地区隆起。

十一 交通运输类

First airlines, then road haulers and railways, were freed from restrictions on what they could carry.

首先是航空，然后是公路和铁路运输，对三者的运输限制先后都放开了。

hauler ['hɔːlə] *n.* 拖曳者（承运人，运输机，运输工），[美] 搬运工

释 a person or a company whose business is transporting goods by road railway / railroad

例 He spent ＄20 and finally found two haulers. 他花了20美元终于找到了两个搬运工。

To search out these answers, I created raised-line drawings of five different wheels, depicting spokes with lines that curved, bent, waved, dashed and extended beyond the perimeter of the wheel.

为了找出这些答案，我画了五个轮子的突起线条，描绘了曲线、斜线、波浪线、虚线和超出轮子周长的射线的轮廓。

depict [dɪˈpɪkt] *vt.* 描述

释 to describe something or someone in writing or speech, or to show them in a painting, picture, etc.

拓 *n.* depiction

用 depict sb. / sth

例 This painting depicts the early age of Shanghai. 这幅画描绘的是早期的上海。

---

extend [ɪkˈstend] *vt.* & *vi.* （空间、时间等）延伸; 延续

释 to make something longer or larger

拓 *a.* extendable; *vt.* & *vi.* extend

例 The hot weather extended into November. 炎热天气一直持续到十一月。

---

perimeter [pəˈrɪmɪtə] *n.* 周长，周界

释 the border around and enclosed area such as a military camp

用 perimeter of; perimeter fence / wall

例 What is perimeter of this polygon? 这个多边形的周长是多少？

The giant trucks rumbled when it finished its job.

巨型卡车完成工作之后发出隆隆的声音。

giant ['dʒaɪənt] *a.* 巨大的

释 extremely big, and much bigger than other things of the same type

例 A giant electronics company has just been established in this area.

该地区刚刚建成一家大型电子公司。

---

rumble ['rʌmbl] *vt.* 隆隆声，辘辘响

释 to make a continuous low sound

拓 *n.* rumbling

例 Please excuse my stomach rumbling — I haven't eaten all day.

请原谅我的肚子发出的咕噜声，我一整天没吃饭了。

Car controlling would be an effective way of reducing emissions as well as easing congestion.

控制汽车是一个有效的减排方法，也可以缓解交通拥堵。

emission [ɪ'mɪʃən] *n.* 发射，射出

释 a gas or other substance that is sent into the air; the act of sending out light, heat, gas, etc

拓 *vt.* emit

例 Britain decided to cut emissions from chemical factories. 英国决定控制化工厂的废气排放。

---

congestion [kən'dʒestʃən] *n.* 拥挤，阻塞

释 a crush or things in a limited space

拓 *a.* congested

例 It is necessary for the government to control the traffic congestion and pollution. 政府控制交通堵塞和污染是必要的。

One solution is car-pooling, all arrangement in which a number of people who share the same destination share the use of one car.

解决办法之一是共用汽车，把去同一目的地的人安排在同一辆车上。

solution [sə'luːʃən] *n.* **解答，解决办法**

释 the answer to a problem

拓 *vt.* solve

用 the solution to the problem

例 Finally I found the solution to the problem. 最后我发现了这个问题的解决方法。

---

destination [ˌdestɪ'neɪʃən] *n.* **目的地，终点**

释 the place where someone is going or where something is being sent or taken

拓 *a.* destined; *vt.* destine

用 destination for

例 We eventually arrived at our destination. 我们终于到达了目的地。

We expect that the work will be completed at this time without further disruption to traffic.

我们期待在交通没有进一步瘫痪的前提下把这份工作完成好。

disruption [dɪs'rʌpʃən] *n.* **分裂，破坏**

释 the act of preventing something, especially a system, process or event， from continuing as usual or as expected

拓 *vt.* disrupt; *a.* disruptive; *ad.* disruptively

例 The whole factory was in disruption. 整个工厂一片混乱。

They are often wealthier than their American counterparts but have not generated the same level of car use.

他们比美国队更加富有，但是在汽车使用上还不在一个档次。

counterpart ['kaʊtəpɑːt] *n.* 对方，极相似的人［物］

释 someone or something that has the same job or purpose as someone or something else in a different place

例 I drained my memory in vain for its counterpart in literature.

我绞尽脑汁也想不出它在文学中的对等物。

---

generate ['dʒenəreɪt] *vt.* 产生，发生

释 to produce or cause something

拓 *n.* generation

例 Steam can generate electricity by turning an electric generator.

蒸汽转动发电机可以发电。

It gauges the pollution from a passing vehicle.

它测算行经车辆的排污剂量。

gauge [geɪdʒ] *n.* 计量器，标准度量；*vt.* 估计；度量（美国英语：gage）

释 an instrument for measuring the size or amount of something; to make judgment about sth.

例 This bank calls 800 customers a night to gauge their experience.

这家银行每天晚上会邀请800位客户评价他们的经历。

---

vehicle ['viːɪkl] *n.* 交通工具，车辆

释 a machine usually with wheels and an engine, which is used for transporting people or goods on land, particularly on roads

用 vehicle for sth.

例 No vehicles are permitted into the park. 公园内禁止任何车辆进入。

十二 建筑类

But do ports all produce a range of common urban characteristics which justify classifying port cities together under a single generic label?

但是否所有的港口都有一系列共同的城市特性，以至于我们可以把港口城市全部归为一类？

characteristic [ˌkærɪktəˈrɪstɪk] *n.* 特性，特色，特征

释 a quality or feature of something or someone that is typical of them and easy to recognize

拓 *ad.* characteristically

用 characteristic of

例 Ambition is a characteristic of all great persons. 雄心勃勃是所有的伟人的共同特点。

---

justify [ˈdʒʌstɪfaɪ] *vt.* 替……辩护；证明，声明

释 to give an acceptable explanation for something that other people think is unreasonable

拓 *a.* justified / justifiable; *ad.* justifiably

用 justify doing sth.

例 The Prime Minister has been asked to justify the decision to Parliament. 首相须就这一决定向议会作出解释。

---

classify [ˈklæsɪfaɪ] *vt.* 分类，分等，归类

释 to decide what group something belongs to; to divide things into groups according to their types

拓 *a.* classifiable; *n.* classification

例 Librarians spend a lot of time classifying books.图书馆工作人员花许多时间将书分类。

---

generic [dʒɪ'nerɪk] *a.* 共有的，一般的，普通的

释 shared by, typical of or relating to a whole group of similar things, rather than to any particular thing

拓 *ad.* generically

用 generic name / term for sth.

例 The generic name for spirits, grape wine and beer is alcoholic beverages. 雪碧、葡萄酒及啤酒通称为酒类饮料。

A new style of architecture emerged to reflect more idealistic notions for the future.

一种新的建筑风格出现了，它更多反映的是对未来的理想主义观念。

emerge [ɪ'mɜːdʒ] *vi.* 浮现，显现出来

释 to appear by coming out of something or out from behind something

拓 *n.* emergence; *a.* emerging

用 emerge from

例 Sea mammals must emerge periodically to breathe fresh air.
海生哺乳动物必须不断地浮出海面呼吸清新空气。

---

reflect [rɪ'flekt] *vt. & vi.* 反射，反映；思考

释 to show, express or be sign of something; to show the image of sb. / sth. on the surface of sth. such as a mirror, water or glass; to think carefully and deeply about sth.

拓 *n.* reflection

用 be reflected in sth.; reflect on; reflect that

例 Snow crystals have many surfaces to reflect sunlight. 雪晶有许多面来反射太阳光。

---

idealistic [ˌaɪdɪəˈlɪstɪk] *a.* 理想主义的

释 believing that you should live according to high standards and principles, even it they cannot really be achieved, or showing this belief

拓 *ad.* idealistically

例 His point was not imperial, but idealistic.他的观点并不傲慢，而是充满理想主义。

---

notion [ˈnəʊʃən] *n.* 观念，主张，想法

释 an idea, belief, or opinion

拓 *a.* notional

用 notion of; notion that

例 The whole notion of admiring Nature is to protect. 主张敬慕大自然就是主张保护它。

The port city provides a fascinating and rich understanding of the movement of people and goods around the world.

港口城市为理解全球人口和货物的流动提供了生动和丰富的依据。

fascinating [ˈfæsɪneɪtɪŋ] *a.* 迷人的

释 extremely interesting and attractive

拓 *vt.* fascinate; *a.* fascinated; *n.* fascination

例 The book contains a fascinating portrait of life. 本书包含着对生活的生动写照。

movement ['muːvmənt] *n.* 活动，运动

释 a group of people who share the same ideas or beliefs and who work together to achieve a particular aim

用 movement to do sth.; movement for

例 The Trade Union Movement works to get much higher salary.
工会运动旨在争取更高的工资。

Newman, however, believes the study demonstrates that the auto-dependent city model is inefficient and grossly inadequate in economic as well as environmental terms.

然而，纽曼认为，这项研究表明，自给自足的城市模型无论在经济还是在环境方面都是行不通的。

grossly [grəʊsli] *ad.* 非常，大体上

释 totally

拓 *a.* / *n.* gross

例 He thought he would be promoted to be the chairman, but he was grossly mistaken. 他认为他将晋升为主席，但是他大错特错了。

---

inadequate [ɪn'ædɪkwɪt] *a.* 不充分的，不适当的

释 not good enough or too low in quality

拓 *n.* inadequacy; *ad.* inadequately

例 He's inadequate for the job. 他不能胜任那个工作。

There are reports of igloos losing their insulating properties as the snow strips and refreezes.

有报道称圆顶建筑可能由于积雪剥落和结冰而失去绝缘性。

igloo ['ɪgluː] *n.* 圆顶建筑

释 a circular house made of blocks of hard snow, especially as built by the Inuit people of northern North America

---

insulate ['insjuleɪt] *vt.* 使……绝缘；隔离；绝缘

释 to protect sth. with a material that prevents heat, sound, electricity, etc. from passing through

拓 *n.* insulation

用 insulate from / against

例 Rubber is used to insulate electric wires. 橡胶被用来使电线绝缘。

---

refreeze [riː'friːz] *vt.* 再结冰（重新冻结，再致冷）

释 to become hard, and often turn to ice, as a result of extreme old

例 It's so cold that even the river has refrozen. 天气太冷，致使河水都结冰了。

The Kansai builders recognized that settlement was inevitable.

关西机场的建筑者认识到地面沉降是不可避免的。

recognize ['rekəgnaɪz] *vt.* 认出，认可，承认

释 to know someone or something because you have seen, heard or experienced them before

拓 *a.* recognizable; *n.* recognition

用 recognize sth. as sth.; recognize that

例 Can you recognize this person? 你能认出这个人吗？

---

inevitable [ɪn'evɪtəbl] *a.* 不可避免的，必然（发生）的

释 certain to happen and unable to be avoided or prevented

拓 *n.* inevitability; *ad.* inevitably

用 it is inevitable (that); inevitable consequence / result

例 It's inevitable that doctors make the occasional operation mistake. 医生出现偶尔的医疗事故是不可避免的。

The proposal advocated the creation of urban villages around railway stations.

该提案主张在火车站旁边建造城中村。

advocate ['ædvəkeɪt] *vt.* 拥护，支持

释 to support sth. publicly

拓 *n.* advocacy

例 Many experts advocate rewarding your child for good behaviour.

很多专家主张对小孩的良好表现加以奖励。

A long cylindrical tube was propped up by two sticks and fastened to the top of launcher.

长圆柱管被根棍子支撑了起来，并系在发射塔的顶部。

cylindrical [sɪ'lɪndrɪkl] *a.* 圆柱的

释 shaped like a cylinder

拓 *ad.* cylindrically; *n.* cylinder

例 He works in that cylindrical office building. 他在那幢圆柱形办公楼里工作。

---

prop [prɒp] *vt.* 支撑，维持

释 to support something physically, often by leaning it against something else or putting something under it

用 prop up

例 It is not the government's policy to prop up declining industries.

资助不景气的工业不是政府的政策。

---

launcher ['lɔːntʃə] *n.* 发射者，发射物，发射台

释 a device that is used to send a rocket, a missile, etc.

例 A medical missile launcher was designed on the principle of the crossbow. 中世纪的火箭发射装置是根据石弓的原理设计而成的。

Building big commercial buildings underground can be a way to avoid disfiguring or threatening a beautiful or environmentally sensitive landscape.

建设大型地下商业大厦是一个可以避免毁损或者威胁一个易受环境影响的地上景观的方法。

disfigure [dɪsˈfɪgjə] *vt.* **使丑陋，损毁(外貌)**

释 to spoil the appearance that something naturally has

拓 *a.* disfigured / disfiguring; *n.* disfigurement

例 Her face had been disfigured in a cosmetic accident. 她的脸在一次化妆的意外事件中被毁坏了。

---

sensitive [ˈsensɪtɪv] *a.* **敏感的**

释 responsive to external conditions or stimulation; able to understand other people's feelings and problems

拓 *ad.* sensitively

用 sensitive to, sensitive about

例 Some people's teeth are highly sensitive to freeze. 一些人的牙齿对冷非常敏感。

Disillusionment at the failure of many of the poor imitations of modernist architecture led to interest in various styles and ideas from the past and present.

人们从现代建筑诸多失败的模仿中觉醒后，其兴趣转向从古到今的各种建筑风格和理念。

disillusionment [ˌdɪsɪˈluːʒənmənt] *n.* **理想破灭，醒悟**

释 the state of being disillusioned

拓 *vt.* / *n.* disillusion; *a.* disillusioned

例 This state of discontent and disillusionment created a real crisis for the country. 怨声载道和理想破灭的现状给这个国家造成了极为严重的危机。

---

imitation [ˌɪmɪˈteɪʃən] *n.* 模仿，仿效

释 an attempt to imitate someone or something, or the act of doing this

拓 *n.* imitator; *vt.* imitate; *a.* imitative

例 Children learn language by imitation. 孩子通过模仿学习语言。

The rediscovery of quick-and-easy-to-handle reinforced concrete and an improved ability to prefabricate building sections meant that builders could meet the budgets of commissioning authorities and handle a renewed demand for development quickly and cheaply.

快捷、简易的钢筋混凝土和预先制造建筑结构的能力的提高这一重新发现，意味着建筑者们可以达到委托管理局的预算，也会解决对快捷、便宜的房屋的再次需求问题。

reinforce [ˌriːɪnˈfɔːs] *vt.* 增援，加强

释 to give support to an opinion, idea, or feeling, and make it stronger

拓 *n.* reinforcement

例 Our defences must be reinforced against attack. 我们必须加强防御设施，以抵御进攻。

---

prefabricate [priːˈfæbrɪˌkeɪt] *vt.* 预先制造；预先构思

释 to make the parts of a building, ship, etc. in a factory in standard sizes, so that they can be fitted together somewhere else

拓 *a.* prefabricated; *n.* prefabrication

例 There is a prefabricated home. 一个预先组合的房子。

A large pane of toughened glass in the roof of a shopping center at bishops walk shattered without warning and fell from its frame.

主教大街购物中心的屋顶上加固的玻璃片毫无征兆地突然从框上掉下来，砸碎了。

toughen ['tʌfn] *vt. & vi.* **使……坚韧，使……顽固**

释 to become tougher, or to make someone or something tougher

拓 *a.* tough; *ad.* toughly; *n.* toughness

例 The government wants to toughen (up) the existing drug laws.

政府想要加强现存的毒品法案建设。

---

bishop ['bɪʃəp] *n.* **主教**

释 a priest with a high rank in the Christian religions, who is the head of all the churches and priests in a large area

例 The bishop conducted a number of confirmations at the service.

主教在仪式上为许多人施行了坚信礼。

---

shatter ['ʃætə] *vt. & vi.* **打碎，破掉**

释 to break suddenly into very small pieces, or to make something break in this way

用 shatter into

例 The explosion shattered the construction. 爆炸摧毁了建筑物。

Public infrastructure did not keep pace with urban sprawl.

公共基础设施没有跟上城市前进的步伐。

infrastructure ['infrəˌstræktʃə] *n.* **基础结构，基础设施**

释 the basic systems and services, such as transport and power supplies, that a country or organization uses in order to work effectively

例 A country's economic infrastructure is essential for its further development. 一个国家的经济基础结构对其未来发展至关重要。

---

sprawl [sprɔːl] *vi.* 躺卧(蔓延)； *n.* 扩展

释 to spread the arms and legs out carelessly and untidily while sitting or lying down; an act of spreading to cover a large area in an untidy way

拓 *a.* sprawled / sprawling

例 I was sprawling full length on the cargo. 我伸展四肢平躺在装载的货物上。

Closer inspection revealed a chink of sky-light window among the thistles.

走近一看，透过丛生的蓟花，可隐约看到天窗的裂缝。

inspection [ɪnˈspekʃən] *n.* 视察，检查

释 when you look at something carefully, or an official visit to a building or organization to check that everything is correct and legal

拓 *vt.* inspect; *n.* inspector; *a.* inspective

用 on inspection

例 Elevators must under go an annual safety inspection. 电梯必须每年接受一次安全检查。

---

chink [tʃɪŋk] *n.* 裂口，裂缝；叮当响

释 a small narrow crack or opening; a light ringing sound; a clink

拓 *a.* chinky

用 a chink of

例 The inspector found a chink in the wall. 检查人员在墙上发现一条裂缝。

thistle ['θɪsəl] *n.*【植】蓟

释 a wild plant with sharp points on the leaves and typically, purple flowers

例 The thistle is the national symbol of Scotland. 蓟是苏格兰的民族象征。

Originally the exterior was covered in highly polished limestone slabs, all of which have been stolen over the years.

起初外表铺设的是光滑的石灰石隔板，但在这几年中几乎都被盗了。

exterior [eks'tɪərɪə] *n.* 外部，表面，外形；*a.* 外部的，外在的，表面的

释 outer; on or from the outside

例 The exterior of the building needs painting and renovating. 建筑的外观需要粉刷和重新装修一下。

---

polish ['pɒlɪʃ] *vt.* 擦亮，磨光

释 to rub something using a piece of cloth or brush to clean it and make it shine

拓 *a.* polished

用 polish up

例 She polished her glasses with a handkerchief before lecture. 在演讲之前，她用手帕擦拭了一下眼镜。

---

limestone ['laɪmˌstəʊn] *n.* 石灰石

释 a white or light grey rock which is used as a building material and in the making of cement

---

slab [slæb] *n.* 平板；厚的切片

释 a thick flat piece of a solid substance, such as stone, wood, metal, food, etc., which is usually square or rectangular

用 slab of

例 The tomb is covered with a marble slab. 墓穴上盖着一块大理石板。

Seven luxury homes cosseted away inside a high earth-covered noise embankment.

七座豪宅被泥土覆盖着的高大的隔音系统保护着。

cosset [ˈkɒsɪt] *vt.* 宠爱，珍爱，溺爱

释 to give someone as much care and attention as you can, especially too much

例 The students have been cosseted by the parents for so long that they have forgotten how to take responsibility for themselves. 学生长期受家长溺爱，以至于忘记了自己的责任所在。

---

embankment [emˈbæŋkmənt] *n.* 堤防，筑堤

释 a wide wall of earth or stones built to stop water from flooding an area, or to support a road or railway

例 He often promenades his family along the Thames Embankment. 他常常带家人沿着泰晤士河堤散步。

十三 历史文化类

Deeply religious people obediently accepted the supreme authority of their pharaohs.

虔诚的信徒顺从地承认了法老的最高权力。

obediently [əˈbiːdɪəntli] *ad.* 顺从地，服从地

释 always doing what you are told to do, or what the law, a rule, etc.

says you must do

拓 *n.* obedience; *a.* obedient

用 obedient to

例 Residents must be obedient to the law. 居民必须服从法律。

---

supreme authority 最高权力，权威

---

pharaoh ['feərəu] *n.* 法老王

释 a ruler of ancient Egypt; the title of a king of ancient Egypt

The British Academy, established by *Royal Charter* in 1902, is the national academy for the humanities and the social sciences.

英国学术委员会由1902年《皇家宪章》批准建立，它是关于人文和社会科学的全国性委员会。

academy [ə'kædəmi] *n.* 学会，学院

释 an organization intended to protect and develop an art, science, language, etc., or a school which teaches a particular subject or trains people for a particular job

拓 *n.* academician

例 He visited Chinese Academy of Science yesterday. 他昨天访问了中国科学院。

---

humanity [hju:'mænɪti] *n.* 人文学科

释 the study of subjects such as literature, language, history and philosophy, etc.

例 The emphasis is on education, and it is an education that places emphasis on both humanities and technology. 重点就是教育，而且是人文教育与科学技术并重的教育。

While the Inuit may not actually starve if hunting and trapping are curtailed by climate change.

然而，因纽特人不会因为环境变化对狩猎造成的破坏而挨饿。

curtail [kɜːˈteɪl] *vt.* 缩减，剥夺，简略

释 to reduce or limit something

拓 *n.* curtailment

用 severely / drastically curtail

例 Budget cuts have drastically curtailed the programs. 削减预算大幅缩减了项目。

Do you see the role of private and public ceremonies changing in the future?

你认为未来个人礼仪和公共礼仪的角色以后会有变化吗？

ceremony [ˈserɪməni] *n.* 典礼，仪式，礼节，礼仪

释 a public or religious occasion that includes a series of formal or traditional actions

例 The wedding ceremony was held on April 15th. 婚礼在四月十五日举行。

The fact they were grouped into sizes and perforated suggests they were deliberately fashioned into beads.

根据不同尺寸将他们分组并对之穿孔这一事实表明他们是被人有意制成珠子。

perforate [ˈpɜːfəreɪt] *vt.* 穿孔，凿孔

释 to make a hole or holes through sth.

拓 *a.* perforated

例 The target was perforated by bullets. 靶子上全是子弹打穿的孔。

deliberately [dɪˌlɪbəˈreɪtli] *ad.* 故意地

释 done in a way that was planned, not by chance

拓 *a.* deliberate; *n.* deliberation

例 I felt his report was deliberately opaque. 我觉得他的报告故意含糊其辞。

All continents were colonized and evolved into a vast array of shapes and sizes.

各大陆都已被殖民化并形成不同形状和面积的殖民地。

colonize [ˈkɒlənaɪz] *vt.* 开拓殖民地，殖民

释 to establish political control over an area or over another country, and send your citizens there to settle

拓 *n.* colonizer / colonization

例 Britain colonized many countries. 英国将许多国家变为自己的殖民地。

---

evolve [ɪˈvɒlv] *vt. & vi.* 使逐步形成，发展；进化

释 to develop or achieve gradually

拓 *n.* evolution; *a.* evolutionary

用 evolve from; evolve out of; evolve into

例 The British present political system has evolved over several centuries. 英国现行的政治制度是经过几个世纪逐步发展而成的。

---

array [əˈreɪ] *n.* 大批，一系列

释 a group of people or things, especially one that is large or impressive

用 an array of

例 There was a splendid array of flowers on the desk. 桌子上摆放着好多美丽的鲜花。

Life for the descendants of those people is still harsh.

那些人的后代依然生活得很艰苦。

descendant [dɪˈsendənt] *n.* 子孙，后代

释 a person's descendants are all the people who live after them and who are related to them

用 descendant of

例 They claim to be descendants of Confucius. 他们声称是孔子的后代。

---

harsh [hɑːʃ] *a.* 残酷的，严厉的

释 cruel, severe and unkind

拓 *ad.* harshly; *n.* harshness

用 harsh winter / weather / climate; harsh criticism / treatment

例 Expulsion from school is a harsh form of punishment. 开除学籍是一种严厉的惩罚。

Research projects that will impinge too much on their daily lives and traditional activities.

研究项目将会过多地影响他们的日常生活及传统活动。

impinge [ɪmˈpɪndʒ] *vi.* 影响

释 to have a harmful effect on someone or something

拓 *n.* impingement

用 impinge on / upon sth. / sb.

例 Your political opinions will necessarily impinge on your public life. 你的政治观点必然会影响你的社会生活。

The fortunate discovery gave the help to subsequent deciphering the Rosetta Stone.

这个幸运的发现为后来的罗塞纳石碑的破译提供了帮助。

subsequent ['sʌbsɪkwənt] *a.* 随后的，后来的

释 happening or coming after something else

拓 *ad.* subsequently

用 subsequent to sth.

例 Those explosions must have been subsequent to our departure, because we didn't hear anything. 爆炸肯定是在我们离开之后发生的，因为我们什么都没有听到。

As they began to settle / grow plants and herd animals, the need for a sophisticated number system became paramount.

当他们开始定居、种植、放牧的时候，对复杂的计数系统的需要就变得格外重要。

herd [hɜːd] *vt. & vi.* 群集，使……成群；放牧

释 to move or make somebody / something move in a particular direction; to make animals move together as a group

例 A man was herding the goats up the mountain. 一个人正在山上放羊。

---

paramount ['pærəˌmaʊnt] *a.* 极为重要的

释 more important than anything else

拓 *n.* paramountcy

例 The reduction of unemployment should be paramount. 降低失业率应是头等大事。

From the earliest times, people have devised highly ingenious methods for conserving water where it is scarce.

早在远古时期缺水时，人们就发明了一种极具独创性的蓄水方式。

ingenious [ɪn'dʒiːnjəs] *a.* 机灵的，有独创性的；足智多谋的

释 very suitable for a particular purpose and resulting from clever new ideas

拓 *ad.* ingeniously; *n.* ingenuity

例 Many animals have ingenious ways of protecting their eggs from predators. 许多动物都有很独特的方法来保护它们的蛋不被猎食者所捕获。

---

scarce [skeəs] *a.* 缺乏的，不足的，稀少的，罕见的

释 if something is scarce, there is not very much of it available

拓 *n.* scarcity; *ad.* scarcely

例 Food was often scarce in the rural areas. 农村常常食物不足。

The British Columbia Folklore Society dedicated to the collection and preservation of folk culture.

英国哥伦比亚民俗学会致力于收集和保存民俗文化。

folklore ['fəʊkˌlɔː] *n.* 民间风俗，民间传说，民俗

释 the traditional stories and culture of a group of people

例 Scandinavian folklore offers numerous explanations for the aurora borealis. 关于北极光，斯堪的那维亚的民间传说对此有着诸多解释。

---

preservation [ˌprezə'veɪʃən] *n.* 保护，维护，维持

释 the act of keeping something the same or preventing it from being damaged

拓 *n.* preservationist; *vt.* preserve; *a.* preservative

用 preservation of

例 The aim of the issue is the preservation of peace. 这一政策旨在维护和平。

This place occasionally superseded theatres and opera-houses in terms of opulence and splendor.

就奢华和辉煌而言，这个地方有时候都可以取代剧院和歌剧院了。

occasionally [ə'keɪʒənəli] *ad.* **偶尔地**

释 sometimes, but not regularly and not often

拓 *n.* occasion; *a.* occasional

例 Due to the long distance, we see each other very occasionally. 因为离得很远，我们只是偶尔见一见彼此。

---

supersede [ˌsjuːpə'siːd] *vt.* **代替，取代**

释 if a new idea, product, or method supersedes another one, it becomes used instead because it is more modern or effective

例 Their map has been superseded by the latest one. 他们的地图已经被最新版所取代。

---

opulence ['ɒpjuləns] *n.* **奢华，富丽堂皇**

释 wealth as evidenced by sumptuous living

拓 *a.* opulent; *ad.* opulently

例 The opulence of the hall impressed every guest. 奢华的礼堂给每位来宾留下了深刻的印象。

Native people encourage tourists to visit their pueblos and reservations to purchase high-quality handicrafts and artwork.

本地人鼓励游客参观他们的印第安人村庄和保留居所，以购买那些高质量的手工艺品和艺术品。

pueblo [pʊ'ebləʊ] *n.* 印第安人村庄

释 a permanent village or community of any of the Puebl people, typically consisting of multilevel adobe or stone apartment dwellings of terraced design clustered around a central place

---

handicraft ['hændɪkrɑːft] *n.* 手工艺

释 activities such as sewing and weaving that use skill with your hands and artistic ability to make things

例 Her hobby is handicraft. 她的爱好是手工艺。

Our ancestors had little use for actual numbers.

我们的祖先很少使用真实的数字。

ancestor ['ænsɪstə] *n.* 祖宗，祖先

释 a person, plant, animal or object that is related to one existing at a later point in time

拓 *a.* ancestral; *n.* ancestry

例 He is sprung from noble ancestor. 他出身名门。

Such anticipation is constructed and sustained through a variety of nontourist practices.

这种预期是通过各种非旅游做法来建造和维持的。

anticipation [æn,tɪsɪ'peɪʃən] *n.* 预期，预料

释 the fact of seeing that something might happen in the future and perhaps doing something about it now

拓 *vt.* anticipate; *a.* anticipatory

用 do sth. in anticipation of sth.

例 He waited in eager anticipation for Jim to arrive. 他急切等待着吉姆的到来。

---

sustain [sə'steɪn] *vt.* 承受，支持，经受，维持

释 to undergo; to make something continue to exist or happen for a period of time

拓 *a.* sustainable; *n.* sustainability

例 She was incapable of sustaining relationships with her boyfriend. 她无法和她的男朋友再维持这种关系了。

Egyptians lived in comparative security, prosperity and peace for thousands of years.

几千年来，埃及人生活得相对比较安全、富有、和平。

comparative [kəm'pærətɪv] *a.* 比较的，相对的

释 that is quite good when compared to how comfortable, free, or rich, etc. something or someone else is

拓 *ad.* comparatively

用 comparative study / analysis; comparative beginner / newcomer

例 She majored in comparative literature. 她主修比较文学。

---

prosperity [prɒs'perɪti] *n.* 繁荣，兴旺

释 the condition of prospering; having good fortune

拓 *a.* prosperous

用 prosperity of

例 The Chinese people are endeavoring to build a harmonious world of common prosperity. 中国人始终为建立一个共同繁荣的和谐世界而努力。

The compiling of dictionaries has been historically the provenance of studious professorial types — usually be spectacled — who love to pore over weighty tomes and make pronouncements on the finer nuances of meaning.

有史以来，辞典的编纂工作大多出自勤奋好学的学家之手，那些人通常戴着眼镜，喜欢埋头于繁重的大部头书籍，即使对一些词条的意义上的微小差别都会做出宣告。

compile [kəm'paɪl] *vt.* 汇编；编辑，编纂

释 to make a book, list, record, etc, using different pieces of information, music, etc.

用 compile sth. from / for sth.

例 The document was compiled by the Department of English. 这份文件是由英语系汇编的。

---

provenance ['prɒvənəns] *n.* 出处，起源

释 the place that something originally came from

例 I'm not quite clear about the provenance of the work. 我不太清楚这个作品的出处。

---

pronouncement [prə'naʊnsmənt] *n.* 宣布，宣告，声明

释 an official public statement

拓 *vt.* pronounce

例 There has been no official pronouncement yet on the state of the president's health. 官方尚未就总统的健康状况发表任何声明。

---

nuance ['njuːˌɑːns] *n.* （色调、音调、意义等的）细微差别

释 a very slight difference in color, tune, meaning, etc.

例 Linguists explore the nuances of language. 语言学家探究的是语言的细微差别。

Having survived there for centuries, they believe their wealth of traditional knowledge is vital to the task.

经过几个世纪的洗礼，他们相信自己所拥有的传统知识对这项任务是至关重要的。

survive [sə'vaɪv] *vi.* 生存，生还

释 to continue to live after an accident, war, or illness

拓 *n.* survival

用 survive on

例 The plants cannot survive in very cold conditions. 植物在非常冷的条件下无法生存下去。

---

vital ['vaɪtl] *a.* 至关重要的

释 extremely important and necessary for something to succeed or exist

用 vital to / for; it is vital (that); it is vital to do sth.

例 This matter is of vital importance to us. 这件事对我们来说至关重要。

People generally pay deference to the superior genius.

人们一般比较尊重天才。

genius ['dʒiːnjəs] *n.* 天才

释 a very high level of intelligence, mental skill, or ability, which only a few people have

用 a stroke of genius = a very clever idea; a genius at (doing) sth.; a genius for (doing) sth.

例 Einstein was a maths genius. 爱因斯坦是位数学天才。

We shall be known and cherished better than any preceding generations.

我们会被铭记，并且会比先辈们得到更多的敬爱。

preceding [ˌprɪ'siːdɪŋ] *a.* 在前的，在先的

释 existing or happening before someone or something

拓 *vt.* & *vi.* precede

用 preceding days / weeks / months / years

例 I hope the preceding arguments have convinced you of the need for action. 我希望之前的证据可以使你信服有必要实施行动。

---

generation [ˌdʒenə'reɪʃən] *n.* 一代，一辈

释 all the people of the same age within a society or within a particular family

用 generations of

例 There were at least four generations — great grandparents, grandparents, parents and children — at the wedding. 婚庆典礼上至少是四世同堂，曾祖父母，祖父母，父母和孩子。

This involves the investigation of bizarre and idiosyncratic social practices.

这包括对奇特的社会习俗的调查。

bizarre [bɪ'zɑː] *a.* 奇异的

释 very strange and unusual

拓 *ad.* bizarrely; *n.* bizarreness

例 The tale has a certain bizarre interest. 这个童话听起来有一种奇特的趣味。

---

idiosyncratic [ˌɪdɪəsɪŋ'krætɪk] *a.* 独特的

释 peculiar to the individual

拓 *n.* idiosyncrasy

The hostility of the indigenous population to North American influences the development of the country.

土著人口对北美人民的敌意影响了国家的发展。

hostility [hɒs'tɪlɪti] *n.* 敌意

释 unfriendly and not liking or agreeing with something

用 hostility to / towards

例 I feel no hostility towards anyone. 我对任何人均无敌意。

The archaeological evidence shows that the natural history of Amazonian is to a surprising extent tied to the activities of its prehistoric inhabitants.

考古方面的证据表明，亚马逊人的自然史与史前居民的活动有着异同寻常的联系。

archaeological [ˌɑːkiə'lɒdʒɪkl] *a.* 考古学的

释 related to or dealing with or devoted to archaeology

拓 *n.* archaeology / archaeologist / ethnoarchaeology

---

inhabitant [ɪn'hæbɪtənt] *n.* 居民；栖居动物

释 a person or an animal that lives in a particular place

拓 *vt.* inhabit

例 His grandfather is said to be one of the oldest inhabitants of the town. 据说他的祖父是这个城镇最早的居民之一。

Archaeologists in recent decades have developed "ethno-archaeology", where, like ethnographers, they live among contemporary communities.

考古学家在最近几十年里发展了“民族考古学”，他们就像民族志学者一样，生活在当代社会里。

ethnographer [eθ'nɒgrəfə] *n.* 民族志学者

释 an expert specializing in a scientific description of the culture of a society by someone who has lived in it, or a book containing this

拓 *n.* ethnography; *a.* ethnographic; *ad.* ethnographically

---

contemporary [kən'tempərəri] *a.* 属同时期的，当代的

释 belonging to the same time

拓 *ad.* contemporarily

例 Life in contemporary Britain impressed me most. 当代英国的生活给我留下了很深的印象。

---

community [kə'mjuːnɪti] *n.* 社区，团体

释 the people living in one particular area or people who are considered as a unit because of their common interests, background or nationality

例 He's well known in the local community. 他在当地非常有名。

Archaeology makes clear that with judicious management selected parts of the region could support more people than anyone thought before.

考古学明确指出，通过明智的管理，该地区的被选定部分可以养活比以往任何人所能想到的更多的人。

archaeology [ˌɑːkɪ'ɒlədʒi] *n.* 考古学

释 the study of the buildings, graves, tools and other objects which belonged to people who lived in the past, in order to learn about their culture and society

拓 *a.* archaeological; *ad.* archaeologically; *n.* archaeologist

例 *Brief History of Chinese Archaeology* contains many interesting stories. 《中国考古学简史》里有很多有趣的故事。

---

judicious [dʒuːˈdɪʃəs] *a.* 明智的，贤明的，判断正确的

释 having or showing reason and good judgement in making decisions

拓 *ad.* judiciously; *n.* judiciousness

例 Judicious lying sounds believable. 明智的谎话听起来就像真的一样。

Evidence of early stages of arithmetic can be readily found.

早期算法的证据很容易找到。

arithmetic [əˈrɪθmətɪk] *n.* 算术

释 the part of mathematics that involves the adding and multiplying, etc. of numbers

拓 *a.* arithmetical; *ad.* arithmetically

例 Her arithmetic is good. 她的算术很好。

One of the earliest dissertations on the subject of tourism is written by Boorstin.

关于旅游这个主题，最早的论文之一是由布尔斯廷写的。

dissertation [ˌdɪsəˈteɪʃən] *n.* 论文

释 a long piece of writing on a particular subject, especially one that is done as a part of a course at college or university

拓 *a.* dissertational

例 One has to write a dissertation for a degree. 必须撰写一篇学术论文才能获得学位。

Office signs and furniture are often used as role signs.

办公室标志及用品往往被当做地位的象征。

furniture ['fɜːnɪtʃə] *n.* 家具

释 items such as chairs, tables, beds, cupboards, etc. which are put into a house or other building to make it suitable and comfortable for living or working in

用 an article of furniture; a piece of furniture

例 They only got married recently and they haven't got much furniture. 他们才结婚不久，因此家里没有什么家具。

It reveals the remarkable ingenuity and the great organizing ability of the ancient Egyptians.

它揭示了古埃及人非凡的才智和伟大的组织能力。

ingenuity [ˌɪndʒɪ'njuɪti] *n.* 才能；心灵手巧；足智多谋

释 the ability to invent things or solve problems in clever new ways

拓 *a.* ingenious; *ad.* ingeniously

例 The small boy has an extraordinary ingenuity of invention. 小男孩具有非凡的发明才能。

To this day, many of the Egyptian artistic creations display the wealth, splendor and talent of this great civilization.

迄今为止，许多埃及的艺术作品中展示了这一伟大文明的富足、辉煌和才华。

splendor ['splendə] *n.* 光辉，壮丽，显赫

释 great beauty which attracts admiration and attention

拓 *a.* splendid; *ad.* splendidly; *n.* splendidness

例 The furniture in majestic splendor strikes people as gorgeous.

华丽的家具给人富丽堂皇的感觉。

---

civilization [ˌsɪvɪlaɪˈzeɪʃən] *n.* 文明；文化

释 human society with its highly developed social organizations, or the culture and way of life of a society or country at a particular period in time

拓 *vt.* civilize; *a.* civilized

例 Chinese civilization is one of the oldest in the world. 中国文明是世界上最古老的文明之一。

The design of these tombs developed into the stepped pyramid.

这些坟墓的设计已发展成为阶梯形金字塔了。

pyramid [ˈpɪrəmɪd] *n.* 金字塔

释 a solid object with a flat square base and four flat triangular sides which slope toward each other and meet to form a point at the top

拓 *a.* pyramidal

例 The Pyramids were among the seven wonders of the world. 古埃及金字塔是世界七大奇观之一。

The museum should acquire materials representing people whose art or material culture, ritual or political structures were on the point of irrevocable change.

博物馆应征集一些材料，这些材料代表了人们所创造的昭示着不可逆转变化的艺术或物质文化、仪式或政治结构。

ritual [ˈrɪtʃʊəl] *a.* 仪式的

释 done as part of a ritual or ceremony

拓 *a.* ritualistic; *ad.* ritualistically

例 Now, the concept of ritual impurity was a central and integral feature of most, of not all, ancient religions. 现在，仪式上的不洁这个概念已经是大部分宗教主要的，而且不可分割的一个特点了。

---

irrevocable [ɪ'revəkəbl] *a.* 不能唤回的，不能取消的，不能变更的

释 impossible to change

拓 *ad.* irrevocably

例 The court made an irrevocable judgement. 法庭做出了一项不可撤销的判决。

To early man, fire was a divine gift randomly delivered in the form of lightning, forest fire or burning lava etc.

对于早期人类来说，火是一种神圣的礼物，它以雷电、森林大火和岩浆等形式任意传递。

divine [dɪ'vaɪn] *a.* 神的，神圣的

释 connected with a god, or like a god

拓 *ad.* divinely; *n.* divination

例 Jesus is believed by Christians to have been divine. 基督教徒们相信耶稣是神圣的。

---

randomly ['rændəmli] *ad.* 任意地，随便地，胡乱地

释 in a random way, happening, done or chosen by chance rather than according to a plan

拓 *a.* random

例 The winning numbers are randomly selected by computer. 获奖号码是由电脑随机选取的。

Experimenting further, Von Frisch unraveled the mystery of the first two related types, the round and the sickle dances.

通过进一步研究，冯·弗里希揭开了前两类相关类型——圆舞和镰刀形舞姿的谜团。

experiment [ɪks'perɪmənt] *vi.* 实验，尝试

释 to try something in order to discover what it is like

拓 *a.* experimental; *ad.* experimentally; *n.* experimentation

用 experiment with / on / in

例 The teacher provided some different materials and left the children to experiment. 老师提供不同的材料，留给学生做实验。

---

unravel [ʌn'rævəl] *vt.* 解开；阐明，解释

释 to disentangle; to understand or explain something that is mysterious or complicated

拓 *a.* unraveled / unraveling

例 The legal tangle was never really unraveled. 这起法律纠葛从来没有真正解决。

The long-lasting nature of their monuments and carved inscriptions in the form of hieroglyphics attracts people from afar.

纪念碑的持久性和用象形文字题词的碑铭吸引了远方的人。

monument ['mɒnjumənt] *n.* 纪念碑

释 a statue or building that is built to honour a special person or event

拓 *a.* monumental; *ad.* monumentally

用 be a monument to sth.

例 This monument was set up in memory of World War II. 这座碑是为纪念二战而建立的。

---

inscription [ɪn'skrɪpʃən] *n.* 题词，碑铭

释 words that are written or cut in something

例 The inscription above the door was in English. 门上方的文字是用英文刻印的。

---

hieroglyphic [ˌhaɪərəˈglɪfɪk] *n.* 象形文字

释 a system of writing which uses pictures instead of words, especially as used in ancient Egypt

例 Hieroglyphics is a great contribution of people to ancient civilization. 象形文字是人们对古代文明的伟大贡献。

Few mortals could stick to that harsh regime.

几乎没有几个人能忍受那种残酷的政治体制。

mortal [ˈmɔːtəl] *n.* 凡人

释 *n.* a human being

拓 *n.* mortality; *ad.* mortally

例 We're all mortals, with our human faults and weaknesses. 我们都是凡人，有着人类的过错和缺点。

---

regime [reɪˈʒiːm] *n.* 政体

释 the organization that is the governing authority of a political unit

例 The regime ruthlessly suppresses all dissent. 这个政权残酷地压制所有不同意见。

On 1 April 1993, it became independent of the local authority and adopted its new title.

1993年4月1日，它从地方当局中独立出来，采用了自己的新名称。

authority [ɔːˈθɒrɪti] *n.* 权力，权威；当局

释 the power you have because of your official position; an administrative unit of government

拓 *vt.* authorize; *a.* authorized

用 in authority; authority over; authority to do sth.

例 The government is the highest authority in the country. 政府是国家的最高权力机构。

---

adopt [ə'dɒpt] *vt.* 采用，接受

释 to choose a new name, country, custom, etc., especially to replace a previous one

拓 *n.* adoption

例 One should disregard shortcomings and adopt good points. 人应该取长补短。

Evolutionarily retarded, prehistoric Amazonian people developed technologies and cultures that were advanced for their time.

由于进化滞后，史前亚马逊人所形成的技术和文化在那个时期是先进的。

retard [rɪ'tɑːd] *vt. & vi.* 妨碍，迟延，迟缓

释 to delay the development of something, or to make something happen more slowly than expected

拓 *a.* retarded

例 Writing may retard the process of language change under certain conditions. 在某些情况下，文字可能会延缓语言变化的进程。

---

prehistoric [ˌpriːhɪ'stɔːrɪk] *a.* 史前的，远古的

释 relating to the time in history anything was written down

用 *n.* prehistory

例 It's a fossil of a prehistoric or primitive human living in caves.

这是一块史前穴居人或居于洞中的原始人的化石。

The critically endangered languages are those that are only spoken by the elderly.

濒临消失的语言是那些只有老人才用的语言。

critically ['krɪtɪkəli] *ad.* 批评性地；精密地；重要地

释 extremely serious or dangerous, in a way that is very important

拓 *a.* critical

例 This is a critically important meeting. 这是个极其重要的会议。

---

endangered [ɪn'deɪndʒəd] *a.* 有危险的，有灭绝危险的，将要绝种的

释 to put someone or something in danger of being hurt, damaged, or destroyed

用 *n.* endangerment

例 Scientists think that the Arctic is endangered by contamination.

科学家们认为北极面临着被污染的危险。

Saving languages from extinction is not a difficult task.

保护语言不遭受灭亡并不是件难事。

extinction [ɪk'stɪŋkʃən] *n.* 消失，消减；废止

释 a particular type of animal or plant stops existing

拓 *a.* extinct

用 on the verge / edge / of extinction

例 Conservationists are trying to save the whale from extinction.

自然资源保护者正试着保护鲸类免遭灭绝。

Such objects can include both the extraordinary and the mundane, the beautiful and the banal.

这些事物既包括特别的也包括世俗的，既包括美丽的也包括平庸的。

extraordinary [ɪks'trɔːdnəri] *a.* **非常的，特别的**

释 beyond what is ordinary or usual; highly unusual or exceptional or remarkable

拓 *ad.* extraordinarily

例 Her voice had an extraordinary hypnotic quality. 她的声音有一种特别的催眠作用。

---

mundane [mʌn'deɪn, 'mʌnˌdeɪn] *a.* **现世的，世俗的**

释 ordinary and not interesting or exciting

例 Mundane matters such as watching TV and shopping for food do not interest me. 像看电视和购买食品这些世俗的事情我都不太感兴趣。

---

banal [bə'nɑːl] *a.* **陈腐的；平庸的**

释 ordinary and not interesting, because of a lack of new or different ideas

拓 *n.* banality

例 The report has a banal remark or statement. 报告中全是陈腐的评论和陈述。

The general submission which religious vow to God, is obedience and voluntarily promise to superiors.

信徒对上帝的誓言是绝对的服从和顺从。

obedience [ə'biːdjəns] *n.* **服从，顺从**

释 when someone does what they are told to do, or what a law, rule, etc. says they must do

拓 *a.* obedient; *ad.* obediently

用 obedience to; in obedience to sth.

例 As a Christian, obedience to God, is the first and foremost.

作为一个基督徒，服从上帝是最重要的。

---

voluntarily ['vɒləntərɪli] *ad.* 自愿地

释 without compulsion; willingly

拓 *a.* voluntary

例 The government calls on the young generation to donate their blood voluntarily. 政府号召年轻人自愿献血。

College encourages and promotes interaction between students and teaching and non-teaching staff.

学院鼓励并促进学生与教职和非教职员工之间的互动。

interaction [ˌɪntə'rækʃən] *n.* 互动；相互作用，相互影响

释 a mutual or reciprocal action; a process by which two or more things affect each other

拓 *vi.* interact; *a.* interactive; *ad.* interactively

用 interaction of; interaction with / between

例 English language games are usually intended to encourage student interaction. 英语游戏通常用来鼓励学生参与互动。

---

staff [stɑːf] *n.* 全体人员；同事

释 personnel who assist their superior in carrying out an assigned task，the group of people who work for an organization

例 The entire staff of the company has done an excellent job.

公司的所有员工都出色地完成了一项工作。

The Egyptian people showed reverence towards natural objects such as the lotus flower, the scarab beetle, the falcon, the lion, the sun and the River Nile.

埃及人对自然界中的事物，如莲花、圣甲虫、猎鹰、狮子、太阳和尼罗河表示出很大的敬畏。

reverence ['revərəns] *n.* 敬畏，尊敬

释 a feeling of great or admiration for somebody / something

拓 *vt.* revere; *a.* reverent / reverential; *ad.* reverently

用 reverence for; reverence to

例 The professor shows great reverence for culture and tradition.

教授对文化和传统表示出极大的尊敬。

---

scarab ['skærəb] *n.* 圣甲虫

释 scarab beetle considered divine by ancient Egyptians, a type of large black beetle

---

falcon ['fælkən] *n.* 猎鹰

释 a bird with pointed wings and a long tail which can be trained to hunt other birds and small animals

十四 医疗保健类

Health in this sense has been defined as the absence of disease or illness and is seen in medical terms.

从这个意义上讲，健康被定义为没有疾病，而且是个医学术语。

absence ['æbsəns] *n.* 缺乏；缺席

释 a lack of something; the state of sb. or sth. being away from a place where they are usually expected to be

拓 *a.* absent; *n.* absentee / absenteeism

用 in / during someone's absence; absence from; absence of

例 A new supervisor was appointed during his absence. 他不在期间一个新主管上任了。

---

medical ['medɪkəl] *a.* 医疗的，医学的

释 relating to medicine and the treatment of disease or injury

拓 *ad.* medically

用 medical care / attention / treatment

例 His legs got timely medical treatment. 他的腿得到了及时的治疗。

It has been calculated that 17 per cent of cases of lung cancer can be attributed to high levels of exposure to second-hand tobacco smoke during childhood and adolescence.

据计算，17%的肺癌病例可以归因于童年和青春期接触了二手烟。

calculate ['kælkjuleɪt] *vt. & vi.* 计算

释 to find out how much something will cost, how long something will take etc., by using numbers

拓 *n.* calculation / calculator

用 calculate that; calculate sth. on sth.

例 Engineers calculate the stresses and stains of a suspension bridge. 工程师们计算一个吊桥的受压力度。

---

attribute [ə'trɪbjuːt] *vt.* 属于，归于

释 *vt.* to say or believe that sth. is the result of a particular thing

拓 *n.* attribution

用 attribute sth. to sb. / sth.

例 He attributes his success to the teacher's encouragement. 他把成功归因于老师对他的鼓励。

---

adolescence [ˌædəʊˈlesəns] *n.* 青春期，青春

释 the period of time in a person's life when they are developing into an adult, usually between the ages of 12 and 18

例 The film is about the troubles and tribulations of adolescence. 这部电影讲述了青春期的麻烦和苦恼。

Sugar's connection with AGE formation may be one reason caloric restriction might delay aging.

糖与高聚糖最终产物之间的紧密关系可能能够解释为什么减少热量（卡路里）的摄入可能会延缓老化过程。

caloric restriction 减少热量（卡路里）

---

caloric [kəˈlɒrɪk] *a.* 卡路里的，热的，热量的

释 of or relating to calories in food

---

restriction [rɪˈstrɪkʃən] *n.* 限制，约束

释 an act of limiting or restricting

拓 *vt.* restrict; *a.* restricted / restrictive

例 The government has an issue on restriction of immigration. 政府出台了限制移民的法案。

The accepted golden standard of evidence is a randomised control trial, in which a new drug is compared with the best existing therapy.

公认的作为证据的黄金标准是一个随机控制试验，这个试

验是对一种新药物和目前最好的治疗方法进行对比的方法。

randomise [ˈrændəmaɪz] *vt.* 形成不规则分布，使……随机化

释 to choose things in a way that is not carefully controlled or planned in order to do a scientific test

拓 *a.* random; *ad.* randomly

例 The numbers have been randomized. 号码被随机化了。

---

compare [kəmˈpeə] *vt. & vi.* 比较，相比

释 to examine or judge two or more things in order to show how they are similar to or different from each other

拓 *a.* comparative; *ad.* comparatively

用 compare to / with sth.

例 The present cannot compare with the past. 今非昔比。

---

therapy [ˈθerəpi] *n.* 疗法，治疗

释 a treatment which helps someone feel better, grow stronger, etc., especially after an illness

拓 *n.* therapist

用 a therapy for

例 The doctor said she should be given a physical therapy. 医生说她应该进行理疗。

All deaths from cancer clearly represent the most important preventable cause of cancer.

所有因癌症死亡的人都明确表明了癌症可预防的最重要原因。

cancer [ˈkænsə] *n.* 癌症

释 a serious disease that is caused when cells in the body grow in a way that is uncontrolled and not normal, killing normal cells and often causing death

拓 *a.* cancerous

例 He has received many honours for his research into cancer. 他因从事癌症方面的研究工作而得到了许多荣誉。

---

preventable [prɪ'ventəbl] *a.* 可防止的，可预防的

释 able to be prevented

拓 *vt. & vi.* prevent; *n.* prevention; *a.* preventive

例 Are most accidents preventable? 大多数意外是可以避免的吗？

It would be possible to administer a curative drug to that girl.

有可能采用一种疗效显著的药物为那女孩治病。

curative ['kjʊərətɪv] *a.* 治病的，有治病效力的

释 able to cure or cause to get better

拓 *n.* / *vt.* cure

例 We are confident in the curative properties of the bottle of medicine. 我们对这种瓶装药品的疗效很有信心。

American researchers identified the genetic defect underlying one type of muscular dystrophy.

美国研究人员识别出了一种导致肌肉萎缩症的遗传缺陷。

identify [aɪ'dentɪfaɪ] *vt.* 识别，认明，鉴定

释 to recognise someone or something and say or prove who or what they are

拓 *a.* identifiable; *n.* identification

用 identify sb. / sth. (as sb. / sth.); be identified with sb. / sth.

例 One cannot identify happiness with wealth. 幸福和财富不能混为一谈。

muscular ['mʌskjulə] *a.* 肌肉的，肌肉发达的

释 of or relating to or consisting of muscle

拓 *ad.* muscularly; *n.* muscularity

例 He seems to be the most muscular guy. 他看起来似乎是肌肉最发达的一个人。

---

dystrophy ['dɪstrəfi] *n.* 萎缩

释 any of several hereditary diseases of the muscular system characterized by weakness and wasting of skeletal muscles

例 Diseases like multiple sclerosis, muscular dystrophy or polio can leave people disabled. 像多发性硬化症、肌肉萎缩或小儿麻痹症等疾病会使人残疾。

Nicotine, however, is only a small component of cigarette smoke.

然而，尼古丁只是香烟成分中的一小部分。

nicotine ['nɪkəti:n] *n.* 尼古丁

释 poisonous substance in tobacco that people become addicted to, so that it is difficult to stop smoking

例 Many smokers who are chemically addicted to nicotine cannot cut down easily. 许多有尼古丁瘾的抽烟者不容易把烟戒掉。

The study suggests that people who smoke cigarettes are continually damaging their cardiovascular system.

研究表明，吸烟者在逐渐损害他们自己的心血管系统。

cardiovascular [ˌkɑ:di:əʊ'væskjulə] *a.* 心血管的

释 of or pertaining to or involving the heart and blood vessels

例 They are used to measure the presence and development of cardiovascular disease. 它们被用来估量心血管疾病的存在和发展。

But the medical world continues to be heavily scrutinized for their sales and marketing strategies.

但是，医学领域的销售和市场策略继续面临严格的检查。

scrutinize ['skruːtɪnaɪz] *vt.* 仔细检查

释 to examine someone or something very carefully

拓 *n.* scrutiny

例 He scrutinized the English graduate students' thesis. 他仔细看了英语研究生的论文。

---

strategy ['strætɪdʒi] *n.* 战略，策略

释 a planned series of actions for achieving something

拓 *a.* strategic; *ad.* strategically; *n.* strategist

用 strategy for doing sth.; strategy to do sth.

例 The government adopted a strategy of massive deflation. 政府采取了大规模通货紧缩的策略。

In 1983 national health survey, 1.9% of people said they had contacted a chiropractor, naturopath, osteopath, acupuncturist or herbalist in the two weeks prior to the survey.

在1983年全国健康调查中，1.9%的人表示，他们在调查之前的两个星期之内接触过按摩师、理疗家、整骨医师、针灸医生或草药医生。

chiropractor ['kaɪrəˌpræktə] *n.* 按摩师，脊椎指压治疗者，（脊柱）按摩疗法医生

释 someone who treats physical problems using chiropractic

---

naturopath ['neɪtʃərəpæθ] *n.* 自然疗者，理疗家

释 someone who tries to cure illness using natural things such as plants, rather than drugs

---

osteopath ['ɒstɪəʊpæθ] *n.* 整骨疗法家，整骨医生

释 a therapist who manipulates the skeleton and muscles

---

acupuncturist ['ækjpʌŋktʃərɪst] 针灸医生

释 a person who is trained to perform acupuncture

---

herbalist ['hɜːbəlɪst] *n.* 草药医生

释 someone who grows, sells, or uses herbs, especially to treat illness

Melatonin pills contain a synthetic version of the hormone and are commonly used for sleep disturbance.

褪黑激素药丸含有一种合成激素，常被有睡眠障碍的人服用。

version ['vɜːʃən] *n.* 版本

释 a copy of something that has been changed so that it is slightly different from an earlier form or from other forms of the same thing

用 the… version of sth.

例 The new version of English text book will be put into use next year. 明年将启用新版英语教科书。

---

disturbance [dɪs'tɜːlbəns] *n.* 心神不安(身心等方面的障碍)；扰乱，骚动

释 mental or emotional unbalance or disorder; the act of disturbing somebody / something or the fact of being disturbed

拓 *vt.* disturb; *a.* disturbing / disturbed

例 Residents are fed up with the disturbance caused by disco club. 居民们对迪斯科俱乐部的干扰烦不胜烦。

Chronically high levels of these hormones have been linked to heart disease.

这类荷尔蒙长期处于高水平的状态是与心脏病息息相关。

chronically ['krɒnɪkli] *ad.* 长期地

释 (especially of a disease or something bad) continuing for a long time

拓 *a.* chronic / chronical

例 We should not neglect the harm of chronically ill. 我们不能忽视慢性病的危害性。

---

hormone ['hɔːˌməʊn] *n.* 荷尔蒙，激素

释 the secretion of an endocrine gland that is transmitted by the blood to the tissue on which it has a specific effect

拓 *a.* hormonal

例 The doctor told her that her disease was caused by unbalanced hormone. 医生说，她的病是由荷尔蒙失衡引起的。

It is legitimate for drug companies to make money.

制药公司赢利是合法的。

legitimate [lɪ'dʒɪtɪmɪt] *a.* 合法的，正当的

释 allowed by law

拓 *vt.* legitimize; *n.* legitimacy; *ad.* legitimately

例 I'm not sure that his business is legitimate or not. 我也不确定他的生意是否合法。

They commented that they liked the holistic approach of their alternative therapist.

他们说，他们倾向于那个临床医学家的综合治疗法进行治疗。

therapist ['θerəpɪst] *n.* 临床医学家

释 a specialist who treats a particular type of illness or problem, or who uses a particular type of treatment

拓 *n.* therapy

例 He is a therapist who heals by the use of herbs. 他是使用草药治病的临床医学家。

Medication is regarded by many as a last resort and often takes the form of sleeping pills, normally benzodiazepines, which are minor tranquilizers.

很多人认为去医院治疗是最后一步棋，病人经常只是吃点安眠药，如苯二氮这样的轻度镇定剂来缓解病情。

medication [ˌmedɪ'keɪʃ ən] *n.* 药物治疗，药物处理；药物

释 a way to treat an illness by using drugs; a drug or another form of medicine that you take to prevent or to treat an illness

拓 *a.* medical

用 be on medication (for sth.)

例 He's on medication for high blood pressure. 他正在用药物来治疗高血压。

---

benzodiazepine [ˌbenzəʊdaɪ'æzəˌpiːn] *n.* 苯二氮

释 any of several similar lipophilic amines used as tranquilizers or sedatives or hypnotics or muscle relaxants; chronic use can lead to dependency

---

tranquilizer ['træŋkwɪˌlaɪzə(r)] *n.* 镇定剂

释 a drug used for making someone feel less anxious

New discovery may revolutionize treatment for pain related to surgery, illness and injury.

新的发现会改革外科、疾病、受伤时引起的疼痛治疗。

surgery [ˈsɜːdʒəri] *n.* 外科手术；外科

释 the treatment of injuries or diseases in people or animals by cutting the body and removing or repairing the damaged part; the branch of medicine connected with this treatment

拓 *a.* surgical

用 surgery on

例 She is a plastic surgery specialist. 她是个整形外科医生。

---

injury [ˈɪndʒəri] *n.* 损害，伤害

释 physical harm or damage to someone's body caused by an accident or an attack

用 injury to

例 Jim suffered serious injuries to the arms and legs. 吉姆的双臂和双腿受到了严重伤害。

The smoke is enough to produce substantial adverse effects on a person's heart and lungs.

吸烟对人体的心脏和肺足以产生大量不利的影响。

substantial [səbˈstænʃəl] *a.* 大量的

释 large in amount or number

拓 *ad.* substantially

例 We have the support of a substantial number of residents. 我们赢得了很多居民的支持。

adverse ['ædvɜːs] *a.* 不利的

释 having a negative or harmful effect on something

拓 *ad.* adversely

例 They are afraid that it could have an adverse effect on global markets. 他们担心这种行为会对国际市场产生不利影响。

---

lung [lʌŋ] *n.* 肺

释 one of the two organs in your body that you breathe with

拓 Smoking is harmful to lung. 吸烟对肺部有害。

It was a terrible experience to suffer from a life-threatening illness such as cystic fibrosis.

遭受类似囊肿性纤维化这样的致命疾病是一种可怕的经历。

life-threatening ['laɪfθretnɪŋ] *a.* 危及生命的

释 a fatal situation, illness, or injury which could cause a person to die

例 Cancer is a life-threatening illness, however, the patients are becoming more and more optimistic. 虽然癌症是绝症，但是患者对这种病越来越乐观了。

---

cystic fibrosis ['sɪstɪ'kˌfaɪ'brəʊsɪs] *n.* 囊肿性纤维化

A recent experimental study demonstrates that passive smoking can affect children in varying degrees of learning and memory ability.

最近的试验研究表明，被动吸烟在很大程度上会影响孩子的学习和记忆能力。

passive smoking 被动吸烟

释 the act of breathing in smoke that is in the air around you when someone else is smoking cigarettes

例 It is said that passive smoking is more harmful than smoking.
据说，被动吸烟要比主动吸烟更有害健康。

Several comparable cases have been reported.
几个可比病例报告已经出来了。

comparable ['kɒmpərəbl] *a.* 可比较的，比得上的

释 similar to something else in size, number, quality etc., so that you can make a comparison

拓 *n.* comparability; *vt. & vi.* compare

用 comparable with / to

例 His English is not bad, but it's hardly comparable with yours.
他的英语不错，但是很难比得上你。

A mold might prove to be a successful antidote to bacterial infection.
霉菌被证实为可能是一种针对细菌感染的有效解药。

antidote ['æntɪˌdəʊt] *n.* 解毒剂，解药

释 a substance that stops the effects of a poison

用 antidote to

例 There is no known antidote to this poison. 这种毒药没有解药。

---

bacterial [bæk'tɪrɪəl] *a.* 细菌的；细菌引起的

释 relating to bacteria; caused by bacteria

拓 *n.* bacteria

例 Bacterial reproduction is accelerated in weightless space. 在失重的空间内，细菌繁殖的速度加快。

infection [ɪnˈfekʃən] *n.* 传染，感染；传染病

释 the act or process of causing or getting a disease; a disease caused by bacteria or a virus that affects a particular part of your body

用 mild / slight / severe infection

例 This new type of infection is resistant to antibiotics. 这种新型的传染病对抗生素有抗药性。

The survey suggested that complementary medicine is probably a better term than alternative medicine.

调查表明，补充性医疗这个名称或许比可替代药物治疗更恰当。

complementary [ˌkɒmplɪˈmentəri] *a.* 补充的，互补的

释 making someone or something better or more attractive by emphasizing its good qualities or having qualities that the other person or thing lacks

拓 *vt.* complement; *n.* complementariness; *ad.* complementarily

例 The computer and the human mind are complementary. 电脑和人脑是互补的。

---

alternative [ɔːlˈtɜːnətɪv] *a.* 两者择一的；替代性的

释 allowing a choice; necessitating a choice between mutually exclusive possibilities

拓 *ad.* alternatively

用 alternative approach / road / method; alternative medicine

例 We returned by the alternative road. 我们是从另外一条路回来的。

67 percent of nurses felt that administration was not sympathetic to the problems of shift work.

百分之六十七的护士表示管理部门对她们的轮班问题不够理解。

sympathetic [ˌsɪmpəˈθetɪk] *a.* 表示同情的；赞同的，支持的

释 kind to somebody who is hurt or sad, showing that you understand and care about their problems; showing that you approve of somebody / something or that you share their views and are willing to support them

拓 *n.* sympathy; *ad.* sympathetically

用 sympathetic to / towards

例 Such requests shall be accorded sympathetic consideration. 我们应对此类请求给予理解支持。

---

shift [ʃɪft] *n.* 轮班

释 if workers in a factory, hospital etc. work shifts, they work for a particular period of time during the day or night, and are then replaced by others, so that there are always people working

例 He works on the night shift. 他上晚班。

Nicotine and other toxins in cigarette smoke activate small blood cells called platelets.

烟草中的尼古丁和其他毒素可以激活血液中的血小板。

toxin [ˈtɒksɪn] *n.* 毒素，毒质

释 a poisonous substance, especially one that is produced by bacteria and particular disease

例 The cake on analysis was found to contain traces of toxin. 经分析发现这块蛋糕里含有微量毒素。

---

activate [ˈæktɪveɪt] *vt.* 刺激，激活，使……活动

释 to make an electrical system or chemical process start working

拓 *n.* activation

例 We must activate the young to study. 我们要激励年轻人去学习。

---

platelet ['pleɪtlɪt] *n.* 血小板

释 a very small cell in the blood that makes the blood thicker and more solid to stop bleeding caused by an injury

Vaccine is the pre-eminent invention. It serves as an interface between academics.

疫苗是一项伟大的发明。它可作为学术之间的一个接口。

vaccine [væk'siːn] *n.* 疫苗

释 a substance which contains a weak form of the bacteria or virus that causes a disease and is used to protect people from the disease

拓 *vt. & vi.* vaccinate; *n.* vaccination

例 This vaccine protects against some kinds of the bacteria which cause HIV. 疫苗可以抵御某些种类的引起艾滋病的病毒。

---

pre-eminent(=preeminent) [prɪ'emənənt] *a.* 卓越的，优秀的

释 much more important, more powerful, or better than any others of its kind

拓 *n.* pre-eminence; *ad.* pre-eminently

例 He is the pre-eminent authority in English language teaching. 他是英语教学方面的权威。

---

interface ['ɪntəfeɪs] *n.* 界面，分界面；【计算机】接口

释 the point where two subjects, systems, etc. meet and affect each other; a connection between two pieces of electronic equipment, or between a person and a computer

用 interface between; interface with sb./ sth.

例 Can you give me an explanation of the man-machine interface?

你能给我解释一下什么是人机接口吗?

---

academic [ˌækəˈdemɪk] *a.* 学院的；学术性的

释 relating to education，especially at college or university level; involving a lot rending and studying rather than practical or technical skills

拓 *ad.* academically

例 IELTS speaking part is mainly about academic background.
雅思口语考试主要是关于学术背景的。

These aids would have been indispensable to very early people who could have found the process impossible without some form of mechanical aid.

这些援助对于早期患有艾滋病但却不能通过医疗器械查明的人是不可缺少的。

indispensable [ˌɪndɪsˈpensəbl] *a.* 不可缺少的

释 too important to be without

拓 *n.* indispensability

例 A good dictionary is indispensable for learning a foreign language.
一本好的字典对学习外语来说是不可或缺的。

---

mechanical [mɪˈkænɪkəl] *a.* 机械的，力学的；呆板的

释 connected with machines and engines; (of people's behavior and actions) done without thinking, like a machine

拓 *n.* machine / machinery / mechanic / mechanics / mechanism; *a.* mechanical / mechanized; *ad.* mechanically

例 The teacher was asked the same question so many times that the answer became mechanical. 同样的问题学生向老师问了太多次了，所以答案也是千篇一律。

In many other industrialized countries, orthodox and alternative medicines have worked "hand in glove" for years.

在其他许多工业化国家，传统医学和替代疗法结合在一起使用已经有很多年了。

industrialize [ɪnˈdʌstrɪəlaɪz] *vt. & vi.* (使)工业化

释 to develop industry

拓 *n.* industry / industrialisation; *a.* industrial; *ad.* industrially

例 Many towns in the coastal area have begun to industrialize. 沿海地区的许多城镇已开始工业化了。

---

orthodox [ˈɔːθədɒks] *a.* 正（传）统的

释 (of beliefs, ideas or activities) considered traditional, normal and acceptable by most people

拓 *n.* orthodoxy

例 He is a very orthodox young man. 他是一个非常传统的年轻人。

So are doctors to blame for the escalating extravagance of pharmaceutical marketing?

所以医生是否应该为药物销售的泛滥负责任呢?

blame [bleɪm] *vt.* 责备

释 to find fault with; to censure

拓 *a.* blamed

用 be to blame for

例 The driver was not to blame for the accident. 这次事故不能责怪司机。

---

escalate [ˈeskəleɪt] *vt. & vi.* 扩大，升级

释 to make or become greater or more serious

拓 *n.* escalation / escalator

用 escalate into

例 We do not want to escalate the war. 我们不想扩大战争。

---

extravagance [ək'strævəgəns] *n.* 奢侈，浪费；奢侈品

释 spending, using or doing more than necessary in an uncontrolled way; something that you buy it costs a lot of money, perhaps more than you can afford or than it necessary

拓 *a.* extravagant

例 Her latest extravagance is a hand-made carpet. 她最近买的一件奢侈品是件手工地毯。

---

pharmaceutical [ˌfɑːmə'suːtɪkəl] *a.* 药物的(医药的)

释 connected with the production of medicines

The data confirms that the rate at which these diseases are declining continues to accelerate.

数据证明，这些一直持续下降的疾病发病率又开始上升了。

confirm [kən'fɜːm] *vt.* 确定，批准，证实

释 to state or show that something is definitely true or correct, especially by providing evidence

拓 *n.* confirmation; *a.* confirmed

用 confirm that

例 Tom looked around to confirm that he was alone. 汤姆四处张望，想确定周围确实没人。

---

decline [dɪ'klaɪn] *vi.* 降低

释 to gradually become less, worse, or lower

用 decline to do sth.; decline that

例 I wish prices would decline. 我希望物价会下降。

In Germany, plant remedies account for 10% of the national turnover of pharmaceuticals.

在德国，植物医疗占了全国药物成交量的10%。

remedy ['remɪdi] *n.* 治疗法；补救

释 a treatment or medicine to cure a disease or reduce pain that is not very serious; a successful way of curing an illness or dealing with a problem or difficulty

拓 *n.* remedial

用 remedy for

例 Her illness is beyond remedy. 她的病不可治愈。

It presents fundamental strategies and approaches in achieving health for all.

它涵盖了基本的策略和方法，以实现人人都可以享有医疗保健的目标。

fundamental [ˌfʌndə'mentəl] *a.* 基本的；根本的

释 forming the base, from which everything else originates; more important than anything else

拓 *n.* fundamental; *ad.* fundamentally

例 A knowledge of economics is fundamental to any understanding of this problem. 掌握经济学知识是理解这个问题的基本。

The American Medical Association(AMA) represents about half of all US doctors and is a strong opponent of smoking.

美国医学协会(AMA)代表美国几乎半数的医生，强烈反对吸烟。

represent [ˌreprɪˈzent] *vt.* 代表

释 to speak, act or be present officially for another person or people

拓 *n.* representation; *a.* representative / representational

例 The rose represents England. 玫瑰花是英格兰的象征。

As treatment for back pain the Clinic mainly recommends relaxation therapy.

至于背痛的治疗，临床主要推荐放松疗法。

treatment [ˈtriːtmənt] *n.* 治疗

释 care by procedure or applications that are intended to relieve illness or injury

拓 *vt.* treat; *a.* treatable

例 He is in a bad way after treatment. 经过治疗他尚未痊愈。

Research in 1999 said arthritis, high blood pressure and circulation problems ect.

1999年的研究报告说了关节炎、高血压和血液循环等问题。

arthritis [ɑːˈθraɪtɪs] *n.* 关节炎

释 a serious condition in which a person's joints become painful, swollen and stiff

拓 *a.* arthritic

---

circulation [ˌsɜːkjuˈleɪʃən] *n.* 流通，循环

释 when something such as information, money or goods passes from one person to another; the movement of blood around the body

拓 *n.* circular; *vt.* & *vi.* circulate

例 Many forged notes are in circulation. 许多假钞在流通。

Causes can be pregnancy or heart disease.

可能是由于怀孕或心脏病造成的。

pregnancy ['pregnənsi] *n.* 怀孕

释 having young developing inside the womb

拓 *a.* pregnant

The diseases associated with old age are afflicting fewer and fewer people and when they do strike, it is much later in life.

与年龄相关的疾病所危害的人数越来越少，而且通常是在晚年时期发病。

associate [ə'səʊʃɪeɪt] *vt.* 联系，联想；*vi.* 结交，交往

释 to make a connection between people or things in your mind; to spend time with somebody, especially a person or people that somebody else does not approve of

拓 *a.* associated; *n.* association

用 associate sb. / sth. with

例 I always associate the happiness with my childhood. 一提到幸福我就想起了童年。

---

afflict [ə'flɪkt] *vt.* 折磨，使痛苦

释 to affect sb. / sth. in an unpleasant or harmful way

拓 *n.* affliction

例 She was afflicted with conscience. 她受良心的折磨。

An increase in some cancers and bronchitis may reflect changing smoking habits and poorer air quality.

某些癌症和支气管炎的增加可能会反映出不断变化的吸烟习惯以及越来越糟的空气质量。

bronchitis [brɒnˈkaɪtɪs] *n.* 支气管炎

释 an illness that affects the bronchial tubes leading to the lungs

拓 *a.* bronchial

例 He was suffering from chronic bronchitis. 他患有慢性支气管炎。

Carbon monoxide competes with oxygen in red blood cells and interferes with the blood's ability to deliver life-giving oxygen to the heart.

一氧化碳在红血球中和氧气竞争，并妨碍血液向心脏输送生命必需氧气的能力。

carbon monoxide [ˈkɑːbən əˈnɒkˌsaɪd] *n.* 一氧化碳

释 the poisonous gas formed by the burning of carbon, especially in the form of car fuel

例 The result is that unburned gasoline or carbon monoxide come out of the tail pipe. 结果是尚未燃烧的汽油或一氧化碳从排气尾管排出。

---

interfere [ˌɪntəˈfɪə] *vi.* 妨碍，干涉

释 to involve yourself in a situation when your involvement is not wanted or is not helpful

拓 *n.* interference; *a.* interfering

用 interfere in; interfere with sth. / sb.

例 If you had not interfered, I should have finished my work by now. 要不是你打扰我的话，我现在早已完成我的工作了。

life-giving ['laɪfˌgɪvɪŋ] *a.* 赋予生命的

释 necessary for life or giving energy

例 The best type of affection is reciprocally life-giving. 最好的那种爱是彼此愉悦的爱。

The creation of health must include addressing issues such as poverty, pollution, urbanization, natural resource depletion, social alienation and poor working conditions.

改善人口健康必须关注以下话题：比如贫困、污染、城市化进程、自然资源消耗、社会异化以及糟糕的工作条件。

issue ['ɪsjuː] *n.* 话题，争论点

释 a subject or problem which people are thinking and talking about

用 issue of; take issue with sb. over sth.

例 There was no issue at all between us. 我们之间毫无争议。

---

poverty ['pɒvəti] *n.* 贫穷，贫困

释 the condition of being extremely poor

用 poverty of

例 Idleness tends to poverty. 懒惰易导致贫穷。

---

urbanization [ˌɜːbənaɪ'zeɪʃən] *n.* 城市化

释 the process by which more and more people leave the countryside to live in cities

拓 *a.* urban; *vt.* urbanize

例 Urbanization level reflects the development of a country. 城市化水平反映了一个国家的发展水平。

---

depletion [dɪ'pliːʃən] *n.* 消耗

释 reduction

拓 *vt.* deplete; *a.* depleted

用 depletion of / in

例 Increased consumption of water has led to rapid depletion of groundwater reserves. 用水量增加导致了地下水贮备迅速枯竭。

---

alienation [ˌeɪljəˈneɪʃən] *n.* 疏远

释 making someone feel that they are different and do not belong to a group

拓 *vt.* alienate; *n.* alien

用 alienation of

例 Alcoholism often leads to the alienation of family and friends. 酗酒常常导致家庭和朋友的疏远。

In 1845, match-makers exposed that its fumes succumbed to necrosis, a disease that eats away jaw-bones.

1845年，火柴商揭露说，其烟雾会引起骨疽——一种会导致下颚骨头坏死的疾病。

expose [ɪksˈpəʊz] *vt.* 暴露，揭穿

释 to remove what is covering something so that it can be seen; to make public know something bad or dishonest

拓 *n.* exposition; *a.* exposed

用 expose sb. to sth.

例 Their scheme was exposed. 他们的阴谋被揭露了。

---

fume [fjuːm] *n.* 烟

释 strong, unpleasant and sometimes dangerous gas or smoke

例 Tobacco fumes filled the air in the room. 室内充满了香烟的烟雾。

succumb [sə'kʌm] *vi.* 屈服，服从；死

释 to lose the determination to oppose something; to accept defeat; to die

用 succumb to

例 The government succumbed to public pressure. 政府屈服于公众的压力。

---

necrosis [ne'krəʊsɪs] *n.* 坏疽，骨疽，坏死

释 death of cells or tissues through injury or disease, especially in a localized area of the body

例 Due to necrosis, she had to quit her job. 由于身患坏疽病，她不得不把工作辞了。

Orthodox doctors could learn a lot about bedside manner and advising patients on preventative health from alternative.

传统型医生知道该如何对待病人，并能就如何选择性地预防疾病而给病人提供建议。

preventative [prɪ'ventətɪv] *a.* 预防性的

释 intended to stop something before it happens

拓 *n.* prevention; *a.* preventable; *vt.* prevent

例 Usually, people pay too little attention to preventative measures, especially that concerning lung diseases. 通常，人们对于疾病——特别是肺病的预防措施关注很少。

Other side-effects are dizziness or headaches, and indigestion or stomachache.

其他副作用是头晕、头痛、消化不良或胃疼。

side-effect ['saɪdˌɪ'fekt] *n.* 副作用

释 an unpleasant effect of a drug that happens in addition to the main effect

例 This medicine has no side-effect. 这种药没有副作用。

---

dizziness [ˈdɪzinɪs] *n.* 头晕

释 feeling as if everything is spinning round and being unable to balance and about to fall down

拓 *a.* dizzying / dizzy; *ad.* dizzily

例 He had a sensation of dizziness. 他有一种眩晕的感觉。

---

indigestion [ˌɪndɪˈdʒestʃən] *n.* 消化不良

释 pain caused by difficulty in digesting food

拓 *n.* indigestibility; *a.* indigestible

例 Jim was suffering from a slight case of indigestion. 吉姆得了轻度消化不良症。

Those suffering from respiratory complaint represent 7% of their patients.

在他们的病人当中，有7%的人遭受呼吸道疾病的困扰。

respiratory [ˈrespərətri] *a.* 呼吸的

释 connected with breathing

例 Smoking can cause respiratory diseases. 吸烟会引起呼吸道疾病。

They may request brief details of your symptoms or illness—this enables the doctors to assess the degree of urgency.

他们可能需要大致了解你的症状或病情，这有助于医生们评估病情的紧急程度。

symptom [ˈsɪmptəm] *n.* 症状；征兆

释 a change in your body or mind that shows that you are not healthy; sign that something exists, especially something bad

用 symptom of

例 Common symptoms of diabetes are fatigue and weight loss. 糖尿病的一般症状是身体虚弱、体重减轻。

---

assess [ə'ses] *vt.* 评估，评定

释 to make a judgment about a person or situation after thinking carefully about it

拓 *n.* assessment / assessor

例 They should assess the performance of college graduates every two years. 他们应该每两年就对大学毕业生的工作表现进行一次考核。

---

urgency ['ɜːdʒənsi] *n.* 紧急

释 the state of being urgent, needing attention very soon

拓 *a.* urgent; *ad.* urgently

例 This is a matter of great urgency. 这是一件十分紧急的事情。

As it was always a collection of dubious repute, one is obliged to reflect upon the standards that the Zoo Federation sets when granting membership.

由于动物保护协会常遭人怀疑，所以就有必要考虑一下他们授予会员权利的标准是否正确。

dubious ['djuːbjəs] *a.* 怀疑的，可疑的

释 not certain and slightly suspicious about something

拓 *ad.* dubiously

例 He deals with the problem in a dubious manner. 他处理问题的方式令人怀疑。

repute [rɪˈpjuːt] *n.* 名望，名气，声望

释 the state of being held in high esteem and honor

拓 *a.* reputed; *ad.* reputedly

例 By repute means according to general belief. 根据名声就是根据人们一般的信任程度。

---

oblige [əˈblaɪdʒ] *vt.* & *vi.* 强制

释 If you are obliged to do something, you have to do it because the situation, the law, a duty etc. makes it necessary.

拓 *n.* obligation

用 oblige sb. to do sth.; feel obliged to

例 She feels obliged to cancel the contract. 她认为有必要取消合同。

---

federation [ˌfedəˈreɪʃ ən] *n.* 联邦，联合，联盟；联合会

释 a country consisting of a group of individual states that have control over their own affairs but are controlled by a central government for national decisions; a group of organizations, clubs, or people that have joined together to form a single group

例 European Federation 欧洲联盟

---

grant [grɑːnt] *vt.* 授予，同意

释 to give someone something or allow them to have something that they have asked for

用 grant sth. to sb.

例 They got a document granting exclusive right to publish and sell literary or musical or artistic work. 他们获得了授予出版和销售文学、音乐或艺术品的独有权的证书。

Yogurt is easier to digest than milk. Many people cannot tolerate milk, either because of a protein allergy or lactose intolerance.

酸奶比牛奶更容易消化。很多人不能喝牛奶是因为对蛋白质或乳糖过敏。

yogurt ['jəʊgət] *n.* 酸奶

释 a thick liquid food that tastes slightly sour and is made from milk，or an amount of this food

---

tolerate ['tɒləreɪt] *vt.* 忍受，容忍

释 to allow people to do，say, or believe sth. without criticizing or punishing them

用 tolerate doing sth.

例 I will not tolerate that sort of behaviour in my class. 我不能容忍学生在课堂上的这种不良表现。

---

protein ['prəʊtiːn] *n.* 蛋白质

释 one of several natural substances that exist in food such as meat, eggs, and beans, and which your body needs in order to grow and remain strong and healthy

---

lactose ['læktəʊs] *n.* 乳糖

释 a type of sugar found in milk, sometimes used as a food for babies and sick people

---

intolerance [ɪn'tɒlərəns] *n.* 不容忍

释 unwillingness to accept ways of thinking and behaving that are different from your own

用 intolerance of

例 The government is determined to make racial intolerance a thing of the past. 政府决定废除种族歧视。

There will be new hope of liberation from the shadows of cancer, heart disease, autoimmune diseases such as rheumatoid.

现在把人们从癌症、心脏病以及像风湿病这样的自身免疫疾病的阴影中解放出来是有希望的。

autoimmune [ˌɔːtəuɪˈmjuːn] *a.* 自身免疫的

释 relating to a condition in which someone's antibodies attack substances that naturally found in the body

例 It is a chronic autoimmune disease with inflammation of the joints and marked deformities. 这是一种慢性自身免疫疾病，会导致关节发炎及明显的身体畸形。

---

rheumatoid [ˈruːməˌtɔɪd] *n.* 风湿病

释 a disease that continues for many years and makes your joints painful and stiff, and often makes them lose their proper shape

例 Inflammation means local reaction of living tissues to injury or illness, including burns, pneumonia, leprosy, tuberculosis, and rheumatoid. 炎症泛指活组织对损伤的局部反应，包括烧伤、肺炎、麻风病、结核和风湿病。

十五 教育培训类

To make the process of note-taking more efficient, it is important to abbreviate and to make use of symbols. The following suggestions will help you to do just that.

为了提高记笔记的效率，使用缩写和符号是很重要的。下面的这些建议对你会很有帮助。

abbreviate [ə'briːvɪeɪt] *vt.* 缩写，简略

释 to make a word or expression shorter by not including some letters or using only the first letter of each word

拓 *a.* abbreviated; *n.* abbreviation

用 abbreviate sth. to sth.

例 "Information technology" is usually abbreviated to "IT".信息技术通常简写为"IT"。

---

symbol ['sɪmbəl] *n.* 符号，象征，标志

释 a sign, shape or object which is used to represent something else

拓 *a.* symbolic / symbolical; *ad.* symbolically

用 symbol of; symbol for

例 The dove is a peaceful symbol. 鸽子是和平的象征。

---

suggestion [sə'dʒestʃən] *n.* 建议，意见，提议

释 an idea, plan, or possibility that someone mentions, or the act of mentioning it

拓 *vt.* suggest; *a.* suggestive; *ad.* suggestively

用 suggestion that; suggestion of

例 We are quite agreeable to your suggestion. 我们十分赞成你的建议。

Its accredited vocational training courses are designed to meet the needs of individual students and industry.

被认可的职业培训课程是专为满足学生和企业的独特需求所设计的。

accredit [əˈkredɪt] *vt.* 归功于

释 to believe that sb. is responsible for doing or saying sth.

拓 *a.* accredited; *n.* accreditation

用 accredit sth. to sb. / accredit sb. with sth.; accredit sb. to

例 We accredit the invention of the telephone to Bell. 我们把电话的发明归功于贝尔。

---

vocational [vəʊˈkeɪʃ ənl] *a.* 职业的

释 relating to the skills you need to do a particular job

拓 *ad.* vocationally

例 We'll provide you with vocational training. 我们将为你提供职业培训。

---

individual [ˌɪndɪˈvɪdjʊəl] *a.* 个人的，独特的

释 being or characteristic of a single thing or person

拓 *n.* individualism; *vt.* individualize; *ad.* individually; *a.* individualized

例 She has her own individual style of doing things. 她有自己独特的行事风格。

It is hard to wean children off picture books when pictures have played a major part.

如果图画书的确起到了举足轻重的作用，那就很难杜绝孩子们去看这些书。

wean [wiːn] *vt.* 戒掉，摆脱；断奶

释 to make somebody gradually stop doing or using something; to gradually stop feeding a baby or young animal with its mother's milk

拓 *n.* weaning

用 wean sb. off / from sth.

例 Tess was trying to wean herself from the old life. 苔丝那时正努力使自己摆脱过去的生活。

The universities of Oxford and Cambridge recently held joint conferences to discuss the noticeably rapid decline in literacy among their undergraduates.

近年牛津大学和剑桥大学召开联合会，讨论两校本科生读写能力明显急速下滑的问题。

noticeably ['nəʊtɪsəbli] *ad.* 显而易见地

释 easy to notice

拓 *n.* notice; *a.* noticeable

例 Crime has decreased noticeably. 犯罪活动明显地减少了。

---

literacy ['lɪtərəsi] *n.* 读写能力，识字

释 the state of being able to read and write

例 We want to promote literacy on a mass scale. 我们要大规模地提高文化水平。

Remember that a student permit is not valid when you have finished your studies.

记住，一旦你完成学业，学生证件就失效了。

permit ['pɜːmɪt] *n.* 许可证，执照

释 a legal document giving official permission to do something.

拓 *n.* permission; *a.* permissive

用 permit of

例 I haven't got a driving permit. 我还没有取得驾驶执照。

Experiments demonstrate these pictures are detrimental to beginning readers' understanding.

实验证明这些图片不利于初学者对此的理解。

detrimental [ˌdetrɪˈmentl] *a.* **有害的**

释 causing harm or damage

拓 *n.* detriment

用 be detrimental to

例 Smoking is detrimental to health. 吸烟有害健康。

It gives lexicographers access to a more vibrant, up-to-date vernacular language.

这给辞典编纂者提供了更加鲜活时新的方言词汇。

lexicographer [ˌleksɪˈkɒgrəfə] *n.* **辞典编纂者**

释 a compiler or writer of a dictionary

拓 *n.* lexicography

---

vibrant [ˈvaɪbrənt] *a.* **充满生机的，生机勃勃的**

释 full of activity or energy in a way that is exciting and attractive

拓 *n.* vibrancy; *ad.* vibrantly

例 Shanghai is a vibrant city. 上海是一个充满生机的城市。

---

vernacular [vəˈnækjələ] *n.* **本土话，方言**

释 a form of a language that ordinary people use, especially one that is not the official language

例 He decided to write the novel in the vernacular in order to reach a larger audience. 为了吸引更多读者，他决定用方言写小说。

There is ample space for quiet independent study and there are also areas for group work.

这儿既有充足安静的独立学习区，又有小组工作区。

ample [ˈæmpl] *a.* **充足的，丰富的**

释 more than enough in size, scope or capacity

拓 *ad.* amply

例 The house has an ample parlor. 这所房子客厅的空间宽敞充足。

---

independent [ˌɪndɪˈpendənt] *a.* 独立的

释 not depending on the help, advice, or opinions of others; habitually taking actions or decisions alone

拓 *n.* independence; *ad.* independently

用 independent of; independent opinion / inquiry / advice

例 You should learn to be independent. 你应该学会独立。

With a bilingual informant, or through use of an interpreter, it is possible to use translation techniques.

运用双语提供者或者运用口译员，都可以利用翻译技术。

bilingual [ˌbɪlɪŋgwəl] *a.* 双语的

释 written or spoken in two languages

例 A bilingual dictionary is indispensable in our foreign language study. 双语词典是我们外语学习中不可或缺的工具。

---

informant [ɪnˈfɔːmənt] *n.* 通知者，密告者，消息（或情报）提供者

释 someone who gives information to another person or organization

拓 *vt.* inform; *n.* information; *a.* informative

例 The correspondent does not want to reveal the identity of his informant. 那个记者不想透露消息提供人的身份。

---

interpreter [ɪnˈtɜːprɪtə] *n.* 译员，口译者

释 one who translates orally from one language into another

拓 *n.* interpretation

例 Simultaneous interpreter must be quick in thinking and skillful in language. 同声传译员必须思维敏捷，语言纯熟。

translation [trænsˈleɪʃən] *n.* 翻译；译文

释 the process of changing sth. that is written or spoken into another language; a text or work that has been changed from one language into another

拓 *vt.* & *vi.* translate; *n.* translator

用 translation of

例 Sometimes we have to combine literal translation and liberal translation. 有时候我们需要把直译与意译结合起来。

---

technique [tekˈniːk] *n.* 技术

释 a way of doing an activity which needs skill

拓 *n.* technician

例 We need to learn modern management techniques. 我们需要学习现代管理技术。

You need to present your linguistic credentials to academic institutions or potential employers.

你需要把你的语言水平证书展示给学术机构或潜在雇主。

linguistic [ˈlɪŋˈgwɪstɪk] *a.* 语言的，语言学的

释 related to language, words, or linguistics

拓 *n.* linguistics / linguist; *ad.* linguistically

例 She is particularly interested in the linguistic development of young children. 她对儿童的语言发展非常感兴趣。

---

potential [pəˈtenʃəl] *a.* 可能的，潜在的

释 likely to develop into a particular type of person or thing in the future

拓 *n.* potentiality; *ad.* potentially

用 potential for

例 The dispute has scared away potential investors. 这种争端吓走了潜在的投资者。

After about hours of training they are generally sufficiently fluent to transmit the language to the next.

经过数小时的培训，他们可以流畅地把语言信号传递给下一个人了。

sufficiently [sə'fɪʃ əntli] *ad.* 足够地

释 enough for a particular purpose

拓 *a.* sufficient; *n.* sufficiency

例 It turned out he had not insured the house sufficiently. 原来他没有给房投足保险。

---

transmit [trænz'mɪt] *vt.* & *vi.* 传播，传送

释 to broadcast something, or to send out or carry signals using radio, television, etc.

拓 *n.* transmission / transmitter

用 transmit from / through / to

例 They are trying to find a better way of transmitting signal. 他们正设法寻找一种更好的方法来传送信号。

Amazingly, there is virtually no empirical evidence to support the use of illustrations in teaching reading.

令人惊讶的是，实际上并没有经验证据去支持在阅读教学中使用插图。

empirical [em'pɪrɪkəl] *a.* 经验主义的

释 based on scientific testing or practical experience, not on ideas

拓 *ad.* empirically

例 Empirical studies show that some experienced mottos are extremely useful. 经验主义研究表明一些古老箴句是很有用的。

---

illustration [ˌɪlə'streɪʃ ən] *n.* 插图；例证

释 artwork that helps make something clear or attractive; the process of illustrating something

拓 *vt.* illustrate; *a.* illustrative

例 The examples are included, by way of illustration. 例子已经有了，是以插图的形式出现的。

The key to fostering diversity is for people to learn their ancestral tongue.

培育多元化的关键是要人们学习他们祖先的语言。

foster ['fɒstə] *vt.* 培养；养育，收养

释 to help a skill, feeling, idea etc. develop over a period of time; to take another person's child into your home for a period of time without becoming his or her legal parents

例 Concerts foster interest in music. 听音乐会可以培养对音乐的兴趣。

---

ancestral [æn'sestrəl] *a.* 祖先的，祖传的

释 inherited or inheritable by established rules (usually legal rules) of descent

拓 *n.* ancestor / ancestry

例 My ancestral home is China. 中国是我的祖国。

This is much more holistic involving guesses, corrections.

加上猜测和校订就更全面了。

holistic [həʊ'lɪstɪk] *n.* 整体的，全面的

释 considering a person or thing as a whole, rather than as separate parts

拓 *ad.* holistically

用 holistic medicine / treatment / approach

例 Dr. Smith gave us a holistic approach to art design. 史密斯博士给了我们一个整体的艺术设计方案。

---

correction [kə'rekʃən] *n.* 订正，改正

释 a change made in something in order to make it right or better

拓 *vt.* / *a.* correct; *ad.* correctly

例 The correction of the composition took me nearly an hour. 我用了将近一个小时才改完这篇作文。

Most publications in the national languages were popular works ,encyclopedias, educational textbooks and translations.

民族语言出版物主要涉及了畅销书、百科全书、教科书和译著。

encyclopedia [enˌsaɪkləʊ'piːdjə] *n.* 百科全书

释 a book or CD, or a set of these, containing facts about many different subjects, or containing detailed facts about one subject

拓 *a.* encyclopedic / encyclopaedic

例 I bought the encyclopedia on a whim. 我凭一时的兴致买了这本百科全书。

They endeavored to use as much as their skill would permit during the experimental year.

在做实验的一年里，他们尽可能使用自己所学的技能。

endeavor [ɪn'devə] *vt. & vi.* 努力，尽力

释 to try one's best to do something

用 endeavour to do sth.

例 He endeavored to streamline the plant organisation. 他努力使工厂组织简化而有效地运作。

---

experimental [ɪksˌperɪ'mentl] *a.* 实验（性）的，试验（性）的

释 used for, relating to, or resulting from experiments

拓 *n.* experiment / experimentation; *ad.* experimentally

例 This is an experimental form of teaching. 这是一种实验性的教学形式。

Marketing Outrageously: How to Crank up Your Revenue?

残酷的营销：如何提升你的收入？

outrageously [aʊt'reɪdʒəsli] *ad.* 令人震怒地，令人震惊地

释 very shockingly and extremely unfairly or offensively

拓 *a.* outrageous

例 This is an outrageously high price. 这是个天价。

---

crank up 使……提高效率

释 to make a machine, etc. work or work at a higher level

例 The manager wants us to crank up the production line. 经理希望我们提高生产线作业速度。

---

revenue ['revənjuːː] *n.* 收入，税收

释 money that a business or organization receives over a period of time, especially from selling goods or services

例 Tax payers provided most of the government's revenue. 纳税人是政府财政收入的磐石。

Atlas's teaching methodology is constantly revised as more is discovered about the process of learning a new language.

Atlas的教学方法在不断地进行修正，更重要的是他发现了学习一种新语言的过程。

revise [rɪ'vaɪz] *vt.* 校订，修正，校正

释 to look at or consider again an idea, piece of writing, etc. in order to correct or improve it

拓 *a.* revised; *n.* revision

用 revise sth. upwards / downwards

例 You should revise your mind about him. 你应该改变对他的看法。

With the exception of applications for scholarship category E,all newly enrolled international students are automatically considered for these scholarships.

除了对E类奖学金的申请，所有新登记的国际学生都将会自动被考虑到奖学金候选名单中来。

exception [ɪk'sepʃən] *n.* 例外

释 someone or something that is not included in a rule, group or list or that does not behave in the expected way

拓 *prep. / conj.* except; *a.* excepted / exceptionable / exceptional; *ad.* exceptionally

用 exception to; with the exception of

例 There is always an exception to any rule. 任何规律总有例外。

---

category ['kætɪgəri] *n.* 种类，类别

释 (in a system for dividing things according to appearance, quality, etc.) a type, or a group of things having some features that are the same

拓 *vt.* categorize; *n.* categorization; *a.* categorical

例 There are three categories of accommodation. 这里有三种住宿方式。

---

automatically [ˌɔːtə'mætɪkəli] *ad.* 自动地，机械地

释 sth. done without thinking or mechanically without intervention

例 The supermarket doors shut automatically. 超级市场的门是自动关闭的。

Certain approaches can be useful in changing the behavior of bullying pupils without confronting them directly.

某些办法是不用直接面对，就对改变那些恃强凌弱的学生的行为有帮助。

bully ['bʊli] *vt.* 威胁，恐吓，欺负

释 to hurt or frighten someone who is smaller or less powerful than you, often forcing them to do something they do not want to do

拓 *n.* bullying

用 bully sb. into doing sth.

例 Don't let anyone bully you into doing something you don't want to do. 不要让任何人恐吓你做任何你不想做的事情。

---

confront [kən'frʌnt] *vt.* 面对，对抗，遭遇

释 to face，meet or deal with a difficult situation or person

拓 *n.* confrontation; *a.* confrontational

用 confront sb. with sth.

例 The manager often has to confront all risks. 经理经常要面对各种各样的风险。

Pupils are likely to be filled with boredom or frustration.

小学生们很可能会感到无聊或沮丧。

boredom ['bɔːdəm, 'bəʊr-] *n.* 无聊，乏味

释 the state of feeling bored

拓 *vt.* bore; *a.* bored / boring; *ad.* boringly

例 He started to drink because of boredom. 因为无聊，他开始喝酒。

---

frustration [frʌs'treɪʃən] *n.* 挫折；沮丧

释 the fact that sth. is preventing sth./ sb. from succeeding; a feeling of annoyance at being hindered or criticized

拓 *vt.* frustrate; *a.* frustrated / frustrating

用 frustration at

例 He vented his frustration on his wife. 他受到挫折却把气发泄到妻子身上。

They opt for smaller classes, learn modern childcare techniques more quickly.

他们选择较小的班级以能够更快地学到现代育儿技巧。

opt [ɒpt] *vi.* 选择

释 to make a choice, especially for one thing or possibility in preference to any others

拓 *n.* option; *a.* optional

用 opt for / to

例 I think I'll opt out of this game. 我不想参加这场比赛。

---

childcare ['tʃaɪldkeə] *n.* 幼托

释 a service of caring for children provided by either the government, an organization or a person, while parents are at work or are absent for another reason

例 Since we both worked, childcare might be a problem. 我们俩都工作，儿童保育是个问题。

Assertiveness training for pupils who are liable to be victims is worthwhile.

坚定自信技巧训练对于那些可能会成为受害者的学生而言是非常重要的。

assertiveness [ə'sɜːtɪvnɪs] *n.* 自信，魄力

释 a state of expressing opinion or desires strongly and with confidence, so that people take notice of it

拓 *a.* assertive; *ad.* assertively

例 Her assertiveness was starting to be seen as arrogance. 她的自信开始被看作是自负了。

---

liable ['laɪəbl] *a.* 有……倾向的；有（法律）责任的，有义务的

释 likely to do something; legally responsible for paying the cost of something; likely to be punished by law for something

拓 *a.* liable; *n.* liability

用 be liable for; be liable to do sth.; be liable to

例 We're all liable to make mistakes when we're tired. 人在疲劳时都可能犯错。

---

worthwhile [ˌwɜːˈθwaɪl] *a.* 重要的，令人愉快的，有趣的；值得的

释 important, enjoyable, interesting, etc.; worth spending time, money or effort on something

拓 *a.* worth / worthy / worthless

用 be worthwhile to do / doing sth.

例 It is worthwhile writing all the facts out. 把全部的事实写出来是值得的。

There are tremendous advantages to involving parents in the program.

把家长纳入到这个项目中来是有很多优点的。

involve [ɪnˈvɒlv] *vt.* 包含，含有；使陷入，使卷入，牵涉

释 to include someone or something in something; or to make them take part in or feel part of it

拓 *a.* involving / involved； *n.* involvement

用 be involved with / in

例 That's no concern of mine. I'm not involved. 那与我无关，我根本没参与。

The cost of the programme, exclusive of accommodation, is built into your tuition fees.

这门课程的开销，除了住宿费外都被算在学费里了。

exclusive [ɪksˈkluːsɪv] *a.* 独占的，唯一的；排外的

释 limited to only one person or group of people; not divided or shared with others; excluding much or all

拓 *ad.* exclusively; *n.* exclusiveness / exclusivity

用 exclusive of sth.

例 This room is for the exclusive of guests. 这个房间是专门为客人准备的。

---

tuition [tjuˈɪʃən] *n.* 学费

释 a fee paid for instruction (especially for higher education)

用 tuition in

例 My family cannot afford the tuition fee in university. 我们家无法支付我上大学的学费。

In fact, about eight percent of its students come from continental Europe and further afield.

事实上，8%的学生来自欧洲大陆和比较远的地方。

continental [ˌkɒntəˈnentl] *a.* 大陆的

释 of or relating to or characteristic of a continent

拓 *n.* continent

例 The country features a continental climate. 该国的气候特点是大陆性气候。

---

afield [əˈfiːld] *ad.* 远离着，在远处

释 a long distance away

例 To discuss them in this book would take us too far afield. 在这本书中讨论它们会使我们离题千里。

A prevalent attitude amongst many nurses in the group selected for study was that there was no reward or recognition for not utilizing the paid sick leave entitlement allowed them in their employment conditions.

被选中参加学习的很多护士都持有这样一种普遍的观点：即使不行使雇佣条件中赋予他们的请病假的权利，也不会得到奖励或认可。

prevalent ['prevələnt] *a.* 流行的，普遍的

释 existing or is very common at a particular time or in a particular place

拓 *n.* prevalence

例 Bilingual classes are more prevalent. 双语教学班更为流行。

---

utilize ['juːtɪlaɪz] *vt.* 利用

释 to use something in an effective way

拓 *n.* utilization; *a.* utilizable

例 Scientists are trying to find more efficient ways of utilizing solar energy. 科学家们正在寻找能更有效地利用太阳能的方法。

---

entitlement [ɪn'taɪtlmənt] *n.* 权利，资格

释 something that you have right to do or have, or when you have the right to have something

拓 *a.* entitled; *vt.* entitle

用 entitlement to

例 This may affect your entitlement to compensation. 这可能会影响你索赔的权利。

Based on a professional experience as a teacher, here comes highlight, a small and simple piece of software that allows you to put an invisible drawing.

在教师专业方面的经验基础上，创作了这一最精彩的部分：这个软件小巧、便捷，可以生成无形图像。

highlight ['haɪlaɪt] *n.* 要点

释 the most interesting or memorable part

例 Without doubt the 2008 Olympics are the highlight of this year.

毫无疑问，2008年奥运会是今年最精彩的一幕。

---

invisible [ɪn'vɪzəbl] *a.* 看不见的，无形的

释 something that cannot be seen, impossible to see

拓 *n.* invisibility; *ad.* invisibly

用 invisible to

例 Germs are invisible to the naked eye. 细菌是肉眼所看不见的。

Counseling and welfare association is willing to listen, and advise or arranse a referral.

辅导和福利机构愿意听取、建议和安排推荐。

counsel ['kaʊnsəl] *vt.* 商议；劝告

释 give advice to somebody; to listen to and give support to professional advice to sb. who needs help

用 counsel for

例 I counselled your trying once again. 我建议你再试一次。

---

referral [rɪ'fɜːrəl] *n.* 推荐

释 the act of sending someone or something to another person to be helped or dealt with

拓 *vt. & vi.* refer；*n.* reference

用 referral to

例 The placement rate through school referral is usually much higher than other means. 经学校推荐的毕业生成功率通常高于其他渠道。

Today, however, I found exuberant, a library which can be used to generate an index file mapping language objects to source files.

然而，令我特别高兴的是现在图书馆可以利用索引地图方便读者找到需要的资料。

exuberant [ɪg'zju:bərənt] *a.* 充满活力的，旺盛的

释 of people and their behaviour very energetic; happy and full of energy and excitement

拓 *n.* exuberance; *ad.* exuberantly

例 Her husband is characterized by a lightly pert and exuberant quality. 她丈夫有着稍显鲁莽而又充满活力的个性。

---

index ['ɪndeks] *n.* 索引，指针，指数

释 an alphabetical list, such as one printed at the back of a book showing which page a subject, name, etc. is found on

拓 *n.* indexation

例 Author and subject index are available on a library database. 作者索引和学科索引可在图书馆的数据库中找到。

In formal contexts, the use of feasible to mean "likely" or "probable" should be avoided.

在正式语境中，feasible的"likely"或"probable"语义项应当避免使用。

feasible ['fi:zəbl] *a.* 可行的，可能的

释 a plan, idea, or method that is feasible is possible and is likely to work

拓 *ad.* feasibly; *n.* feasibility

用 feasible to; feasible that

例 It's not feasible to follow your proposals. 按照你的建议去做是行不通的。

---

probable ['prɒbəbl] *a.* 很可能的

释 likely to be true or likely to happen

拓 *n.* probability

用 it is probable that

例 Rain is possible but not probable this evening. 今晚可能有雨，但不一定会下。

Great collection of famous quotations, and quotes are sorted by categories and subjects, including authors, biographies, and quotes citings.

大量名言和引语按类别和主题整理起来，还包括作者、传记和引证。

quote [kwəʊt] *n.* 引用

释 a passage or expression that is quoted or cited

拓 *n.* quotation

用 quote from

例 This is a quote from the Bible. 这是引自《圣经》的语句。

---

biography [baɪˈɒgrəfi] *n.* 传记

释 the life story of a person written by someone else

拓 *n.* biographer; *a.* biographical

用 biography of

例 The *Bible* as it has come down to modern times is composed of biography, history, legend, genealogy. 流传至今的《圣经》包括传记、历史、传说和宗谱（家系）。

It is critical for all the training programs including the development of basic business and life skills.

对于所有培训项目来说（包括开发基本的商业和生活技能），这是至关重要的。

critical [ˈkrɪtɪkəl] *a.* 决定性的，极重要的，关键性的

释 extremely important because a future situation will be affected by it

拓 *ad.* critically

用 critical of; critical to

例 It is a critical time in the nation's history. 这是涉及国家命运的一个关键时刻。

Given the prominence of scientific English today, it's promising.

科技英语现今的重要性使它很有发展前途。

prominence ['prɒmɪnəns] *n.* 重要，突出，出名

释 the state of being important, well known or noticeable

拓 *a.* prominent; *ad.* prominently

例 Bob was one of the comedians who gained prominence. 鲍勃是其中一个著名的喜剧演员。

十六 体育类

Polymeric exercises help athletes make the best use of this brief interval.

复合性练习帮助运动员能够充分利用这段间隔时间。

polymeric [ˌpɒlɪ'merɪk] *a.* 聚合(物)的

释 of or relating to or consisting of a polymer

---

interval ['ɪntəvəl] *n.* 间隔

释 the period of time between two events，activities etc.

用 interval between

例 He left the room, returning after a short interval with a book. 他离开了房间，很快拿了本书又回来了。

They are developing unobtrusive sensors that will be embedded in an athlete's clothes or running shoes to monitor heart rate.

他们正在开发一种不引人注目的传感器，它将被安放在运

动员的衣服或跑鞋里，以监测其心率。

unobtrusive [ˌʌnəbˈtruːsɪv] *a.* 不引人注目的

释 not noticeable

拓 *ad.* unobtrusively

例 She's a quiet unobtrusive student, but always does well in the exam. 她是个沉默寡言、不引人注目的学生，但考试成绩总是很优异。

---

embed [ɪmˈbed] *vt.* 使插入，使嵌入；深留脑中

释 to put something firmly and deeply into something else, or to be put into something in this way; live a deep impressive in one's mind

用 be embedded in sth.

例 Feelings of guilt are deeply embedded in his personality. 罪恶感深深地根植于他的个性中。

---

monitor [ˈmɒnɪtə] *vt.* 监视，监听，监督

释 to carefully watch and check a situation in order to see how it changes over a period of time

例 This instrument monitors the patient's heartbeats. 这台仪器用来监听病人的心跳。

The AIS unveiled the jackets for endurance athletes.

AIS展示了专为耐力运动员设计的夹克。

unveil [ʌnˈveɪl] *vt.* 揭开，揭幕；使公之于众

释 to remove a curtain-like covering from a new statue, etc. at a formal ceremony in order to show the opening or completion of a new building or work of art; make visible

例 She unveiled her plan of reform. 她首次公开了她的改革计划。

---

endurance [ɪnˈdjuərəns] *n.* 忍耐，忍耐力，耐性

释 the ability to keep doing something difficult, unpleasant or painful for a long time

拓 *vt.* endure; *a.* endurable / enduring

例 He came to the end of his endurance. 他终于忍无可忍了。

For both men and women, running was good for our health and they received no monetary reward.

不论男女，跑步对我们的身体都有好处，而不是金钱方面的回报。

monetary [ˈmʌnɪtəri] *a.* 货币的，金融的

释 relating to the money in a country

拓 *n.* money

例 She was in complete charge of all monetary matters affecting the household. 她全权负责有关家庭的一切财政事宜。

---

reward [rɪˈwɔːd] *n.* 报酬，酬谢，赏金

释 something given in exchange for good behaviour or good work

拓 *a.* rewarding

用 reward for / with

例 It is unfair that he gets very little in reward for his hard work. 他工作很辛苦，报酬却很少，这是不公平的。

The first matches resembling those use today were made in 1827 by John Walker.

第一届与现在形式相似的比赛最早是由约翰·沃克在1827年设计的。

resemble [rɪˈzembl] *vt.* 相似，类似，像

释 to look like or be like someone or something

拓 *n.* resemblance

例 She was not beautiful; she did not resemble her mother. 她不漂亮，不像她的母亲。

十七 经济贸易类

In many countries deregulation has influences on the economy.

在很多国家，撤销管制规定是对国家经济有一定影响的。

deregulation [ˌdiːˌregju'leɪʃən] *n.* 撤销管制规定

释 the act of freeing from regulation(especially from governmental regulations)

拓 *vt.* deregulate; *a.* deregulatory

例 Deregulation of Japan airlines resulted in fierce competition and price-cut. 撤销对日本航班的管制规定导致了激烈的竞争和价格的下跌。

Sears also noted a positive trend from the recession.

西尔斯从经济衰退中仍看到了积极的趋势。

recession [rɪ'seʃən] *n.* 不景气，经济衰退

释 a difficult time for the economy of a country, when there is less trade and industrial activity than usual and more people are unemployed

拓 *a.* recessionary

例 Recession could cause the increase of unemployment. 经济衰退会导致失业量增多。

Research in Britain has shown that green consumers' continue to flourish as a significant group amongst shoppers.

一项英国研究表明，作为一个重要的消费群体，绿色消费者的规模在继续扩大。

flourish ['flʌrɪʃ] *vi.* 繁荣，茂盛

释 to develop well and be successful and active

拓 *a.* flourished / flourishing

例 My tomatoes are flourishing this summer. 今年夏天，我的西红柿长得非常茂盛。

---

significant [sɪɡ'nɪfɪkənt] *a.* 有意义的，重要的，重大的

释 having an important effect or influence, especially on what will happen in the future

拓 *ad.* significantly; *n.* significance

用 significant for; it is significant that

例 His most significant political achievement was the abolition of the slave ruling. 他最重要的政治成就是废除了奴隶制度。

Theoretically, in the world of trade, shipping costs are cheaper than others.

理论上讲，在世界贸易中，船运的价格相对比较便宜。

theoretically [θɪə'retɪkəli] *ad.* 理论上

释 in a theoretical manner

拓 *a.* theoretical; *n.* theory

例 I'll explain how it works theoretically. 我将解释它在理论上如何运作。

Huge investments have been made in new systems, information technology and amassing quality assurance accreditations.

新系统、信息技术和越来越多的质保认证领域都获得了巨大投资。

amass [ə'mæs] *vt.* 收集，积聚

释 to collect something, especially in large quantities

例 He amassed a big fortune after 40. 他40岁以后积累了一大笔财富。

assurance [əˈʃuərəns] *n.* 保证；自信

释 a statement that sth. will certainly be true or will certainly happen, particular when there has been doubt about it; belief in your own abilities or strengths

拓 *vt.* assure

用 assurance that

例 In spite of my repeated assurances, Bob still looked very nervous. 尽管我再三保证，鲍勃看起来还是非常紧张。

---

accreditation [əˌkredɪˈteɪʃən] *n.* 达到标准，证明合格

释 the act of granting credit or recognition (especially with respect to educational institution that maintains suitable standards)

拓 *vt.* accredit; *a.* accredited

例 The manufacture offered the accreditation of its products. 生产商提供了其产品合格证书。

Please fill in the Safety Return Questionnaire, print it and attach it to the product before shipping.

在运输之前请填写安全返回问卷，并打印好附在商品上。

questionnaire [ˌkwestʃəˈneə] *n.* 调查表

释 a list of questions that a number of people are asked so that information can be collected and analyzed

拓 fill in / out a questionnaire; complete a questionnaire

例 All workers were asked to fill in a questionnaire about their occupation. 所有的员工都要填写工作调查问卷。

---

attach [əˈtætʃ] *vt. & vi.* 附上，系上，贴上

释 to fasten, join or connect one thing to another; to place or fix in position

拓 attach sth. to sth.

例 This middle school is attached to a normal university. 这所中学附属于一所师范大学。

There are branches around the world and 57 reciprocal clubs world-wide.

他们的分公司遍及全球57个互惠俱乐部。

branch [brɑːntʃ] *n.* 分支，分部；树枝

释 a local office or shop / store belonging to a large company or organization; a part of a tree that grows out from the main stem

例 The supermarket has branches all over the country. 这家超市在全国各地都设有分部。

---

reciprocal [rɪˈsɪprəkəl] *a.* 互惠的，相应的

释 to behave or feel toward someone in the same way as they behave or feel towards you

拓 *vt.* & *vi.* reciprocate; *n.* reciprocity / reciprocation

例 They have a reciprocal loathing for each other. 他们互相憎恨。

They import goods from Singapore rather than purchasing them on the domestic market.

他们从新加坡进口货物，而不是在国内市场上采购。

purchase [ˈpɜːtʃəs] *vt.* 购买

释 to buy

拓 *n.* purchaser / purchasing

例 He purchased this stamp at an auction. 他在拍卖会中购得这枚邮票。

---

domestic [dəˈmestɪk] *a.* 国内的；家庭的

释 of or inside a particular country, not foreign or international; belonging or relating to the home, house or family

拓 *vt.* domesticate; *ad.* domestically; *n.* domesticity

例 Her domestic troubles have ended. 她的家庭烦恼结束了。

In recent years, advertising has been more preoccupied with grabbing attention.

近年来，广告更加注重于吸引人们的注意力。

preoccupy [priˈɒkjupaɪ] *vt.* 先占领，先取；迷住

释 to fill or use a space, an area or an amount of time; to be the main thought in someone's mind, causing other things to be forgotten

拓 *a.* preoccupied; *n.* preoccupation

用 be preoccupied with

例 The seats have been preoccupied. 座位已被人家先占了。

---

grab [græb] *vt. & vi.* 抓取，抢去

释 to take hold of something or someone suddenly and roughly

拓 *a.* grabby / grabbing

例 The thief grabbed the purse and ran away with it. 这贼猛地一把抓住钱包逃跑了。

Visit the beneficial homepage and find more information on mortgage refinancing, debt consolidation, and online services.

访问益友主页可以找到更多关于按揭、债务合并及网上服务的信息。

beneficial [ˌbenɪˈfɪʃəl] *a.* 有益的，有利的

释 having a helpful or good effect, or intending to help

拓 *n. / vt. & vi.* benefit

用 beneficial to

例 Sunshine and moisture are beneficial to living things. 阳光和水分对生物有益。

mortgage [ˈmɔːɡɪdʒ] *n.* 抵押，按揭贷款

释 an agreement which allows you to borrow money from a bank or similar organization, especially in order to buy a house or apartment, or the amount of money that you borrowed

拓 *n.* mortgagee

例 Most people buy a flat on a mortgage. 大多数人都是按揭购房。

---

refinancing [rɪfɪˈnænsɪŋ] *n.* 重新筹集资金

释 borrowing money to pay a debt

例 The company has been troubled by refinancing of debt service payments. 公司正在为偿还债务再筹划资金而发愁。

---

consolidation [kənˌsɒlɪˈdeɪʃən] *n.* 巩固，合并

释 the action of becoming, or causing something to become stronger and more certain; the act of combining into an integral whole

拓 *vt. & vi.* consolidate; *a.* consolidated

例 The consolidation of knowledge is essential for further progress. 知识的巩固对取得更大的进步非常关键。

The only practicable ways to resolve this problem in the longer term are economic pricing in conjunction with conservation measures.

从长远来看，解决这个问题最实际的方法是实现经济定价与保守措施的并轨。

resolve [rɪˈzɒlv] *vt.* 解决

释 to find a satisfactory solution to a problem or difficulty

拓 *n.* resolution

用 resolve that; resolve against; resolve to

例 Have you resolved the problem of traffic congestion yet? 你已经解决交通堵塞这个问题了吗?

The language barrier presents itself in stark form to firms who wish to market their products in other countries.

语言障碍使那些希望在国外销售产品的公司陷入了一个严酷的处境。

stark [stɑːk] *a.* 严酷的，严格的

释 unpleasant; real and impossible to avoid

拓 *ad.* starkly; *n.* starkness

例 The young man is faced with a stark choice. 这位年轻人面临着严峻的抉择。

Glass as instant curtains is available now, but the cost is exorbitant.

现在我们已经可以用玻璃做瞬间拉开的幕布，但其价格却异常高昂。

instant [ˈɪnstənt] *n.* 立即，瞬间； *a.* 立即的，即时的

释 an extremely short period of time; a moment; happening or produced immediately

拓 *ad.* instantly

例 Achieve immediate victory; win instant success. 马到成功。

---

exorbitant [ɪgˈzɔːbɪtənt] *a.* 过高的，高昂的

释 (of a price) much too high

拓 *ad.* exorbitantly

例 The practice of lending money and charging the borrower interest, especially at an exorbitant or illegally high rate must be forbidden. 借给他人钱并要求偿还很高的利息，尤其是利息高得离谱或者非法的做法必须被禁止。

In economics, utility is a measure of the relative satisfaction from consumption of goods.

在经济学中，实用性是用于衡量商品消费所带来的相对满意感的标尺之一。

utility [ju:'tɪlɪti] *n.* **实用品，实用性；公共设施**

释 the quality of being useful; a service such as gas or electricity for people to use

拓 *vt.* utilize; *a.* utilizable

例 The supermarket deals in objects of domestic utility. 那家超市出售家庭用品。

The Credential Select Balanced Portfolio aims to provide reasonable current income and growth of your investment over the long term by investing.

证书选择平衡的证券投资组合意在提供合理的收入以及增长的长期投资。

credential [krɪ'denʃəl] *n.* **凭据；印信；证书**

释 a document attesting to the truth of certain stated facts; someone's education, achievements, experience etc. that prove they have the ability to do something

用 credentials for / as

例 All the interviewees had excellent academic credentials. 所有的面试者都有很好的学术背景。

---

balanced ['bælənst] *a.* **均衡的，平衡的**

释 keeping or showing a balance so that different things or different parts of sth. exist in equal or correct amounts

拓 *n.* / *vt.* & *vi.* balance

例 A balanced diet provides nutrition for your body. 均衡的饮食能为你的身体提供营养。

portfolio [pɔːt'fəʊljəʊ] *n.* **文件夹；证券投资组合**

释 a large flat case used especially for carrying pictures, documents; the combination of shares

例 First we should build up a portfolio of work. 首先，我们要建立一个工作文件夹。

---

reasonable ['riːznəbl] *a.* **合理的；有道理的**

释 based on or using good judgement and therefore fair and practical

拓 *n.* reasonableness; *ad.* reasonably

用 It is reasonable to do sth.; a reasonable explanation

例 The management took all reasonable safety precautions. 管理部门采取了一切合理的安全预防措施。

---

investment [ɪn'vestmənt] *n.* **投资；投入；投资额**

释 the act of investing; laying out money or capital in an enterprise with the expectation of profit

拓 *vt. & vi.* invest; *n.* investor

用 investment in; investment of

例 Stocks and funds are regarded as good long-term investments. 股票和基金被视为很好的长期投资。

British industry, in particular, has in recent decades often been criticized for its insularity.

近几十年来，特别是英国产业，因其孤立化而受到批评。

criticize ['krɪtɪsaɪz] *vt. & vi.* **批评；评论**

释 to express your disapproval of someone or something, or to talk about their faults

拓 *n.* criticism

用 criticize sb. / sth. for doing sth.

例 Jim does nothing but criticize and complain all the time. 吉姆每天

无所事事，就是批评和抱怨。

---

insularity [ˌɪnsjʊ'lærəti] *n.* 思想偏狭；孤立

释 thoughts of interested only in your own country or group and not willing to accept different or foreign ideas; isolated from others

拓 *a.* insular

例 Insularity knowledge of culture difference causes "culture shock". 对文化差别的无知会引起"文化休克"。

The pragmatic need to find acceptable substitutes for dwindling supplies of "luxury" materials such as tortoiseshell and ivory.

实用主义者需要找到一种代替品来减少昂贵的材质，比如玳瑁和象牙的使用。

pragmatic [præg'mætɪk] *a.* 实际的；实用主义的

释 dealing with problems in a sensible, practical way instead of strictly following a set of ideas

拓 *ad.* pragmatically

例 The pragmatic way to problems is to find the solution. 最实际的是找到解决问题的方法。

---

dwindle ['dwɪndl] *vt. & vi.* （使）减少，缩小

释 to gradually become less and less or smaller and smaller

拓 *a.* dwindling

用 dwindle to

例 Drought has dwindled the quantity of crop production. 干旱减少了农作物的产量。

---

luxury ['lʌkʃəri] *n.* 奢侈，豪华

释 a thing that is expensive and enjoyable but not essential

拓 *a.* luxurious; *ad.* luxuriously

用 in luxury

例 The government has imposed strict controls over the import of luxury goods. 政府对奢侈品的进口采取了严格的管制。

---

tortoiseshell ['tɔːtəsʃel] *n.* 龟甲，玳瑁

释 a hard shiny brown and white material made from the shell of a tortoise

例 Researchers found a synthetic imitation of natural tortoiseshell. 研究者发现了一种模仿自然玳瑁制作的人工仿造品。

---

ivory ['aɪvəri] *n.* 象牙；乳白色

释 the hard yellowish-white substance that forms the tusks of some animals such as elephants, used especially in the past to make decorative object; a yellowish white color

例 In ancient Greece, some jewels were made of gold and ivory, as certain pieces of sculpture or artwork. 在古希腊，有些珠宝由黄金和象牙制成，如一些雕刻作品或工艺品。

十八 娱乐休闲类

Hollywood settled upon the novel-length narrative that remains the dominant cinematic convention of today.

好莱坞选用了至今在电影惯例中占主导地位的叙事型长篇小说。

cinematic [ˌsɪnɪ'mætɪk] *a.* 电影的

释 relating to films / cinema

拓 *n.* cinema

例 He is trying to capture a poem in a cinematic visual. 他正试着用电影画面来传达一首诗的意境。

convention [kən'venʃən] *n.* 惯例，大会；协定

释 a large formal meeting for people who belong to the same profession or organization or who have the same interests the way in which sth. is done that most people in a society expect and consider to be polite or the right way to do it

拓 *a.* conventional

用 by convention; convention on

例 The town's new convention center is located in the new district. 这个城市的新会议中心坐落在新区中。

A popular explanation of play has been that it helps juveniles develop the skills they will need to hunt, mate and socialize as adults.

对游戏的一种普遍解释就是：它帮助青少年发展成年后所需的猎食、择偶和社交的能力。

juvenile ['dʒuːvənaɪl] *n.* 青少年；*a.* 少年的；未成熟的

释 a child or a young person who is not yet old enough to be considered as an adult; childish

例 He wrote down to the juvenile reader. 他的作品面向青少年读者。

The star as magnified human self is one of cinema's most strange and enduring legacies.

明星作为被夸大了的人类自身而成为电影最奇特、最持久的遗产之一。

magnify ['mægnɪfaɪ] *vt. & vi.* 放大；夸张

释 to make something look larger than it is, especially by looking at it through a specially cut piece of glass; to make it seem more important or serious than it really is

拓 *n.* magnification

例 Tom wanted to magnify that picture. 汤姆要把那张照片放大。

endure [ɪn'djuə] *vt. & vi.* **耐久，忍耐，容忍；持久，持续**

释 to suffer something difficult, unpleasant or painful; continue to live

拓 *n.* endurance; *a.* endurable

例 The old man had to endure a toothache. 这位老人不得不忍受牙痛。

---

legacy ['legəsi] *n.* **祖先传下来之物，遗赠物**

释 money or property that you receive from someone after they die

用 legacy of

例 His aunt left him a legacy of $50,000. 他阿姨给他留下五万美元遗产。

But in cinema, the real, objective flow of time was captured.

在电影院，真实客观的剧情深深地吸引了观众。

objective [əb'dʒektɪv] *a.* **客观存在的；客观的；** *n.* **目的，目标**

释 existing; outside the mind, real; the goal intended to be attained and which is believed to be attainable

拓 *n.* objectivity; *ad.* objectively

例 Try to be more objective about it. 尽量更客观地对待此事。

---

capture ['kæptʃə] *vt.* **抓取；获得；迷住**

释 to catch a person or an animal; to take control of a place, building, etc. using force; make sb. interested in sth.

用 capture sb's attention / imagination / interest

例 The story captured the imagination of thousands of readers.
这部小说吸引了成千上万的读者。

It was no more than a gimmick, a fairground attraction.

这只不过是一个小花招，一个游乐场吸引观众的手段而已。

gimmick ['gɪmɪk] *n.* **骗局；花招**

释 something which is not serious or of real value that is used to attract people's attention or interest temporarily, especially to make them buy something

拓 *n.* gimmickry; *a.* gimmicky

例 They give away free presents with children's meals as marketing gimmick. 他们给购买儿童餐的人们赠送礼物，以作为他们市场营销的一个策略。

---

fairground ['feəgraʊnd] *n.* 游乐场

释 a large outside area used for a fair

例 There was a fairground near the square. 广场旁边有一个游乐场。

A substantial proportion of the population of modern societies engages in such tourist practices.

现代社会中的大部分人都会加入这一旅游实践。

proportion [prə'pɔːʃən] *n.* 比例；部分

释 a part of a number or amount, considered in relation to the whole; the correct relationship in size, degree, importance, etc. between one thing and another or between the parts of a whole

拓 *a.* proportional; *ad.* proportionally

用 proportion of; proportion to; the proportion of sth. to sth.; in proportion to sth.

例 The proportion of fresh graduates has increased in recent years. 最近几年应届毕业生人数越来越多。

---

engage [ɪn'geɪdʒ] *vt.* 吸引； *vi.* 从事，参加

释 to succeed in attracting and keeping sb.'s attention and interest; to become involved with and try to understand sth./ sb.

拓 *n.* engagement

用 engage as; engage with; engage in / upon

例 To engage in the hunting of whales is illegal. 参与捕鲸活动是非法的。

Tourism and travel in these days are more significant social phenomena than most commentators have considered.

如今，旅游度假作为一种社会现象，其重要性超乎了大多数评论员的想象。

significant [sɪg'nɪfɪkənt] *a.* 有意义的，重要的，重大的

释 having an important effect or influence, especially on what will happen in the future

拓 *n.* significance; *ad.* significantly

用 significant for; it is significant that; significant of

例 Penicillin is a new significant discovery. 青霉素是一个非常重要的发现。

---

commentator ['kɒmənteɪtə] *n.* 时事评论者；实况播音员

释 someone who knows a lot about a particular subject, and who writes about it or discusses it on the television or radio; someone on television or radio who describes an event as it is happening

拓 *vt. & vi.* commentate

例 Several news commentators hit out at the president on his foreign policy. 有几位时事评论员猛烈抨击总统的对外政策。

I believe that 10,000 is a serious underestimate of the total number of masquerading.

我相信，参加化装舞会的人数远远不止一万。

masquerade [ˌmæskə'reɪd] *vi.* 化装；参加化装舞会；
n. 化装舞会；伪装

释 to pretend to be something or someone different; to attend a masked ball; a masked ball; pretense; a way of behaving that hides the truth or a person's true feelings

用 masquerade as

例 A number of police officers masqueraded as the poor. 很多警察都

装扮成穷人。

The history of the cinema in its first thirty years is one of major and unparalleled expansion and growth.

电影史中的头三十年是其发展是最主要、最快的阶段之一。

unparalleled [ʌn'pærəˌleld] *a.* **无比的，优良无比的，空前的**

释 bigger, better, or worse than anything else

例 The scene of this country is unparalleled. 这个国家的风景无与伦比。

---

expansion [ɪks'pænʃ ən] *n.* **扩大，膨胀**

释 an act of increasing or marking sth.; increase in size, amount or importance

拓 *vt.* & *vi.* expand; *n.* expansionist

用 expansion of; expansion in

例 This book is an expansion of the play he wrote before. 这本书是他以前写的剧本的扩充。

Hollywood films appealed because they had better-constructed narratives and their special effects were more impressive.

好莱坞影片的吸引人之处在于它构思精巧的叙事和令人印象深刻的特效。

appeal [ə'pi:l] *vt.* & *vi.* **有吸引力；诉诸，呼吁**

释 to attract, please, stimulate, or interest; to make a serious and urgent request; to change with a crime

拓 *a.* appealing; *ad.* appealingly

用 appeal for; appeal to; appeal to sb. to do sth.; appeal against

例 Do these paintings appeal to you? 这些画对你有吸引力吗?

---

narrative ['nærətɪv] *n.* **叙述，故事**

释 a description of events in a story, especially in a novel

拓 *n.* narration / narrator

例 The writer had great skill in narrative. 这位作家极擅长叙事。

---

impressive [ɪm'presɪv] *a.* 给人深刻印象的

释 making you feel admiration, because they are very large, good, skillful, etc.

拓 *vt.* impress; *ad.* impressively

例 There are some very impressive constructions in the city. 这个城市里面的建筑给人留下了深刻的印象。

Now you can enjoy more of the mind-bending game with tons of enjoyable jumble merchandise.

你可以随心所欲地使用橡皮泥做任何稀奇古怪令人费解的东西。

jumble [dʒʌmbl] *vt. & vi.* 掺杂，混杂；*n.* 混杂，混乱

释 to mix things together in a confused or untidy way; a lot of different things mixed together in an untidy way, without any order

用 jumble of

例 There is a jumble of books and papers on the table. 桌上凌乱地放着一堆书和报纸。

---

merchandise ['mɜːtʃəndaɪz] *n.* 商品，货物

释 goods that are being sold; things you can buy that are connected with or that advertise a particular event or organization

例 A range of official English book merchandise was on sale. 一些官方英语书在出售。

Zealous is an independent record label based in New York City, dedicated to the development of raw, honest, and powerful rock and roll bands.

Zealous是纽约市独立的唱片品牌，致力于发展原生态，真诚而又有影响力的摇滚乐队。

dedicate [ˈdedɪˌkeɪt] *vt.* 指定；奉献

释 to describe sth. that is made, built, or designed for one particular purpose or thing; to describe someone who is dedicated works very hard at what they do because they care a lot about it

拓 *vt.* dedicate

用 dedicated to

例 The ancient Greek dedicated many shrines to Aphrodite. 古希腊人为爱神阿佛洛狄特建造了许多神庙。

---

raw [rɔː] *a.* 天然的，未加工的；无经验的；生的

释 not processed; lacking experience; not cooked

拓 *n.* rawness

例 Cocoa is very bitter in its raw state. 未加工的可可是非常苦的。

Film personalities have such an immediate presence that, inevitably, they become super-real.

电影有快速出现画面的特点，因此才不可避免地变得非常真实。

inevitably [ɪnˈevɪtəbli] *ad.* 不可避免地

释 certain to happen and unable to be avoided or prevented

拓 *a.* inevitable

例 Inevitably, the two sides began to fight. 双方随后不可避免地打了起来。

There were also increasing audiences for films which were artistically more adventurous.

越来越多的观众喜欢看在艺术上更勇于尝试创新的影片了。

artistically [ɑːˈtɪstɪkəli] *ad.* 艺术地，艺术家地

释 connected with art or artists

拓 *a.* artistic

例 The room is luxuriously and artistically decorated. 房间装饰得十分豪华雅致。

---

adventurous [əd'ventʃ ərəs] *a.* 有冒险精神的，新奇的

释 willing to take risks and try new ideas; enjoying being in new, exciting situations, including new and interesting things, methods and ideas

拓 *n.* adventure / adventurer / adventurism

例 Many teachers would like to be more adventurous and creative. 许多教师更愿意去冒险，去创新。

To understand the initial shock is to understand the power and magic of cinema, the unique, hypnotic quality that has made film the most dynamic.

要想理解电影最初的震撼力就要理解电影的魔力，也就是使电影极富动态性的那种独特的让人易被催眠的特质。

initial [ɪ'nɪʃ əl] *a.* 开始的，最初的

释 happening at the beginning

拓 *ad.* initially; *vt.* initialize / initiate; *n.* initiation

例 His initial reaction was one of shock. 他最初的反应是震惊。

---

hypnotic [hɪp'nɒtɪk] *a.* 催眠的，催眠术的，易于催眠的

释 caused by hypnosis; making you feel as if you are going to fall asleep, especially because of a regular, repeated noise or movement

拓 *vt.* hypnotize; *n.* hypnotism / hypnotist / hypnosis

例 The story read before bedtime has hypnotic effect. 睡前读的那个故事有催眠效果。

---

dynamic [daɪ'næmɪk] *a.* 动态的，有活力的，有力的

释 relating to energy or objects in motion or characterized by continuous change, activity or progress

拓 *ad.* dynamically

例 The present economy needs a dynamic market. 目前经济需要一个有活力的市场。

The artwork is often marvelous, but the pictures make the language redundant.

艺术作品往往是传神非凡的，但是照片上的语言显得多余冗长了。

marvelous ['mɑːvɪləs] *a.* **很好的，非凡的**

释 extremely good, wonderful

拓 *n.* / *vt.* & *vi.* marvel

例 This will be a marvelous opportunity for him. 这对他来说可是千载难逢的机会啊。

---

redundant [rɪ'dʌndənt] *a.* **多余的，冗长的**

释 not needed or useful

拓 *n.* redundancy; *ad.* redundantly

例 The essay has too many redundant words. 这篇论文有很多废话。

The mass tourist finds pleasure in authentic contrived attractions, gullibly enjoying the pseudo-events and disregarding the real world outside.

大量游客都能从设计得十分逼真的景点中找到乐趣，心甘情愿地被骗，享受虚假的事物，全然不顾外面真实的世界。

authentic [ɔː'θentɪk] *a.* **逼真的，真正的，可信的**

释 known to be real, true and accurate

拓 *vt.* authenticate; *n.* authentication

例 Autumn is also the authentic season of renewal. 秋天也是真正的万象更新的季节。

contrive [kən'traɪv] *vt. & vi.* **计划，企图；发明，设计**

释 to arrange a situation or an event, or arrange for something to happen, using clever planning; to invent and / or make a device or other objects in a clever and possibly unusual way

拓 *n.* contrivance

用 contrive to

例 The writer contrived a happy ending for the book. 作者为这本书安排了一个大团圆的结局。

---

disregard [ˌdɪsrɪ'gɑːd] *vt.* **无视，不顾**

释 to ignore something

拓 *a.* disregarded

用 disregard for

例 You can't just disregard the security problem! 你绝对不能无视安全问题！

The German cinema, relatively insignificant in the pre-war years, exploded on to the world scene after 1919.

战前微不足道的德国电影在1919年以后却在世界银幕上大为轰动。

insignificant [ˌɪnsɪg'nɪfɪkənt] *a.* **微不足道的，无关紧要的**

释 not important or thought to be valueless, especially because of being small

拓 *n.* insignificance; *ad.* insignificantly

例 This problem was insignificant compared to others she faced. 较之她面临的其他问题，这个问题是微不足道的。

---

pre-war [ˌpriː'wɔː] *a.* **战前的**

释 happening before a war

例 The front door of my pre-war terrace house has just been painted red. 我住的地方是战前建的排屋，其大门刚刚刷上红色。

explode [ɪksˈpləʊd] *vt. & vi.* 引爆，爆炸

释 to (cause to) burst violently

拓 *n.* explosion; *a.* explosive; *ad.* explosively

用 explode into

例 The terrorists exploded a bomb in a store. 恐怖分子在一家商店里引爆了一枚炸弹。

Social activities include a welcome buffet and a half-day excursion round Bingham.

社交活动包括一个欢迎宴会和一个半天的环宾厄姆短途旅行。

buffet [ˈbʌfeɪ] *n.* 自助餐

释 a meal at a party or other occasions, in which people serve themselves at a table and then move away to eat

用 buffet breakfast / lunch / supper

例 This buffet offers you a easeful enjoyment. 本自助餐厅为您提供无拘无束的享受。

---

excursion [ɪksˈkɜːʃən] *n.* 远足，短途旅行

释 a short journey arranged so that a group of people can visit a place, especially while they are on holiday

用 excursion to

例 The excursion was rounded off with a short visit to the school. 集体游览在参观学校后圆满结束。

Gospel music is a musical genre characterized by dominant vocals referencing lyrics of a religious nature.

福音音乐是一种大量采用和声的音乐形式，其歌词具有宗教色彩。

gospel [ˈgɒspəl] *n.* 福音，福音书；真理

释 one of the four books in the Bible about Christ's life; the complete truth

例 *The Gospel of St. John* has more idiosyncrasies and is colored by theology of a strongly Hellenic type. 《约翰福音》具有更多的特性，而且具有强烈的希腊式神学色彩。

---

genre [ʒɑːnrə] *n.* 类型，体裁

释 a particular type of art, writing, music etc., which has certain features that all examples of this type share

用 genre of

例 Superficially, this Shakespeare's work seems to fit into the same genre. 表面上看，莎士比亚的这个剧本似乎属于同一类型。

---

vocal [ˈvəʊkəl] *a.* 声音的；*n.* 声乐作品

释 connected with the voice; the part of a piece of music that is sung

拓 *ad.* vocally

例 They played a piece of vocal music. 他们演奏了一曲声乐作品。

---

lyric [ˈlɪrɪk] *n.* 抒情诗；歌词

释 poems that expressing strong personal emotions such as love, in a way that is similar to music in its sounds and rhythm; the words of a song

例 Selina wrote the lyrics for the song. 塞琳娜为该曲谱写了歌词。

---

religious [rɪˈlɪdʒəs] *a.* 宗教的

释 connected with religion or with a particular religion

拓 *n.* religiosity / religion

例 In the old days, the government opposes religious freedom and persecutes religious people. 在旧社会，政府反对宗教自由，迫害宗教人士。

Early cinema audiences often experienced the same confusion.

早期电影院的观众往往经历了同样的困惑。

confusion [kənˈfjuːʒən] *n.* 混乱；混淆

释 a state of uncertainty about what is happening; the fact of making a mistake about who sb. is or what sth. is

拓 *vt.* confuse; *a.* confused / confusing

例 The room was in confusion after the Christmas party. 圣诞晚会之后，房间里一片混乱。

Some countries developed distinctive national cinemas.

一些国家建立了非常有特色的国家电影院。

distinctive [dɪ'stɪŋktɪv] *a.* 有特色的，出众的

释 easy to recognize because it is different from other things

拓 *a.* distinct; *ad.* distinctly; *n.* distinction / distinctiveness

例 The book is said to have distinctive features. 据说这本书特色鲜明。

十九 企业管理类

No attempt was made to place a division in the programme that would best fit its habitual methods of supervision used by the manager, assistant managers, supervisors an assistant supervisors to solve the problems.

他们没有尝试对程序进行划分，使其与经理、经理助理、监督人惯常使用的监督方法相配合。

habitual [hə'bɪtjuəl] *a.* 惯常的，习惯的

释 doing something from habit, and unable to stop doing it, usual or repeated

拓 *ad.* habitually

例 Excessive or habitual indulgence in alcoholic liquor is harmful to people's health. 过度酗酒或习惯性地大量饮酒对人体健康有害。

---

supervision [ˌsjuːpə'vɪʒən] *n.* 监督，管理

释 when you supervise someone or something; when someone

watches a person or activity and makes certain that everything is done correctly, safely, etc.

拓 *n.* supervisor; *vt. & vi.* supervise

用 under sb.'s supervision

例 Statistical work shall be subject to public supervision. 统计工作应当接受社会公众的监督。

Job descriptions eliminate role ambiguity for managers.

职位描述使经理的角色不再模棱两可。

eliminate [ɪ'lɪmɪneɪt] *vt.* 除去，排除，剔除

释 to completely get rid of something that is unnecessary or unwanted

拓 *n.* elimination

用 eliminate from

例 Let us eliminate all uncertain thought. 让我们从思想上消除一切疑惑。

---

ambiguity [ˌæmbɪ'gjuːɪti] *n.* 不明确，含糊，模棱两可

释 the state of having more than one possible meaning

拓 *a.* ambiguous; *ad.* ambiguously

例 The dispute resulted from ambiguities in the contract. 争议是由合同中模棱两可的词句引发的。

Chicago Mercantile Exchange Inc. (CME) has approximately 200 technology employees and approximately 100 consultants working on more than 300 technology.

芝加哥商业交易有限公司拥有约200名技术员工以及100名左右的工作顾问来解决300多个技术难关。

mercantile ['mɜːkəntaɪl] *a.* 贸易的，商业的

释 related to trade or business

例 Dun & Bradstreet is the largest mercantile agency in the United

States. 丹·布瑞斯追特公司是美国最大的商业征信所。

She cites both quantitative and qualitative studies that show increased productivity for part-time workers.

她用定性和定量两种研究结果来说明兼职工作者的生产力有所提高。

quantitative ['kwɒntɪtətɪv] *a.* 数量的，定量的

释 measured by the quantity of something rather than to its quality

拓 *ad.* quantitatively

用 quantitative data / analysis

例 He said it was only a quantitative difference. 他说这仅仅是数量上的差别。

---

qualitative ['kwɒlɪtətɪv] *a.* 性质上的，质的

释 relating to the quality or standard of something rather than the quantity

拓 *ad.* qualitatively

用 qualitative analysis / study

例 Qualitative analysis shows that water is made up of hydrogen and oxygen. 定性分析表明水是由氢和氧结合而成的。

---

productivity [ˌprɒdʌk'tɪvɪtɪ] *n.* 生产率，生产能力

释 the rate at which goods are produced, and the amount produced, especially in relation to the work, time and money needed to produce them

拓 *n.* product / production; *vt.* & *vi.* produce; *a.* productive

用 improve / increase / raise productivity

例 There have been tremendous increases in agricultural productivity. 农业生产率已得到极大提高。

It is our belief that this improvement alone, while not tangibly measurable, has increased the ability of management to manage the effects of absenteeism more effectively since this study.

我们相信，虽然效果还不太明显，但单是这一方面的提高，就能有效提高对缺勤率的管理能力。

tangibly ['tændʒɪbli] *ad.* 明白地，可触知地

释 able to be shown, touched or experience

拓 *a.* tangible

例 The development of the economy has tangibly improved the lives of all people in China. 经济发展显著改善了中国居民的生活水平。

---

measurable ['meʒərəbəl] *a.* 可测量的；重大的，重要的

释 large or important enough to be measured; noticeable; important

拓 *ad.* measurably; *n.* / *vt.* & *vi.* measure

例 I really don't see a measurable risk from the products we are selling. 我实在看不出我们目前正在贩售的产品中，有任何大的风险。

This means that employees must have the capability of doing the job and must regard the appraisal process as valid.

这就意味着所有的员工必须具备从事这类工作的能力，还必须认同这种评定的标准。

capability [ˌkeɪpə'bɪlɪti] *n.* 能力，才能

释 ability to do things effectively and skilfully, and to achieve results

拓 *a.* capable

用 have the capability to do sth.

例 As an interpreter, he has the capability to do important meetings. 作为一个口译员，他具有从事重要会议翻译的能力。

appraisal [ə'preɪzəl] *n.* **估计，估量，评价**

释 a statement or opinion judging the worth, value, or condition of sth.

拓 *vt.* appraise; *n.* appraisee / appraiser

用 appraisal of

例 The collector made an appraisal of $2, 000 on the drawing. 收藏家对那幅画的估价是2000美元。

---

valid ['vælɪd] *a.* **有确实根据的；有效的；正当的**

释 based on truth or reason; able to be accepted; acceptable

拓 *ad.* validly; *n.* validity

用 be valid for

例 My passport is valid for two years. 我的护照有效期是两年。

Estimates of the ratio of basic to service workers range from 1:4 to 1:8.

估计基本工人和服务人员的比例从1:4到1:8不等。

range [reɪndʒ] *vt.* & *vi.* **排列；变化；包括（从……到……）之间的各类事物**

释 to place or arrange in a row or rows or in a specified order; to vary or extend between specified limits

用 rang from… to…; range between… to…

例 Estimates of the damage range between $1 million and $5 million. 估计损失在100万到500万元之间。

Members of staff who have paid the requisite fee and display the appropriate permit may bring a vehicle into the grounds.

付了必要费用并得到许可的员工可以将车开进广场。

requisite ['rekwɪzɪt] *a.* **必要的，需要的**

释 needed for a particular purpose

用 requisite of / for

例 He hasn't got the requisite qualifications for this job. 他不具备这项工作所需要的资格。

---

appropriate [ə'prəʊprɪət] *a.* 适当的

释 suitable, acceptable or correct for the particular circumstances

拓 *n.* appropriateness; *ad.* appropriately

用 appropriate to / for; it is appropriate (for sb.) to do sth.

例 Clothes appropriate for a job interview would give the interviewer a good impression. 穿着得体会给面试官留下一个好印象。

Services will depend on personal circumstances and discretion of bank managers.

服务取决于个人情况和银行经理的判断。

circumstance ['sɜːkəmstəns] *n.* 环境，状况

释 a fact or event that makes a situation the way it is

用 in... circumstances; under... circumstances

例 In normal circumstances， John would have resigned immediately. 正常情况下约翰会马上辞职的。

---

discretion [dɪ'skreʃən] *n.* 慎重；辨别力

释 care in what you say or do, in order to keep sth. secret or to avoid causing embarrassment or difficulty for sb.; the ability and right to decide exactly what should be done in a particular situation

拓 *a.* discretional; *ad.* discretionally

用 discretion over; at sb's discretion

例 You must show more discretion in choosing your girlfriends. 你选择女友须更加谨慎。

Employees are likely to perceive the participation process as manipulative and be negatively affected by it.

雇员很可能感受到参与过程的可操作性并且会受到负面影响。

perceive [pə'siːv] *vt.* 察觉，感觉；认知，理解

释 to become aware of sth. through the senses; to understand or think of sth.

拓 *a.* perceptive

用 perceive sth. / sb. as sth.; perceive sth. / sb. to be sth.; perceive that

例 I perceived a man enter the room. 我看到一个人走进房间。

---

manipulative [mə'nɪpjulətɪv] *a.* 操作的；巧妙处理的

释 skillful at influencing sb. or forcing sb. to do what you want, often in an unfair way

拓 *vt.* manipulate; *n.* manipulation

例 The early manipulative techniques of a four-year-old are based on persistent training. 一个四岁小孩的早期操控技巧建立在持续训练的基础之上。

The annual value of these subsidies is immense.

每年的补贴加起来金额巨大。

subsidy ['sʌbsɪdi] *n.* 补助金，津贴

释 money that is paid by government or an organization to reduce the costs of services or of producing goods so that their prices can be kept low

拓 *vt.* subsidize; *n.* subsidization / subsidizer

例 The government should offer more housing subsidies to the poor. 政府应该为穷人提供更多的住房补贴。

---

immense [ɪ'mens] *a.* 巨大的，广大的

释 extremely large or great

拓 *ad.* immensely; *n.* immensity

例 It's almost impossible to find him in the immense ocean. 在无边无际的大海中要找到他几乎是不可能的。

The job to be filed is a managerial post in a large bureaucratic organization.

一家大行政机构中一个管理职位有空缺。

managerial [ˌmænəˈdʒɪərəl] *a.* 管理的

释 connected with the work of a manager

拓 *n.* manager / management; *vt.* manage

例 Do you have any managerial experience? 你有没有管理方面的经验?

---

bureaucratic [bjuəˌrəʊˈkrætɪk] *a.* 官僚的

释 connected with a bureaucracy or bureaucrats and involving complicated official rules which may seem unnecessary

拓 *n.* bureaucrat / bureaucracy; *ad.* bureaucaticrally

例 It is necessary to get rid of bureaucratic practices. 清除官僚习气是必须的。

The study, by recruitment consultants, shows that while one in six men who appear on interview shortlists get jobs, the figure rises to one in four women.

一项由招聘顾问进行的研究表明，面试名单上每六个男人中才有一个能获得工作，而对女人而言，每四个里面就有一个。

recruitment [rɪˈkruːtmənt] *n.* 征募

释 of finding new people to work in a company, join an organization or do a job

拓 *vt.* & *vi.* recruit

例 This has significantly shifted the balance of power is the recruitment process. 这种情况大大转变了人才招聘过程中的均势。

---

consultant [kənˈsʌltənt] *n.* 顾问

释 an expert who gives advice

拓 *vt.* & *vi.* consult; *n.* consultancy

例 The former general manager now serves as a financial consultant. 前任总经理现在成了财政顾问。

Key rewards such as pay increases and promotions or advancements should be allocated for the attainment of the employee's specific goals.

重点奖励(比如增加员工工资和提供晋升机会)应该给完成某一特殊目标的员工。

attainment [ə'teɪnmənt] *n.* 达到，成就，造诣

释 sth. that you learned or achieved; success in achieving sth.

拓 *vt.* & *vi.* attain; *a.* attainable

例 The attainment of wealth did not make her happy. 获得财富并没有使她幸福。

This led to significant improvement in communication between managers and staff.

这一方法显著增强了经理和员工之间的沟通。

improvement [ɪm'pru:vmənt] *n.* 改进，改善

释 the act of improving something or the state of being improved

拓 *vt.* improve

例 I cannot see any improvement in your writing. 我看不出你在写作方面有何提高。

As well be observed, the hierarchically controlled programmes increased productivity by about 2 5%.

观察结果显示，分层控制方案使生产率提高了约25%。

observe [əb'zɜ:v] *vt.* 观察，注意到；遵守

释 to see and notice something; to fulfill or comply with

拓 *n.* observation / observer

用 observe sb. doing sth.; observe that

例 He observed a strange man hanging around the shop. 他看到一个陌生男人在商店附近闲逛。

---

hierarchically [ˌhaɪəˈrɑːkɪkəli] *ad.* **分层地，体系地**

释 if a system, organization etc. is hierarchical, people or things are divided into levels of importance

拓 *a.* hierarchical; *n.* hierarchy

例 France in Middle Age was a hierarchical society. 法国在中世纪是一个等级分明的社会。

In the marketing of their campaign, there are shrewd and skillful image-builders.

在他们的营销活动中，有精明和熟练的形象塑造者。

shrewd [ʃruːd] *a.* **精明的**

释 good at judging what people or situations are really like

拓 *ad.* shrewdly; *n.* shrewdness

例 She was a shrewd business woman. 她是一个精明的商人。

The assessment of clerical workers must consider factors such as quality work performed.

考评文书人员主要看员工的工作绩效等因素。

clerical [ˈklerɪkəl] *a.* **书记的，事务上的，抄写员的**

释 connected with office work

拓 *n.* clerk

例 We should recruit some clerical assistants to finish the proof-reading. 我们招聘一些文书人员来完成这些校对工作。

You should answer the following questions: what is redundancy, and what are your rights if you're made redundant, how should you consult.

你应该明白以下几个问题：什么是裁员，假如被裁员你有哪些权益，你该如何去咨询。

redundancy [rɪˈdʌndənsi] *n.* 裁员；冗余，多余

释 a situation in which someone has to leave their job, because they are no longer needed; when something is not used because something similar or the same already exists

拓 *a.* redundant

例 Three thousand workers now face redundancy. 3000名员工面临着裁员问题。

Employees who had been putting in 12-hour a day, six days a week, found their time on the job shrinking to 10 hours daily.

那些每天工作12小时，一周工作6天的员工发现他们的工作时间缩短到每天10小时。

shrink [ʃrɪŋk] *vt.* & *vi.* 收缩，退缩，萎缩

释 to become smaller, or to make something smaller, through the effects of heat or water

拓 *n.* shrinkage

用 shrink to; shrink from sth.

例 I'm worried about washing that skirt in case it shrinks. 我担心那条裙子洗过之后会缩水。

In order to develop an economically viable hotel organization model. AHI decided to implement some one policies.

为了发展一个经济上可行的酒店管理模式，AHI决定实施新的政策。

viable ['vaɪəbəl] *a.* 可行的

释 a viable idea, plan, or method can work successfully

拓 *n.* viability; *ad.* viably

用 viable alternative / option; economically / financially viable

例 The panel came forward with one viable solution. 专家组想出一个可行的方案。

---

implement ['ɪmplɪmənt] *vt.* 执行，使生效

释 to take action or make changes that you have officially decided should happen

拓 *n.* implementation

用 implement a policy / plan / decision

例 We have decided to implement the committee's plans in full. 我们决定充分实施委员会的方案。

Mediocre record on conservation caused skeptical attitude towards advertisement.

平庸的保护记录引起对广告的怀疑态度。

mediocre ['miːdɪəʊkə] *a.* 平庸的，平凡的

释 not very good; moderate or inferior in quality

拓 *n.* mediocrity

例 I thought the novel was pretty mediocre. 我认为这篇小说很平庸。

---

conservation [ˌkɒnsə'veɪʃən] *n.* 保存，保护

释 the protection of natural things such as animals, plants, forests etc., to prevent them being spoiled or destroyed

拓 *vt.* conserve; *a.* conservative

例 Most people are aware of the conservation of natural resources.

现在大多数人已意识到要保护自然资源。

---

skeptical [ˈskeptɪkəl] *a.* 怀疑的

释 tending to disagree with what other people tell you

拓 *n.* skeptic / skepticism

用 sceptical about / of

例 I'm extremely skeptical about my date of birth. 我非常怀疑我的出生日期是否正确。

Whether the goals should be assigned by a manager or collectively set in conjunction with the employees is a question needs discussion.

由经理制定目标还是由员工集体制定是一个需要讨论的问题。

collectively [kəˈlektɪvli] *ad.* 共同地，集体地，总体来说

释 in conjunction with; combined; as a group

拓 *a.* / *n.* collective; *vt.* & *vi.* collect; *n.* collection

例 She has a staff of four who collectively earn almost $200, 000. 她有4个员工，4个人的工资合起来大概$20万美元。

---

conjunction [kənˈdʒʌŋkʃən] *n.* 结合，联合

释 working, happening, or being used with someone or something else

用 conjunction of; in conjunction with

例 The answer sheets are designed to be used in conjunction with the new English text books. 设计这些答题卡的目的是为了与新的英语教科书配套使用。

During this period, there was an emphasis on providing clean drinking water, improved sanitation and housing.

在这期间，工作的重心应该放在提供干净的饮用水、改善房屋和卫生设施上面。

emphasis ['emfəsɪs] *n.* 强调，重点

释 special attention or importance

拓 *vt.* emphasize

用 emphasis on; put / place emphasis on sth.

例 The course places emphasis on practical knowledge. 这个课程注重实践知识。

---

sanitation [ˌsænɪ'teɪʃ ən] *n.* 环境卫生，卫生设备

释 the equipment and systems that keep places clean, especially by removing human waste

拓 *vt.* sanitize; *a.* sanitary

例 Overcrowding and poor sanitation are common problems in rural areas. 人口过多和卫生条件差是农村地区的普遍问题。

If they see potential clientele going elsewhere, they might want to be able to offer a similar service.

如果看到潜在的主顾去了其他的地方，他们有可能会希望自己能够提供类似的服务。

clientele [ˌklaɪən'tel] *n.* 主顾，客户

释 the customers of a shop, restaurant etc.

拓 *n.* client

例 The Disco nightclub has a very fashionable clientele. 迪厅的客人都很时尚。

I work in local firm of solicitors. It's nearly the end of the year and I am trying to find someone to help us organize our finances.

我在当地律师行上班。快到年底了，我试着找人帮我们整理财务。

solicitor [sə'lɪsɪtə] *n.* 律师

释 a type of lawyer in Britain who gives legal advice, prepares the necessary documents when property is bought or sold, and defends people, especially in the lower courts of law

例 The solicitor is preparing a case in the court tomorrow. 这位律师正在为明天法庭审理的案件做准备。

Allocating annual salary increases in a lump sum rather than spreading them out.

按年薪分发增加了大块资金的数目，而不是将它分散开来。

allocate ['æləkeɪt] *vt.* 分派，分配

释 to give something to someone as their share of a total amount, for them to use in a particular way

拓 *n.* allocation

用 allocate sth. to sb. / sth.; allocate sth. for sth.

例 The government is allocating 20 million for education. 政府拨款2000万用于教育。

---

lump [lʌmp] *n.* 块状

释 a piece of a solid substance, usually with no particular shape

拓 *a.* lumpish

用 lump of; lump sb. / sth. together

例 The artist started with a big lump of clay. 艺术家用一大块粘土开始制作雕塑。

Absence from work is a costly and disruptive problem for any organization.

员工旷工对于任何一个组织而言，都是一个既破费又麻烦的问题。

disruptive [dɪs'rʌptɪv] *a.* 捣乱的，破坏性的，制造混乱的

释 causing trouble and therefore stopping something from continuing as usual

拓 *vt.* disrupt; *n.* disruption; *ad.* disruptively

例 He has a disruptive influence on the other children. 他能带坏别的孩子。

They have been involved in the policy, which needs to be disseminated and implemented effectively.

他们参与了该政策的制定，这一政策需要得到宣传和有效实施。

disseminate [dɪ'semɪneɪt] *vt.* 散播，传播，宣传

释 to spread or give out something，especially news，information，ideas, etc., to a lot of people

拓 *n.* dissemination

例 They use the media to disseminate their own views. 他们利用媒体来传播自己的观点。

Scrapping them offers a two-fold bonus.

除掉他们将提供双倍奖金。

scrap [skræp] *vt.* 抛弃，除掉

释 to not continue with a system or plan; to get rid of something which is no longer useful or wanted, often using its parts in new ways

拓 *a.* scrappy

例 Hundreds of nuclear weapons have been scrapped. 很多核武器已经停止使用了。

---

bonus ['bəʊnəs] *n.* 红利，奖金

释 an extra amount of money that is given to you as a present or reward in addition to the money you were expecting

例 The firm rewarded her hard work with a bonus. 公司发给她奖金以酬谢她工作努力。

Reducing the number of incomplete reservations greatly improved perceptions of service.

减少无竞争力的预定大大提高了客服意识。

reservation [ˌrezəˈveɪʃ ən] *n.* 预定

释 the actions of reserving something

拓 *vt.* reserve

用 make a reservation for

例 Their airline reservation systems were attacked by hackers yesterday. 他们的订票系统昨天遭黑客攻击。

---

perception [pəˈsepʃ ən] *n.* 认识，观念；感知

释 a belief or opinion, often held by many people and based on appearance; a awareness of things through the physical senses, especially sight; someone's ability to notice and understand things that are not obvious to other people

拓 *n.* perceptiveness; *a.* perceptive; *ad.* perceptively

用 perception of

例 People differ a lot in their aesthetic perceptions. 人们在审美观上差别很大。

Managers need to make rewards contingent on performance.

经理奖励员工需要凭其业绩而定。

contingent [kənˈtɪndʒənt] *n.* 分队，代表团；*a.* 依情况而定的

释 a group of people representing an organization or country, or a part of a military force; depending on something that may or may not happen

拓 *n.* contingency

例 Any further payments are contingent upon satisfactory completion dates. 下一步付款要视完工日期是否令人满意而定。

We take a cooperative approach to the assessment of your work and encourage you to contribute to discussion.

我们采取合作的方法来评估你的工作并且鼓励你勇于参与讨论。

cooperative [kəʊ'ɒpərətɪv] *a.* 合作的

释 willing to act or work together for a particular purpose, or to help or do what people ask

拓 *vi.* cooperate; *n.* cooperation; *ad.* cooperatively

例 I've asked them not to play their music so loudly, but they're not being very cooperative. 我让他们别这么大声地演奏音乐，但他们并不是很配合。

---

assessment [ə'sesmənt] *n.* 估计，评估

释 the act of judging or deciding the amount, value, quality or importance of something

拓 *vt.* assess

例 She made a careful assessment of the situation. 她对形势做了细致的评估。

The challenge to management is how to motivate employees under such retrenchment conditions.

管理者所面临的挑战是在这种开支紧缩状况下如何调动员工的积极性。

motivate ['məʊtɪveɪt] *vt.* 给……动机，刺激，激发

释 to give an incentive for action, to make sb. want to do sth. especially sth. that involves hard work and effort

拓 *a.* motive; *n.* motivation

用 motivate sb. to do sth.

例 With counseling and training, managers can motivate problem employees by setting them a goal and encouraging them to achieve it. 通过商议和培训，管理者帮助问题员工设定目标并鼓励他们去实现，由此可以激励他们。

---

retrenchment [rɪ'trentʃmənt] *n.* 紧缩

释 the reduction of expenditures in order to become financial stable

拓 *vt. & vi.* retrench

例 The government had to adopt the policy of financial retrenchment. 政府被迫采取财政紧缩的政策。

China will accelerate the fully listing of its eligible centrally administered state-owned enterprises.

中国将重点加速扶持国有控股企业。

eligible ['elɪdʒəbl] *a.* 有资格的，合格的；（婚姻）合意的

释 having the right to do or obtain something; satisfying the appropriate conditions; desirable or suitable as a partner in marriage

拓 *n.* eligibility

用 eligible for; eligible to do sth.

例 He was not eligible for the examination because he was over age. 他没有考试资格，因为他已超龄。

---

enterprise ['entəpraɪz] *n.* 企业，事业

释 an organization, especially a business, or a difficult and important plan, especially one that will earn money

例 An enterprise should encourage innovation and promote competitive advantage. 企业应该鼓励创新，提高竞争优势。

Indeed AHI is progressively rolling out these initiatives in other hotels in Australia.

在澳大利亚其他酒店，AHI将逐步开展新方案。

initiative [ɪ'nɪʃɪətɪv] *n.* 首创精神；主动权；倡议，新方案

释 the power or opportunity to act and gain an advantage before other people do; the ability to decide and act on your own without waiting for sb. to tell you what to do; a new action or movement, often intended to solve a problem

拓 *a.* initial; *ad.* initially; *vt.* initialize

用 initiative for

例 The United Nations talk about a new peace initiative. 联合国就新的和平倡议进行讨论。

The equity problem will not vanish, even if we quash it or control it.

公平问题不会消失，即使我们镇压或管制它。

vanish ['vænɪʃ] *vi.* 消失，不见了

释 to disappear suddenly, especially in a way that cannot be easily explained

用 vanish without trace

例 Many types of animals have now vanished from the earth. 很多种动物现在已经从地球上绝迹了。

---

quash [kwɒʃ] *vt.* 镇压，压碎，平息

释 to forcefully stop something that you do not want to happen

例 They have their sentence quashed by the appeal court judge.

他们通过上诉，使法院法官撤销了对他们的判决。

Some of the more obvious rewards that managers allocate include pay, promotion, autonomy, job scope and depth.

经理有一些较为明显的奖励办法，包括加薪、晋升、调整自主权和工作范围及深度。

promotion [prə'məʊʃən] *n.* 促进；提升；推广

释 activity that encourages people to believe in the value or importance of sth.; a move to a more important job or position in a company or organization; activities done in order to increase the sales of a product or service

拓 *a.* promotional; *vt.* promote

用 promotion to; promotion of

例 There are good opportunities of promotion in this company.
这家公司里晋升的机会很多。

---

autonomy [ˈɔːtɒnəmi] *n.* 自治

释 the right of a group of people to govern itself, or to organize its own activities

拓 autonomous

例 The separatist is demanding full autonomy for their state.
分裂主义者要求他们的州完全自治。

---

scope [skəʊp] *n.* 范围

释 an area in which something acts or operates or has power or control

用 outside / beyond / within the scope of sth.; scope for

例 Your question is beyond the scope of this English book. 你所问的问题已超出了这本英语书的范围。

---

depth [depθ] *n.* 深度

释 the distance down either from the top of something to the bottom, or to a distance below the top surface of something

用 to / at a depth of sth.

例 There is a sea with an average depth of 40 metres. 这片海的平均深度是40米。

二十 其他类

The city centre is just a five-minute walk from the college, easily accessible in lunch or study breaks.

市中心距离学院步行只需5分钟，特别是在午饭和学习的休憩时间到那里很方便。

accessible [æk'sesəbl] *a.* 可得到的，易接近的

释 that can be reached, entered, used, seen

拓 *n.* access / accessibility; *ad.* accessibly

用 accessible to

例 Attention, medicine should not be kept where it is accessible to children. 注意，药品不应放在儿童容易拿到的地方。

There are also several direct methods of elicitation, such as asking informants to fill in the blanks in a substitution frame.

还有几种直接的诱导方法，比如让被调查者填写替换格。

elicitation [ɪˌlɪsɪ'teɪʃən] *n.* 引出，诱出；抽出

释 the act of getting information or a reaction from sb.; stimulation that calls up (draws forth) a particular class of behaviors

拓 *vt.* elicit

例 Teaching with the method of elicitation proves to be effective. 启发式教学法被证明有效。

The majority of them are fatal; the majority of the victims are children.

它们大多数是致命的；大部分受害者都是孩子。

fatal ['feɪtl] *a.* 致命的，毁灭性的

释 resulting in someone's death

拓 *n.* fate

用 fatal to; fatal accident / injury / illness; fatal mistake / error

例 He committed a fatal mistake. 他犯了一个不可挽回的错误。

victim ['vɪktɪm] *n.* 受害者

释 someone who has been attacked, robbed, or murdered

拓 *vt.* victimize; *n.* victimization; *a.* victimless

用 victim of

例 The victims of the explosion were dead. 爆炸事故的受害者都遇难了。

For larger studies, scrupulous attention has been paid to the sampling theory employed.

对于更广泛的研究来说，需要对所使用的取样理论采取谨慎的态度。

scrupulous ['skru:pjuləs] *a.* 小心谨慎的，细心的

释 very careful to be completely honest and fair

拓 *ad.* scrupulously

用 scrupulous in (doing) sth.; scrupulous about (doing) sth.

例 You must be scrupulous about hygiene when you're preparing a baby's feed. 给婴儿准备食物时，对卫生丝毫马虎不得。

---

theory ['θɪəri] *n.* 理论

释 an idea or set of ideas that is intended to explain something about life or the world, especially an idea that has not yet been proved to be true

拓 *ad.* theoreticelly

用 theory about / on; theory of; theory that

例 There are different theories about how the human brain works. 关于人类大脑的工作原理存在多种不同理论。

Unfortunately, this modernist interest in geometric simplicity and function became exploited for profit.

不幸的是，这种现代的对几何简单性和功能性的兴趣是为了利益而被开发。

geometric [dʒɪə'metrɪk] *a.* 几何学的，几何学图形的

释 of or like the lines, shapes, etc. used in geometry, esp. because of having regular shapes or lines

拓 *n.* geometry; *ad.* geometrically

---

exploit ['eksplɔɪt] *vt.* 开发，利用，开拓

释 to use sth. well in order to gain as much from it as possible; to treat a person or situation as an opportunity to gain an advantage for yourself; to develop or use sth. for business or industry

拓 *a.* exploitable; *n.* exploitation

例 People should read the related provisions before they exploit natural resources. 在开发自然资源前，人们应该先了解相关的规定。

This caused the outer layer of pane to solidify.

这使得窗格的最外层凝固。

layer ['leɪə] *n.* 层

释 a quantity or thickness of sth. that lies over a surface or between surfaces

例 A layer of dust covers everything. 所有的东西都盖了一层灰。

---

solidify [sə'lɪdɪfaɪ] *vt. & vi.* 凝固，巩固

释 to become solid; to make sth. solid

拓 *n.* solidity; *a.* solid; *ad.* solidly

例 They try to solidify their relationship. 他们试图巩固他们的关系。

It is possible that receptions will ask you to explain your problem.

接待处可能要求你解释你的词典。

reception [rɪˈsepʃən] *n.* 接待处；欢迎会，欢迎

释 the area inside the entrance of a hotel, an office building, etc. where guests or visitors go first when they arrived; the type of welcome that is given to sb. / sth.

拓 *n.* receptionist

例 Jim had an enthusiastic reception when he returned home. 吉姆回家时受到了热情的接待。

People state benefits are their only income.

人们说他们得到的权益仅仅是收入本身。

benefit [ˈbenɪfɪt] *n.* 利益

释 an advantage, improvement, or help that you get from something

用 benefit of; on benefit; benefit (BrE) = welfare (AmE)

例 The new credit cards will be of great benefit to our customers. 新的信用卡将给客户带来巨大利益。

The flashy brochures and pamphlets are often seen at expensive restaurants.

我们经常在昂贵的餐厅看到这些华而不实的宣传册。

flashy [ˈflæʃi] *a.* 闪光的，一瞬间的，浮华的

释 attracting attention by being bright, expensive, large

拓 *a.* / *n.* / *vt.* & *vi.* flash; *ad.* flashily; *n.* flashiness

例 I just want a good reliable car, nothing flashy. 我只要一辆性能可靠的轿车，不要华而不实的那种。

---

pamphlet [ˈpæmflɪt] *n.* 小册子

释 a very thin book with paper covers, which gives information about something

例 The pamphlet contains information of political opinion. 这本小册子含有关于政治主张的资料。

Notwithstanding the disappointing results, it is our contention that the strategies were not in vain.

尽管结果令人失望，但是我们认为这些策略并非一无是处。

notwithstanding [ˌnɒtwɪθ'stændɪŋ] *ad.* 尽管；*prep.* 纵使；*conj.* 虽然

释 in spite of something

例 Notwithstanding differences, there are clear similarities. 尽管有区别，但还是有相似的地方。

---

contention [kən'tenʃən] *n.* 论点；争论，争辩

释 a strong opinion that someone expresses; angry disagreement between people

用 one's contention that; in contention

例 Her main contention is that doctors should encourage healthy eating. 她认为医生应该鼓励病人健康饮食。

The emergent nation states of Europe developed competitive interests.

欧洲的新兴国家各有各的竞争利益。

emergent [ɪ'mɜːdʒənt] *a.* 新兴的；处于发展时期的

释 in the early stages of existence or development; now and still developing

拓 *vi.* emerge; *n.* emergence

例 I believe in emergent democracy and the importance of celebrating the whole community. 我坚信民主的新生和展示整个团体的重要性。

---

competitive [kəm'petɪtɪv] *a.* 竞争的，比赛的

释 involving competition

拓 *n.* competition; *ad.* competitively

例 Our price of the goods are competitive. 我们的商品在价格上具有竞争优势。

So Jim concluded that they were incapable of deductive reasoning.

因此吉姆得出结论，他们没有能力进行演绎推理。

incapable [ɪnˈkeɪpəbl] *a.* 无能力的，不能的

释 not able to do something

拓 *n.* incapability; *ad.* incapably

用 incapable of

例 He seemed incapable of understanding what the teacher said in the class. 他似乎无法理解老师上课时讲的东西。

A slight shudder shook her frame, and she said, out of a dry throat, "God forgive me."

一阵轻微的战栗掠过全身，她从干哑的嗓子挤出一句话："上帝饶恕我吧"。

shudder [ˈʃʌdə] *n.* / *vt.* & *vi.* 颤动，发抖

释 a shaking movement you make because you are cold, frightened or disgusted; to shake suddenly with very small movements because of a very unpleasant thought or feeling

拓 a shudder ran / went through sb.

例 The plane is shuddering and lurch in the most terrifying manner. 飞机在震颤摇晃，真让人害怕。

They also show that we may be underestimating the impact of simple factors.

他们也表明，我们可能低估了这些简单因素的影响。

underestimate [ˌʌndərˈestɪmeɪt] *vt.* 低估

释 to think or guess that something is smaller, cheaper, easier, etc. than it really is

拓 *vt. & vi.* estimate / overestimate; *n.* estimation

用 underestimate the importance / effect / power of sth.

例 Never underestimate your opponent. 千万不要低估对手。

---

impact [ˈɪmpækt] *n.* 影响

释 the effect or influence that an event, situation etc. has on someone or something

用 impact on / upon; major / significant impact

例 We shouldn't neglect its impact on climate change. 我们不应该忽略它对天气变化造成的影响。

A natural approach is to impose additional homogeneous assumptions.

一种自然的做法是增加一些额外的同质假设。

homogeneous [ˌhɒməˈdʒiːnɪəs] *a.* 同质的

释 consisting of parts or people which are similar to each other or are of the same type

拓 *n.* homogeneity

例 They are homogeneous people and they get along well with eath other. 他们是同类人，相处得很好。

---

assumption [əˈsʌmpʃən] *n.* 假定，设想

释 something that you accept as true without question or proof

拓 *vt.* assume

例 This theory is based on a series of wrong assumptions. 这一理论建立在一系列错误的假定之上。

Where the mining is underground, the surface can be simultaneously used for forests, cattle grazing and crop raising, or even reservoirs and urban development.

地下有矿产的地方，地上就可用来培育森林、畜牧、种植庄稼，甚至储水和建造城市。

reservoir ['rezəvwɑː] *n.* 水库，蓄水池

释 a lake, especially an artificial one, where water is stored before it is supplied to people's houses

用 reservoir of

例 He found there was a reservoir nearby the river. 他发现河旁边有一个蓄水池。

A collaborative approach to problem solving has facilitated improved cooperation.

用合作的方式解决问题，促进了合作。

collaborative [kə'læbərətɪv] *a.* 协作的，合作的

释 a job or piece of work that involves two or more people working together to achieve something

拓 *vi.* collaborate; *n.* collaboration / collaborator

例 The presentation was a collaborative effort by all the children in the class. 这个演讲是班里所有学生合作的成果。

---

facilitate [fə'sɪlɪteɪt] *vt.* 使……容易，促进

释 to make it easier for a process or activity to happen

拓 *n.* facilitator

例 Computers can be used to facilitate English language learning.
计算机的使用有助于英语学习。

There are a lot of reasons for causing news to be inconsistent with facts, most are subjective reasons.

造成新闻失实的原因很多，但大部分是主观原因。

inconsistent [ˌɪnkənˈsɪstənt] *a.* 不一致的；前后矛盾的

释 not in agreement or harmony; incompatible

拓 *n.* inconsistency

用 inconsistent with

例 The remarks of the witnesses are inconsistent. 证人们的证词不一致。

Skeptics might say that longer exposures to the sunshine.

怀疑者们推测说也许是长时间在阳光下暴晒的原因。

skeptic [ˈskeptɪk] *n.* 怀疑者，怀疑论者，无神论者

释 a person who disagrees with particular claims and statements, especially those that are generally thought to be true

拓 *a.* skeptical; *ad.* skeptically; *n.* skepticism

例 Skeptics argued that the rise in unemployment was temporary. 怀疑者们认为失业率的上升是暂时的现象。

The most important thing is to tackle malicious computer hackers.

最重要的事情是治理恶意的电脑黑客。

tackle [ˈtækl] *vt.* 处理，解决

释 to try to deal with a difficult problem

拓 *n.* tackler

用 tackle sb. about sth.

例 What's the best way to tackle this problem? 解决这个问题的最好方法是什么？

malicious [məˈlɪʃəs] *a.* 怀恶意的，恶毒的

释 very unkind and cruel, and deliberately behaving in a way that is likely to upset or hurt someone

拓 *ad.* maliciously

用 malicious rumor / gossip / words

例 Who wrote these malicious words? 这些恶毒的文字是谁写的?

This policy describes what you can do when you have a dispute with another editor.

这一方针告诉我们当你和其他编辑发生争执时你可以做什么。

dispute [dɪsˈpjuːt] *n.* / *vt.* & *vi.* 争论

释 an argument or disagreement, especially an official one between, for example, workers and employers or two bordering countries; to have a disagreement over something

用 dispute that; dispute over / with / against

例 The dispute was settled last week. 争端在上周解决了。

This basic approach is limited in the range of numbers that it can express, but this range will generally suffice when dealing with the simpler aspects of human existence.

这一基本方法仅限于在可以表达的数字之内，但是当谈论到关于人类生存的几个较简单的方面时，这一方法足够了。

suffice [səˈfaɪs] *vt.* & *vi.* 足够；使……满足

释 to be enough for sb./ sth.

拓 *a.* sufficient; *ad.* sufficiently; *n.* sufficiency

例 An hour should suffice for the tour. 这点路程一小时足够了。

The difficulty lies not in the inferential process which the task demands, but in certain perplexing features of the apparatus and the procedure.

困难不在工作所要求的推理过程中，而是在复杂的装置和其步骤中。

inferential [ˌɪnfəˈrenʃəl] *a.* **推理的，推论的，推理上的**

释 relating to or having the nature of inference

拓 *n.* inference; *ad.* inferentially

例 The validity of inferential form is the key conception of logic. 推理形式的有效性是逻辑学的核心概念。

---

perplex [pəˈpleks] *vt.* **使困惑，使复杂化，使……为难**

释 to confuse and worry someone slightly by being difficult to understand or solve

拓 *a.* perplexed / perplexing; *n.* perplexity

例 Faced with that dilemma, Bob was perplexed. 鲍勃面对进退两难的局面，不知如何是好。

---

apparatus [ˌæpəˈreɪtəs] *n.* **装置，器具；机构**

释 a set of equipment or tools or sometimes a machine which is used for a particular purpose; an organization or system, especially a political one

例 There are some electrical apparatus in the room. 房间里有些电器。

Those for the military, for example, were originally intended to impress and even terrify the enemy.

对于军队而言，例如，首先应该给敌人留下深刻的印象，甚至可以威吓对方。

military [ˈmɪlɪtəri] *n.* **军队；** *a.* **军事的**

释 the armed forces; connected with soldiers or the armed forces

拓 *ad.* militarily; *n.* militarist / militarism

例 I am not interested in military history. 我对军队史没什么兴趣。

intend [in'tend] *vt.* 想要，打算，计划

释 to have a plan or purpose in your mind when you do sth.

拓 *n.* intent / intention; *a.* intentional; *ad.* intentionally

用 intend (sb.) to do sth.

例 We intend to go to the UK next year. 我们打算明年去英国。

---

terrify ['terɪfaɪ] *vt.* 使恐怖

释 to frighten someone very much

拓 *a.* terrifying / terrified / terrific; *ad.* terrifically

例 The girls were terrified out of her wits. 那些女孩们吓得魂不附体。

Now there is widespread speculation about its true beginnings.

现在有关于它真实的开端的推测有很多。

speculation [ˌspekju'leɪʃən] *n.* 推测

释 the act of forming opinions about what has happened or what might happen without knowing all the facts

拓 *vt.* & *vi.* speculate; *a.* speculative; *ad.* speculatively

例 My speculations proved to be totally wrong. 我猜想的全错了。

These misconceptions do not remain isolated but become incorporated into a multifaceted, but organized, conceptual framework, making it and the component ideas, some of which are not only erroneous, but also accessible to modification.

这些误解并不是孤立的而是被纳入一个多方面的、有组织的、有概念的框架之内，使之成为观点的一部分，其中有些是错误的，但同时也是可以修改的。

isolated ['aɪsəleɪtɪd] *a.* 孤立的，单独的

释 far away from any others

拓 *n.* isolation / isolationism / isolationist

例 The radical group in the ruling party is becoming increasingly isolated. 执政党内的激进派日益孤立。

multifaceted [ˌmʌltɪˈfæsətɪd] *a.* **多方面的**

释 having many different parts

例 Robinson was in the religious sense of the performance is multifaceted. 宗教意识在鲁宾逊身上有多方面的表现。

conceptual [kənˈseptjuəl] *a.* **概念上的**

释 based on ideas or principles

拓 *n.* concept / conception; *vt.* & *vi.* conceptualize

例 I was doing more conceptual work, rather than working directly with people. 我做得更多的是概念性工作，而不是直接与他人接触

erroneous [ɪˈrəʊnɪəs] *a.* **错误的，不正确的**

释 wrong or false

拓 *ad.* erroneously; *n.* error

例 An erroneous belief probably lead to a serious mistake. 一个错误观念很可能铸成大错。

modification [ˌmɒdɪfɪˈkeɪʃ ən] *n.* **修正，修改，修饰**

释 the act of changing something such as a plan, opinion, law or way of behaviour in order to improve it or make it more acceptable

拓 *vt.* modify; *n.* modifier

例 The speech added by some modifications will be perfect. 修改后的演讲稿将会更加完美。

A precise definition allows you to do very prescribed things in certain situations.

一个确切的定义可使你在确定的环境下做所规定的事情。

precise [prɪˈsaɪs] *a.* **精确的，准确的**

释 exact and accurate

拓 *ad.* precisely; *n.* precision

用 at the precise moment

例 I am not clear about the precise bearing of the word in this passage. 我说不准这个字在这段文章里的确切意义是什么。

---

prescribe [prɪsˈkraɪb] *vt.* & *vi.* 规定，命令；开药方

释 to say what should be done or how sth. should be done; to say what medical treatment someone should have

拓 *n.* prescription; *a.* prescriptive

用 prescribe for; prescribe that

例 What medicine did doctor prescribe for your illness? 医生开了什么药来治你的病?

If the predictions you make as a result of deducing certain consequences from your hypothesis are not shown to be correct then you modify your hypothesis.

如果你从你的假设中推出的预言是不正确的，那么你应该修改你的假设。

prediction [prɪˈdɪkʃən] *n.* 预言，预报

释 a statement that says what you think will happen; the act of making such a statement

拓 *vt.* & *vi.* predict; *a.* predictable / predictive; *ad.* predictably; *n.* predictability

用 make predictions about sth.; prediction that

例 We all believed in her prediction. 我们都相信她的预言。

---

deduce [dɪˈdjuːs] *vt.* 推论，演绎出

释 to form an opinion about sth. based on the information or evidence that is available

拓 *n.* deduction; *a.* deducible / deductive

用 deduce from

例 From this fact we may deduce that he is sick. 从这个事实来看我们可推断他生病了。

---

hypothesis [haɪˈpɒθɪsɪs] *n.* 假设

释 an idea or explanation for something that is based on known facts but has not yet been proved

拓 *vt & vi.* hypothesize; *a.* hypothetical

例 Several conclusions flow from this hypothesis. 从这项假设中可以得出几个结论。

It can spill over and indicate an obsession with power.

它可以蔓延，并表明对权力的沉迷。

spill [spɪl] *vt. & vi.* 溢出，洒，使(血)流出

释 to (cause to) flow, move, fall or spread over the edge or beyond the limits of something

拓 *n.* spill / spillage

用 spill on / down / over / onto

例 Don't jog me, or you'll make me spill something! 别碰我，不然我就把东西弄洒了。

---

obsession [əbˈseʃən] *n.* 痴迷；困扰；使人痴迷的人(或物)

释 the state in which a person's mind is completely filled with thoughts of one particular thing or person so that they cannot think of anything else; something or someone that you think about all the time

拓 *vt.* obsess; *a.* obsessive; *ad.* obsessively

用 obsession with

例 Her madness is caused or conditioned by compulsion or obsession. 她的精神失常是由强迫或者痴迷造成的。

Those were consecutive laps in less than seconds, which had once been regarded impossible.

这些是在很短的时间内出现的连续圈，曾经被认为是不可能出现的。

consecutive [kən'sekjutɪv] *a.* 连续的，连贯的

释 following one after another in a series, without interruption

拓 *ad.* consecutively; *n.* consecutiveness

例 She has four consecutive gold medals. 她连续获得四枚金牌。

The policy should be developed through consultation rather than imposed from the government.

该政策应通过协商制定而不是由政府强加制定。

consultation [ˌkɒnsəl'teɪʃən] *n.* 协商会；请教，咨询

释 a meeting to discuss something or to get advice; when you discuss something with someone in order to get their advice or opinion about it

拓 *vt.* & *vi.* consult; *a.* consultative; *n.* consultant

用 in consultation of

例 He is in consultation and cannot come to the phone. 他在商议事情，不方便接电话。

---

impose [ɪm'pəʊz] *vt.* 加上，强迫；征收(税款)

释 to officially force a rule, tax, punishment. etc. to be obeyed or received; to force someone to accept something, especially a belief or way of living

拓 *n.* imposition

用 impose on

例 The present trouble was imposed on him. 目前的困难是强加在他身上的。

It may be overly optimistic, which could turn out to be pessimistic.

也许过度乐观就是一种悲观吧。

optimistic [ˌɒptɪˈmɪstɪk] *a.* 乐观的，乐观主义的

释 expecting good things to happen or something to be successful

拓 *n.* optimism / optimist; *ad.* optimistically

用 be optimistic about

例 I'm sufficiently optimistic that I'm inclined to think life's wonderful. 我足够乐观地倾向于认为生活是美好的。

---

pessimistic [ˌpesɪˈmɪstɪk] *a.* 悲观的，悲观主义的

释 expecting bad things to happen or something not to be successful

拓 *n.* pessimism / pessimist; *ad.* pessimistically

用 be pessimistic about / over

例 Now suddenly there's this pessimistic atmosphere because we don't know what's going to happen in london. 忽然之间一片愁云惨淡，我们不清楚伦敦的未来状况会怎样。

But it also needs to be separated into different types and sorted from contaminants such as staples, paperclips, string and other miscellaneous items.

我们还需要把它分成不同种类，并从订书钉、回形针、绳子，还有其他各种各样的杂物中分离出来。

contaminant [kənˈtæmɪnənt] *n.* 杂质，污染物质，沾染物

释 a substance that spoils the purity of something or makes it poisonous

拓 *vt.* contaminate *a.* contaminated; *n.* contamination

例 Carbon dioxide is not a contaminant—it is inevitable by-product of carbon in the coal reacting with oxygen in the air. 二氧化碳并不是污染物质，它是煤炭和氧气在空气中反应后不可避免的副产品。

string [strɪŋ] *n.* 线；一串

释 strong thin cord which is made by twisting very thin fibres together and which is used for fastening and tying things; a set or series of things that are joined together

拓 *a.* stringy

用 a ball / piece of string

例 He found a piece of string to tie this book. 他找到一根细绳把这包书扎起来。

---

miscellaneous [ˌmɪsɪˈleɪnjəs] *a.* 各种的，多方面的

释 consisting of a mixture of various things which are not usually connected with each other

拓 *n.* miscellany

例 He has a miscellaneous talent. 他多才多艺。

This is the situation which now prevails in Sydney.

这是在悉尼盛行的境况。

prevail [prɪˈveɪl] *vt.* 获胜；流行，盛行

释 to defeat an opponent; to get control or influence; to be common among a group of people or area at a particular time

拓 *n.* prevalence; *a.* prevailing / prevalent

用 prevail in / among; prevail over / against; prevail on / upon

例 This custom does not prevail now. 这种风俗现在已经不流行了。

There are two clear divisions and one of these is decidedly more glamorous than the other.

有两个部分非常清楚，其中的一个绝对要比另一个更有魅力。

division [dɪˈvɪʒən] *n.* 区分，分开；公司，部门

释 the process or result of dividing into separate parts; unit or section of an organization

拓 *a.* divisible

例 All universities have Logistics Division. 所有大学都设有后勤处。

---

glamorous ['glæmərəs] *a.* 富有魅力的，迷人的

释 attractive in an exciting and special way

拓 *n.* glamour / glamorousness; *vt.* glamorize; *ad.* glamorously

例 You're looking extremely glamorous. 你看上去真是漂亮极了。

You then proceeded to a strictly logical and rigorous process.

接下来，你将着手进行一个条理分明、组织严密的过程。

proceed [prə'siːd] *vi.* 着手进行；继续进行

释 to continue to do something that has already been started; to do sth. next, after having done sth. else first

用 proceed to do sth.; proceed with

例 They decided to proceed with their research. 他们决定继续进行研究工作。

---

rigorous ['rɪgərəs] *a.* 严厉的，严格的

释 demanding strict attention to rules and procedures, forcefulness or extremely strict obedience of rules

拓 *ad.* rigorously; *n.* rigour

例 The work failed to meet her rigorous standards. 工作没有达到她的严格标准。

The focus is on individuals, tweaking and squeezing the cover.

聚集个体，挤压表面。

tweak [twiːk] *vt.* 扭，拉，拧

释 to suddenly pull or twist something

例 The robber is trying to tweak a girl's hair. 劫匪试图用力拉扯一个女孩子的头发。

squeeze [skwi:z] *vt. & vi.* 紧握，挤；压榨

释 to press sth. firmly, especially with your fingers; to get liquid from sth. by pressing it

例 She squeezed the tube hard and the last of the toothpaste came out.
她用力挤掉牙膏筒，把最后一点牙膏挤了出来。

Democratic centralism is system that integrates centralism on the basis of democracy with democracy under centralized guidance.

民主集中制是民主基础上的集中和集中指导下的民主相结合的制度。

democratic [ˌdeməˈkrætɪk] *a.* 民主的

释 controlled by representatives who are elected by the people of a country

拓 *n.* democracy / democrat / democratization; *ad.* democratically; *vt.&vi.* democratize

例 Many people were elected to take part in democratic involvement.
很多人被选举参与民主管理。

第二章　剑七、剑八词汇精选

Word List 1

- **accommodation** [əˌkɒmə'deɪʃən] *n.* 住所
- **acquire** [ə'kwaɪə] *vt.* 获得，学到
- **approximately** [ə'prɒksɪmətli] *adv.* 大约，近似地
- **available** [ə'veɪləbl] *a.* 可利用的，可得到的
- **be concerned about** 关注
- **be in touch** 联系
- **branch** [brɑːntʃ] *n.* 分支，分系
- **construction** [kən'strʌkʃən] *n.* 建筑
- **defeat** [dɪ'fiːt] *vt.* 击败
- **double** ['dʌbl] *vt.* & *vi.* 翻倍
- **elective** [ɪ'lektɪv] *n.* 选修课
- **era** ['ɪərə] *n.* 时代
- **exaggeration** [ɪgˌzædʒə'reɪʃən] *n.* 夸张；夸张的言语
- **fortune** ['fɔːtʃən] *n.* 财产，财富，巨款
- **in effect** 实质上
- **inhabitant** [ɪn'hæbɪtənt] *n.* 居民，居住者
- **innovate** ['ɪnəʊveɪt] *vi.* 更新，改革，创新
- **justified** ['dʒʌstɪfaɪd] *a.* 合理的，情有可原的
- **maintain** [meɪn'teɪn] *vt.* 养护，维持，保持，使继续
- **massive** ['mæsɪv] *a.* 大规模的
- **nephew** ['nefjuː] *n.* 侄子
- **option** ['ɒpʃən] *n.* 选择；选择权；选修科目

- **overpaid** [ˌəʊvə'peɪd] *a.* 收入过高的
- **predecessor** ['priːdɪsesə] *n.* 早期产品；前辈
- **principal** ['prɪnsəpəl] *a.* 主要的
- **priority** [praɪ'ɒrɪti] *n.* 首要；任务优先权
- **pursue** [pə'sjuː] *vt.* 追逐；*vi.* 追赶
- **quagmire** ['kwægmaɪə] *n.* 泥沼；无法脱身的困境
- **quantify** ['kwɒntɪfaɪ] *vt.* 以数量表示；使量化
- **realistically** [ˌrɪə'lɪstɪkəli] *adv.* 事实上看
- **recession** [rɪ'seʃən] *n.* 衰退，经济不景气
- **relatively** ['relətɪvli] *adv.* 相对地
- **rely on** 依赖
- **remainder** [rɪ'meɪndə] *n.* 剩余部分
- **remaining** [rɪ'meɪnɪŋ] *a.* 剩下的

Word List 2

- **amazing** [ə'meɪzɪŋ] *a.* 令人惊奇的
- **breakdown** ['breɪkdaʊn] *n.* 【化】分解；(机器等的)故障,损坏
- **compared with** 和……相比
- **contentious** [kən'tenʃəs] *a.* 热烈的；爱争论的
- **dominant** ['dɒmɪnənt] *a.* 主导的，占优势的，支配的，统治的
- **dominate** ['dɒmɪneɪt] *vt.* 支配，统治；*vi.* 处于支配地位
- **downward** ['daʊnwəd] *a.* 向下的
- **drastic** ['dræstɪk] *a.* 严厉的；极端的
- **enforce** [ɪn'fɔːs] *vt.* 执行；强制，强迫
- **enviable** ['envɪəbəl] *a.* 令人羡慕的
- **excel** [ɪk'sel] *vt.* 胜过，优于；*vi.* 突出
- **exert** [ɪg'zɜːt] *vt.* 运用，行使，发挥，施加

- **expectedly** [ɪks'pektɪdli] *adv.* 意料之中地
- **flexibility** [ˌfleksə'bɪləti] *n.* 灵活度，灵活性
- **gap** [gæp] *n.* 差距
- **in terms of** 就…… 而言
- **in turn** 依次
- **marked** [mɑːkt] *a.* 明显的
- **motivator** ['məʊtɪveɪtə] *n.* 激励，动因，动力
- **nurture** ['nɜːtʃə] *n.* 食物；培育；*vt.* 养育；培植
- **observe** [əb'zɜːv] *vt.* 注意到；观测；*vi.* 注意，观察
- **on the contrary** 正相反
- **outstanding** [aʊt'stændɪŋ] *a.* 出众的
- **overall** ['əʊvərɔːl] *a.* 全面的
- **predict** [prɪ'dɪkt] *vt.* 预测，预报；*vi.* 作预报
- **prerequisite** [ˌpriː'rekwɪzɪt] *n.* 前提，首要事物
- **rebound** [riː'baʊnd] *n.* 反弹
- **responsive** [rɪ'spɒnsɪv] *a.* 响应的
- **rocket** ['rɒkɪt] *vt.* 用火箭运载；*vi.* 猛涨；飙升
- **roughly** ['rʌfli] *adv.* 大概
- **security** [sɪ'kjuərəti] *n.* 安全
- **senior** ['siːnjə] *a.* 高级的
- **significant** [sɪg'nɪfɪkənt] *a.* 重要的
- **stable** ['steɪbl] *a.* 平稳的
- **stagnancy** ['stægnənsi] *n.* 停滞，萧条，不景气
- **staircase** ['steəkeɪs] *n.* 楼梯间
- **subsequent** ['sʌbsɪkwənt] *adj* 后续的，继……之后的
- **substantial** [səb'stænʃəl] *a.* 极大的，大量的
- **systematic** [ˌsɪstɪ'mætɪk] *a.* 系统的，成体系的
- **tumultuous** [tjuː'mʌltʃuəs] *a.* 激烈的，吵闹的，喧哗的

Word List 3

- **accelerate** [æk'seləreɪt] *vt.* 促进，使增速；*vi.* 加快，增长
- **adjustment** [ə'dʒʌstmənt] *n.* 调整，校正
- **arbitrary** ['ɑːbɪtrəri] *a.* 专断的，独断的
- **at recession** 低迷
- **be supposed to** 应该
- **climb** [klaɪm] *vt.* 攀登，爬；*vi.*（物价）逐渐上升
- **continuously** [kən'tɪnjʊəsli] *adv.* 继续地
- **decade** ['dekeɪd] *n.* 十年
- **deserve** [dɪ'zɜːv] *vt.* 值得，该得；应受赏（罚）
- **deterring** [dɪ'tɜːrɪŋ] *a.* 有震慑力的
- **discrepancy** [dɪs'krepənsi] *n.* 差异，不一致之处
- **esteem** [ɪs'tiːm] *n.* 尊重
- **extreme** [ɪks'triːm] *a.* 极端的
- **frighten** ['fraɪtən] *vt.* 吓坏，吓唬；*vi.* 惊恐
- **glimpse** [glɪmps] *vt. & vi.* 瞥见
- **incentive** [ɪn'sentɪv] *n.* 激励，鼓励；动机
- **indispensable** [ˌɪndɪs'pensəbl] *a.* 必不可少的，必需的
- **inferior** [ɪn'fɪərɪə] *a.* 自卑的；下级的；低于……的
- **insult** ['ɪnsʌlt] *n.* 侮辱，羞辱
- **law-abiding** ['lɔːəˌbaɪdɪŋ] *a.* 遵纪守法的
- **lifespan** ['laɪfspæn] *n.* 生命周期
- **lose sight of** 忽略，不再看见
- **measurement** ['meʒəmənt] *n.* 衡量，测量，测定
- **monotonous** [mə'nɒtənəs] *a.* 单调的，无抑扬顿挫的
- **motivation** [ˌməʊtɪ'veɪʃən] *n.* 动机

- **narrow** ['nærəʊ] *a.* 小的，窄的
- **normally** ['nɔːməli] *adv.* 通常
- **notable** ['nəʊtəbl] *a.* 值得注意的
- **preference** ['prefərəns] *n.* 倾向性，偏爱
- **prime** [praɪm] *a.* 重要的
- **purpose** ['pɜːpəs] *n.* 目的；*vt.* 决意；打算
- **record** [rɪ'kɔːd] *vt.* 记录；*vi.* 进行录音
- **resistance** [rɪ'zɪstəns] *n.* 对立，抵抗，反抗
- **scare off** 吓跑
- **self-defense** [ˌselfdɪ'fens] *n.* 自卫
- **strive** [straɪv] *vi.* 努力
- **superiority** [sjuˌpɪərɪ'ɒrɪti] *n.* 优越，优等；上级
- **survive** [sə'vaɪv] *vt.* 从……中逃出；生存；*vi.* 从幸存；残留
- **throughout** [θruː'aʊt] *prep.* 贯穿
- **unarguably** [ʌn'ɑːgjuəbli] *adv.* 无可争议地
- **various** ['veərɪəs] *a.* 不同的
- **witness** ['wɪtnɪs] *vt.* 目睹

Word List 4

- **absorber** [əb'sɔːbə] *n.* 吸收者；减震器
- **architecture** ['ɑːkɪtektʃə] *n.* 建筑学
- **brick** [brɪk] *n.* 砖
- **buddhism** ['bʊdɪzəm] *n.* 佛教
- **carpenter** ['kɑːpɪntə] *n.* 木匠
- **collapse** [kə'læps] *vt.* 使倒塌；*vi.* 倒塌，崩溃
- **concrete** ['kɒŋkriːt] *n.* 混凝土
- **dampen** ['dæmpən] *vt.* 使潮湿；使沮丧；*vi.* 潮湿；沮丧

- **disastrous** [dɪ'zɑːstrəs] *a.* 灾难性的，损失惨重的
- **dispense** [dɪs'pens] *vt.* 分配，分发
- **erect** [ɪ'rekt] *a.* 直立的
- **flatten** ['flætn] *vt.* （使）变平，展开
- **hesitation** [ˌhezɪ'teɪʃən] *n.* 犹豫，踌躇
- **intertwine** [ˌɪntə'twaɪn] *vt.* 交织
- **magnificent** [mæg'nɪfɪsənt] *a.* 壮丽的，华丽的，宏伟的
- **majestic** [mə'dʒestɪk] *a.* 宏伟的，庄严的，雄壮的
- **masterpiece** ['mɑːstəpiːs] *n.* 名著，杰作
- **mystify** ['mɪstɪfaɪ] *vt.* 使迷惑
- **neighborhood** ['neɪbəhʊd] *n.* 邻近地区
- **pagoda** [pə'gəʊdə] *n.* 宝塔
- **peg** [peg] *n.* 钉，栓
- **reinforce** [ˌriːɪn'fɔːs] *vt.* 加固，补充
- **scholar** ['skɒlə] *n.* 学者
- **sideways** ['saɪdweɪz] *a.* 一旁的，侧面的
- **skyscraper** ['skaɪˌskreɪpə] *n.* 摩天大楼
- **slender** ['slendə] *a.* 苗条的；微弱的
- **soaring** ['sɔːrɪŋ] *a.* 高飞的，翱翔的
- **storey** ['stɔːri] *n.* 层
- **sway** [sweɪ] *vt.* 使摇摆；使倾斜；*vi.* 摇晃，摇动；倾斜
- **topple** ['tɒpl] *vt.* 倾倒，倒塌，推翻
- **undergo** [ˌʌndə'gəʊ] *vt.* 经历
- **unfairness** [ʌn'feənɪs] *n.* 不公平
- **weighty** ['weɪti] *a.* 重要的
- **would-be** ['wʊdbiː] *a.* 潜在的，想要成为的

Word List 5

- **abrupt** [ə'brʌpt] *a.* 突然的，意外的
- **bang into** 撞入，偶尔遇见
- **column** ['kɒləm] *n.* 圆柱
- **consecutive** [kən'sekjutɪv] *a.* 连续的，连贯的
- **constrain** [kən'streɪn] *vt.* 强制，强迫
- **corresponding** [ˌkɒrɪ'spɒdɪŋ] *a.* 相当的，对应的，一致的
- **counterpart** ['kaʊntəpɑːt] *n.* 相对应的人或物
- **craftsman** ['kraːftsmən] *n.* 工匠，手工艺人
- **earthenware** ['ɜːθənweə] *n.* 陶器
- **eave** [iːv] *n.* 屋檐
- **enormous** [ɪ'nɔːməs] *a.* 巨大的，极大的
- **feature** ['fiːtʃə] *n.* 特征，特色
- **flex** [fleks] *vt.* 弯曲
- **gush down** 冲刷
- **individual** [ˌɪndɪ'vɪdjuəl] *n.* 个体，个人
- **massive** ['mæsɪv] *a.* 巨大的
- **overall** ['əʊvərɔːl] *a.* 全部的
- **overhang** [ˌəʊvə'hæŋ] *vt.* 悬垂
- **passion** ['pæʃən] *n.* 激情，热情
- **pendulum** ['pendjuləm] *n.* 钟摆，摆锤
- **pillar** ['pɪlə] *n.* 柱子，栋梁
- **porcelain** ['pɔːslɪn] *n.* 瓷器
- **resilience** [rɪ'zɪlɪəns] *n.* 弹性
- **roof** [ruːf] *n.* 屋顶
- **slither** ['slɪðə] *vi.* 滑动，不稳地滑行

- **stack** [stæk] *n.* 堆叠
- **startling** ['stɑ:tlɪŋ] *a.* 令人吃惊的
- **stationary** ['steɪʃənəri] *a.* 固定的，稳定的，不动的
- **successive** [sək'sesɪv] *a.* 连续的，接连的
- **suspend** [səs'pend] *vt.* 悬挂
- **taper** ['teɪpə] *n.* 锥形物；尖塔
- **tile** [taɪl] *n.* 瓦片
- **trial** ['traɪəl] *n.* 试验；审问
- **trick** ['trɪk] *n.* 诡计；窍门
- **trunk** [trʌŋk] *n.* 树干
- **typhoon** [taɪ'fu:n] *n.* 台风
- **unscathed** [ʌn'skeɪðd] *a.* 没有受伤的
- **upright** ['ʌpraɪt] *a.* 垂直的
- **vertical** ['vɜ:tɪkəl] *a.* 垂直的
- **watchtower** ['wɒtʃtaʊə] *n.* 瞭望塔
- **wedge** [wedʒ] *n.* 楔形物，三角木

Word List 6

- **aesthetic** [i:s'θetɪk] *a.* 美学的
- **algae** ['ældʒi:] (alga的复数) 藻类，海藻
- **anticipate** [æn'tɪsɪpeɪt] *vt.* 预料，预期
- **arable** ['ærəbl] *a.* 适合耕种的，可耕地的
- **battery** ['bætəri] *n.* 电池
- **battlefield** ['bætlfi:ld] *n.* 战场
- **cash** [kæʃ] *n.* 现金
- **challenge** ['tʃælɪndʒ] *n.* 挑战
- **collateral** [kə'lætərəl] *a.* 旁边的，旁系的；间接的

- **colossal** [kə'lɒsəl] *a.* 巨大的
- **concept** ['kɒnsept] *n.* 观念，概念
- **corn bunting** 白颊鸟
- **destruction** [dɪs'trʌkʃən] *n.* 破坏，毁坏
- **enervation** [ˌenɜː'veɪʃən] *n.* 削弱，衰弱
- **equivalent** [ɪ'kwɪvələnt] *a.* 相等的，相当的
- **externality** [ˌekstɜː'nælɪti] *n.* 外形，外在性
- **fertilizer** ['fɜːtɪlaɪzə] *n.* 化肥，肥料
- **filth** [fɪlθ] *n.* 肮脏，污物
- **genetic** [dʒɪ'netɪk] *a.* 基因的
- **graceful** ['greɪsfəl] *a.* 优美的
- **grey partridge** 灰山鹑
- **hectare** ['hektaː] *n.* 公顷
- **hedgerow** ['hedʒrəʊ] *n.* 树篱
- **jolt** [dʒəʊlt] *vt.* 颠簸，摇动
- **lapwing** ['læpwɪŋ] *n.* 田凫
- **livestock** ['laɪvstɒk] *n.* 家畜，牲畜
- **loch** [lɒk] *n.* 【苏格兰】湖；海湾
- **march** [mɑːtʃ] *n.* 行进
- **mechanization** [ˌmekənaɪ'zeɪʃən] *n.* 机械化
- **monoculture** ['mɒnəˌkʌltʃə] *n.* 单一栽培；单一经营
- **pesticide** ['pestɪsaɪd] *n.* 杀虫剂
- **rear** [rɪə] *n.* 后部
- **skylark** ['skaɪlaːk] *n.* 云雀
- **stretch** [stretʃ] *vt.* 伸展，伸长
- **tightrope** ['taɪtrəʊp] *n.* 绳索，钢丝
- **transaction** [træn'zækʃən] *n.* 交易

◆ **vanish** ['vænɪʃ] *vi.* 消失
◆ **yield** [ji:ld] *vt.* 生产；结出（果实）

Word List 7

◆ **agrochemical** ['ægrəˌkemɪkəl] *n.* 农用化学品
◆ **alternative** [ɔ:l'tɜ:nətɪv] *a.* 两者择一的，选择性的
◆ **assumption** [ə'sʌmpʃən] *n.* 假定，臆断
◆ **bug** [bʌg] *n.* 臭虫
◆ **carbon** ['kɑ:bən] *n.* 碳
◆ **competitive** [kəm'petɪtɪv] *a.* 竞争的
◆ **comprise** [kəm'praɪz] *vt.* 包含，构成
◆ **conservative** [kən'sɜ:vətɪv] *a.* 保守的
◆ **conventional** [kən'venʃənl] *a.* 传统的，符合习俗的
◆ **coordinate** [kəʊ'ɔ:dɪneɪt] *vt.* 调节，协调
◆ **cryptosporidium** [ˌkrɪptəʊ'spɒrɪdɪəm] *n.* 隐孢子虫
◆ **diverse** [daɪ'vɜ:s] *a.* 不同的
◆ **emission** [ɪ'mɪʃən] *n.* 发射
◆ **erosion** [ɪ'rəʊʒən] *n.* 腐蚀，侵蚀
◆ **estimate** ['estɪmeɪt] *vt.* 评估
◆ **feasible** ['fi:zəbl] *a.* 切实可行的，可能的，可实行的
◆ **financial** [faɪ'nænʃəl] *a.* 财政的，金融的
◆ **integrated** ['ɪntɪgreɪtɪd] *a.* 整合的，完整的
◆ **intensive** [ɪn'tensɪv] *a.* 精深的，透彻的
◆ **nitrate** ['naɪtreɪt] *n.* 硝酸盐
◆ **norm** [nɔ:m] *n.* 标准，基准，准则
◆ **organic** [ɔ:'gænɪk] *a.* 器官的；有机的
◆ **pasture** ['pɑ:stʃə] *n.* 牧场，草原

- **permanent** ['pɜːmənənt] *a.* 永久的
- **phosphate** ['fɒsfeɪt] *n.* 磷酸盐
- **premium** ['priːmɪəm] *n.* 额外补贴，津贴；酬金；保险费
- **prop** [prɒp] *vt.* 支持，支撑
- **removal** [rɪ'muːvəl] *n.* 移动；清除；拆卸
- **rural** ['rʊərəl] *a.* 乡村的，农村的
- **staggering** ['stægərɪŋ] *a.* 蹒跚的
- **strategy** ['strætɪdʒi] *n.* 战略，策略
- **subsidy** ['sʌbsədi] *n.* 补贴
- **sum** [sʌm] *n.* 金额
- **sustainable** [sə'steɪnəbl] *a.* 可持续的
- **tackle** ['tækl] *vt.* 对付；解决
- **threefold** ['θriːˌfəʊld] *n.* 三倍
- **thriving** ['θraɪvɪŋ] *a.* 兴旺的，繁荣的
- **viable** ['vaɪəbl] *a.* 能养活的
- **virtually** ['vɜːtʃʊəli] *adv.* 实际上，事实上
- **welfare** ['welfeə] *n.* 福利

Word List 8

- **access to** 进入，接近或使用的机会
- **access** ['ækses] *n.* 通道，入口
- **accompany** [ə'kʌmpəni] *vt.* 陪伴，伴随
- **afford** [ə'fɔːd] *vt.* 买得起，担负得起
- **approach** [ə'prəʊtʃ] *n.* 方式，方法
- **arduous** ['ɑːdjuːəs] *a.* 辛劳的，费劲的
- **assistance** [ə'sɪstəns] *n.* 帮助，援助
- **authority** [ɔː'θɒrɪti] *n.* 权威

◆ **awareness** [ə'weənɪs] *n.* 察觉，觉悟，意识
◆ **community** [kə'mju:nɪti] *n.* 社会，团体
◆ **criticize** ['krɪtɪsaɪz] *vt.* & *vi.* 批评
◆ **dedicated** ['dedɪˌkeɪtɪd] *a.* 献身的；热诚的；专注的
◆ **district** ['dɪstrɪkt] *n.* 地区，区域，行政区
◆ **essential** [ɪ'senʃəl] *a.* 重要的
◆ **fluctuate** ['flʌktjueɪt] *vi.* 变动，动摇；波动，涨落
◆ **footbridge** ['fʊtbrɪdʒ] *n.* 人行桥
◆ **handrail** ['hændreɪl] *n.* 扶手，栏杆
◆ **household** ['haʊshəʊld] *n.* 家庭，户
◆ **initiative** [ɪ'nɪʃətɪv] *a.* 开始的，创始的
◆ **institutionalization** [ˌɪnstəˌtju:ʃənəlaɪ'zeɪʃən] *n.* 制度化
◆ **isolate** ['aɪsəleɪt] *vt.* 使隔离，使孤立
◆ **locality** [ləʊ'kælɪti] *n.* 地区，场所
◆ **low-cost** ['ləʊ'kɒst] *a.* 价格便宜的，廉价的
◆ **mechanical workshop** 机械工厂
◆ **poverty** ['pɒvəti] *n.* 贫穷，贫困
◆ **pyramid** ['pɪrəmɪd] *n.* 金字塔
◆ **rare** [reə] *a.* 罕见的，珍贵的
◆ **reference** ['refərəns] *n.* 参考
◆ **refinement** [rɪ'faɪnmənt] *n.* 精致，精确，精细；细微的区别
◆ **restrict** [rɪ'strɪkt] *vt.* 约束，限制，限定
◆ **solution** [sə'lu:ʃən] *n.* 解答；解决(办法)；解释
◆ **supplementary** [ˌsʌplɪ'mentəri] *a.* 补充的，附加的
◆ **wheelbarrow** ['wi:lˌbærəʊ] *n.* 独轮手推车

Word List 9

- **aeronautics** [ˌeərə'nɔːtɪks] *n.* 航空学
- **apparently** [ə'pærəntli] *ad.* 显然的
- **convinced** [kən'vɪnst] *a.* 确信的
- **drag** ['dræg] *vt.* 托，拉
- **evidence** ['evɪdəns] *n.* 证据
- **fascinate** ['fæsɪneɪt] *a.* 迷人的
- **hieroglyph** ['haɪərəglɪf] *n.* 象形文字或符号
- **horizontal** [ˌhɒrɪ'zɒntl] *a.* 水平的
- **initial** [ɪ'nɪʃəl] *a.* 开始的
- **intrigue** [ɪn'triːg] *vt.* 施诡计取得，激起好奇心
- **investigative** [ɪn'vestɪgeɪtɪv] *a.* 调查的
- **magnify** ['mægnɪfaɪ] *vt.* 扩大
- **mechanical system** 机械系统
- **modest** ['mɒdɪst] *a.* 中等的
- **monument** ['mɒnjumənt] *n.* 历史遗迹
- **nylon** ['naɪlən] *n.* 尼龙
- **peruse** [pə'ruːz] *vt.* 细阅，审阅
- **possibility** [ˌpɒsə'bɪlɪti] *n.* 可能性
- **posture** ['pɒstʃə] *n.* 姿势
- **pulley** ['pʊli] *n.* 滑轮
- **reckon** ['rekən] *vt.* 认为，把……看作
- **rectangular** [rek'tæŋgjələ] *a.* 矩形的
- **scaffold** ['skæfəld] *n.* 脚手架；断头台
- **slave** [sleɪv] *n.* 奴隶
- **sledge** [sledʒ] *n.* 雪橇

- **trolley** ['trɒli] *n.* 滚轮
- **wind-tunnel** ['wɪndˌtʌnl] *a.* 风洞的

Word List 10

- **arch** [ɑːtʃ] *n.* 拱门
- **archipelago** [ˌɑːkɪ'peləʊgəʊ] *n.* 群岛
- **artifact** ['ɑːtɪfækt] *n.* 人工制品
- **associate professor** 助理教授
- **bering sea** 白令海
- **bounty** ['baʊnti] *n.* 慷慨，大方，施舍
- **civilization** [ˌsɪvɪlaɪ'zeɪʃən] *n.* 文明
- **coastline** ['kəʊstlaɪn] *n.* 海岸线
- **cod** [kɒd] *n.* 鳕鱼
- **crustacean** [krʌs'teɪʃən] *n.* 甲壳纲动物
- **debris** ['debriː] *n.* 残骸，破瓦，残砾
- **dump** [dʌmp] *vt.* 丢弃，抛弃
- **egyptology** [ˌiːdʒɪp'tɒlədʒi] *n.* 埃及古生物学
- **explorer** [ɪks'plɔːrə] *n.* 探险者，探险家
- **fishery** ['fɪʃəri] *n.* 渔业，渔场
- **flourish** ['flʌrɪʃ] *vi.* 兴旺，繁荣
- **foe** [fəʊ] *n.* 敌人
- **gentle** ['dʒentl] *a.* 轻柔的
- **glider** ['glaɪdə] *n.* 滑翔机
- **ground fish** 底栖鱼
- **herring** ['herɪŋ] *n.* 鲱鱼
- **land mass** 大陆块
- **mollusc** ['mɒləsk] *n.* 软体动物

- **nutrient** ['nju:trɪənt] *n.* 营养品，滋养物
- **perch** [pɜ:tʃ] *n.* 鲈鱼
- **pollock** ['pɒlək] *n.* 青鳕
- **salmon** ['sæmən] *n.* 鲑鱼，大马哈鱼
- **sensible** ['sensəbl] *a.* 明智的
- **sole** [səʊl] *n.* 鲽鱼
- **sophistication** [səˌfɪstɪ'keɪʃən] *n.* (科技产品的)复杂；精密
- **stun** [stʌn] *vt.* 使大吃一惊
- **uncannily** [ʌn'kænɪli] *ad.* 惊异地
- **volcanic** [vɒl'kænɪk] *a.* 火山的；猛烈的

Word List 11

- **benefit** ['benɪfɪt] *n.* 利益，好处；优势
- **biologist** [baɪ'ɒlədʒɪst] *n.* 生物学家
- **certification** [ˌsɜ:tɪfɪkeɪʃən] *n.* 证明
- **certify** ['sɜ:tɪfaɪ] *vt.* 认证，证实
- **Chinook** [tʃɪ'nʊk] *n.* （印第安部落）切努克语
- **chum** [tʃʌm] *n.* 密友
- **constitution** [ˌkɒnstɪ'tju:ʃən] *n.* 宪法，章程
- **crisis** ['kraɪsɪs] *n.* 危机；紧急关头；转折点
- **cumulative** ['kju:mjulətɪv] *a.* 累积的；渐增的
- **declare** [dɪ'kleə] *vt.* 宣布，声明，宣称
- **devastate** ['devəsteɪt] *vt.* 毁坏
- **effect** [ɪ'fekt] *n.* 结果，影响
- **El Nino** [el'ni:njəʊ] 厄尔尼诺
- **exceed** [ɪk'si:d] *vt.* 超过，超越
- **federal** ['fedərəl] *a.* 联邦政府的，联邦的

- **grant** [grɑːnt] *vt.* 授予，同意，准许
- **halt** [hɔːlt] *vt.* & *vi.* 停止，停住，暂停
- **harsh** [hɑːʃ] *a.* 严酷的；刺耳的
- **in excess of** 超过
- **logo** ['ləʊgəʊ] *n.* 标志，商标
- **mandate** ['mænˌdeɪt] *n.* 授权，委任
- **noise** [nɔɪz] *n.* 噪音，喧哗声
- **permission** [pə'mɪʃən] *n.* 允许，许可，同意
- **plausible** ['plɔːzəbl] *a.* 似乎正确的，貌似真实的
- **potential** [pə'tenʃəl] *a.* 潜在的
- **priority** [praɪ'ɒrɪti] *n.* 优先权
- **prosper** ['prɒspə] *vt.* & *vi.* 兴旺，繁荣
- **sonar** ['səʊnɑː] *n.* 声纳
- **spawner** ['spɔːnə] *n.* 产卵鱼
- **standard** ['stændəd] *n.* 标准，规格
- **subsistence** [səb'sɪstəns] *n.* 生存，存在
- **threaten** ['θretən] *vt.* 威胁

Word List 12

- **adapt** [ə'dæpt] *vt.* 使适应，使适合；改编，改写
- **adaptability** [ə'dæptəbɪlɪti] *n.* 适应性
- **capable of** 有……能力的，能……的
- **chronic** ['krɒnɪk] *a.* 长期的，慢性的
- **dial** ['daɪəl] *n.* 钟面，刻度盘，仪表盘
- **distract** [dɪ'strækt] *vt.* 使（人）分心
- **eliminate** [ɪ'lɪmɪneɪt] *vt.* 排除，减少
- **emit** [ɪ'mɪt] *vt.* 发出，散发

- **ethnicity** [eθ'nɪsɪti] *n.* 种族地位
- **fatigue** [fə'tiːg] *n.* 疲劳，劳累
- **individual** [ˌɪndɪ'vɪdjuəl] *n.* 个体，个人
- **interfere with** 干涉，妨碍
- **intrusion** [ɪn'truːʒən] *n.* 干扰
- **last** [lɑːst] *vi.* 持续
- **monitor** ['mɒnɪtə] *n.* 监视，监控
- **negative** ['negətɪv] *a.* 负面的
- **performance** [pə'fɔːməns] *n.* 表现
- **physiological** [ˌfɪzɪə'lɒdʒɪkəl] *a.* 生理的，生理学的
- **piping hot** (口)滚烫的，新鲜的
- **predictable** [prɪ'dɪktəbl] *a.* 可预知的
- **proofread** ['pruːfriːd] *vt.* 校对
- **random** ['rændəm] *n.* 任意行动；随机过程
- **soapy** ['səʊpi] *a.* 涂肥皂的
- **steam** [stiːm] *n.* 蒸汽
- **steering wheel** 方向盘
- **stir** [stɜː] *vt.* 搅拌，搅合
- **subject** ['sʌbdʒɪkt] *n.* 实验对象；主题；学科
- **sufficient** [sə'fɪʃənt] *a.* 足够的，充分的
- **toll** [təʊl] *n.* 代价
- **transient** ['trænsənt] *a.* 短暂的，临时的，过渡的
- **troublesome** ['trʌblsəm] *a.* 令人烦恼的，讨厌的
- **unpredictable** [ˌʌnprɪ'dɪktəbl] *a.* 不可预测的
- **variable** ['veərɪəbl] *n.* 可变物，变量
- **wipe out** 擦干，拭干

Word List 13

- **academic** [ˌækə'demɪk] *a.* 学术的；纯理论的
- **accountancy** [ə'kaʊntənsi] *n.* 会计学
- **ache** [eɪk] *n.* /*vi.* 疼
- **allocation** [ˌælə'keɪʃən] *n.* 分配
- **alter** ['ɔːltə] *vt.* /*vi.* 改变
- **arrange** [ə'reɪndʒ] *vt.* 安排
- **authority** [ɔː'θɒrɪti] *n.* 权威，权力
- **authorized** ['ɔːθəraɪzd] *a.* 权威认证的
- **box office** 售票处
- **cancel** ['kænsl] *vt.* 取消
- **cargo** ['kɑːgəʊ] *n.* 船货，货物
- **casual work** 临时工作
- **cheque** [tʃek] *n.* 支票
- **companion** [kəm'pænjən] *n.* 同伴，陪同人员
- **credit card** 信用卡
- **customer** ['kʌstəmə] *n.* 顾客
- **disability** [ˌdɪsə'bɪlɪti] *n.* 残疾
- **disposal** [dɪ'spəʊzəl] *n.* 支配，控制
- **eligible** ['elɪdʒəbl] *a.* 有资格的
- **entitle** [ɪn'taɪtl] *vt.* 有……资格，授权
- **exactly** [ɪg'zæktli] *ad.* 准确地
- **flexibility** [ˌfleksə'bɪlɪti] *n.* 适应性，弹性
- **grace period** 宽限期
- **internally** [ɪn'tɜːnəli] *ad.* 内部地，内在地
- **landlord** ['lændlɔːd] *n.* 房东，地主

◆ **obstruct** [əb'strʌkt] *n.* 阻碍，障碍物
◆ **physically** ['fɪzɪkəli] *ad.* 身体上地
◆ **praise** [preɪz] *n.* 赞扬
◆ **prospect** ['prɒspekt] *n.* 前景，前途
◆ **rigid** ['rɪdʒɪd] *a.* 严格的，强硬的
◆ **sniff** [snɪf] *vt. &vi.* 闻到，嗅到
◆ **squeeze** [skwiːz] *vt.* 榨出，挤出；塞进
◆ **stamina** ['stæmɪnə] *n.* 持久力，毅力

Word List 14

◆ **alphabetically** [ˌælfə'betɪkli] *ad.* 按字母顺序地
◆ **angle** ['æŋgl] *n.* 角度
◆ **article** ['ɑːtɪkl] *n.* 文章
◆ **author** ['ɔːθə] *n.* 作者
◆ **avoid** [ə'vɒɪd] *vt.* 避免
◆ **bring up** 提出
◆ **comment** ['kɒment] *n.* 评论
◆ **concentrate** ['kɒnsentreɪt] *vt. &vi.* 集中注意力
◆ **consider** [kən'sɪdə] *vt.* 考虑
◆ **consult** [kən'sʌlt] *vt.* 咨询
◆ **conversation** [ˌkɒnvə'seɪʃən] *n.* 谈话
◆ **detail** ['diːteɪl] *n.* 细节
◆ **disorganised** [dɪs'ɔːgənaɪzd] *a.* 杂乱无章的，混乱的
◆ **equipment** [ɪ'kwɪpmənt] *n.* 设备，设施
◆ **especially** [ɪs'peʃəli] *ad.* 特别
◆ **exchange** [ɪks'tʃeɪndʒ] *n.* 交换，交流
◆ **finance** [faɪ'næns] *n.* 金融

- **gift voucher** 礼券
- **hold** [həʊld] *vt.* 保留
- **hospitality** [ˌhɒspɪ'tælɪti] *n.* 款待，好客
- **in advance** 提前
- **inclusive** [ɪn'kluːsɪv] *a.* 包括的，包含的
- **matinee** ['mætɪneɪ] *n.* 日场
- **party** ['pɑːti] *n.* 团体
- **pay off** 回报
- **payable** ['peɪəbl] *a.* 支付的
- **primary school** 小学
- **recreation** [ˌrekrɪ'eɪʃən] *n.* 休闲，娱乐，放松
- **refund** [rɪ'fʌnd] *vt.* 退款
- **reserve** [rɪ'zɜːv] *vt.* 预约
- **schedule** ['ʃedjuːl] *n.* 日程表
- **secondary school** 中学
- **self-employment** [ˌselfɪm'plɔɪmənt] *n.* 个体经营，自己创业
- **set aside** 留出，放在一旁

Word List 15

- **abdomen** ['æbdəmən] *n.* 腹，腹部
- **acceptable** [ək'septəbl] *a.* 能接受的
- **achieve** [ə'tʃiːv] *vt.* 取得，达到
- **advanced** [əd'vɑːnst] *a.* 高级的
- **apply** [ə'plaɪ] *vi.* 申请
- **get back to** 返回，重新
- **guideline** ['gaɪdlaɪn] *n.* 准则
- **height** [haɪt] *n.* 高度

- **insufficient** [ˌɪnsə'fɪʃənt] *a.* 不充分的，不充足的
- **involve** [ɪn'vɒlv] *vt.* 涉及
- **lighting** ['laɪtɪŋ] *n.* 照明
- **log** [lɒg] *vt.* 作记录
- **margin** ['mɑːdʒɪn] *n.* (页面)空白处
- **mark** [mɑːk] *vt.* 做标记
- **mentally** ['mentəli] *ad.* 心理上
- **particular** [pə'tɪkjulə] *a.* 特别的
- **refresh** [rɪ'freʃ] *vt.* 使重新提起精神；使恢复
- **relevant** ['relɪvənt] *a.* 相关的
- **similarly** ['sɪmɪləli] *ad.* 类似地
- **standby** ['stændbaɪ] *n.* 余票；备用物
- **stick to** 坚持
- **tip** [tɪp] *n.* 贴士，建议
- **title** ['taɪtl] *n.* 标题
- **unforeseen** ['ʌnfɔː'siːn] *a.* 不可预见的
- **urgent** ['ɜːdʒənt] *a.* 紧急的
- **vacancy** ['veɪkənsi] *n.* 空缺，空白
- **value** ['væljuː] *n.* 价值，价格
- **wheelchair** ['wiːltʃeə] *n.* 轮椅
- **wonder** ['wʌndə] *n.* 奇迹

Word List 16

- **adapt to** 适合
- **administrative** [əd'mɪnɪˌstrətɪv] *a.* 行政的，管理的
- **aeronautical** [ˌeərə'nɔːtɪkəl] *a.* 航空学的
- **airborne** ['eəbɔːn] *a.* 空运的；空气传播的；空降的

- **anatomist** [ə'nætəmɪst] *n.* 解剖学家；剖析者
- **authentic** [ɔː'θentɪk] *a.* 真实的
- **break the ice** 打破僵局
- **enclosure** [ɪn'kləʊʒə] *n.* 附件
- **essential** [ɪ'senʃəl] *a.* 必要的
- **focus on** 集中
- **forum** ['fɔːrəm] *n.* 论坛
- **heading** ['hedɪŋ] *n.* 标题
- **incorporate** [ɪn'kɔːpəreɪt] *vt.* 使融入，汇入
- **linguistically** [lɪŋ'gwɪstɪkəli] *ad.* 语言方面
- **notification** [ˌnəʊtɪfɪ'keɪʃən] *n.* 通知，通告
- **oral** ['ɔːrəl] *a.* 口头的
- **organizational** [ˌɔːgənaɪ'zeɪʃənəl] *a.* 组织的
- **plagiarize** ['pleɪdʒɪəˌraɪz] *vt.* 剽窃
- **practical** ['præktɪkəl] *a.* 实用的
- **profit** ['prɒfɪt] *vt.* 有益于；*vi.* 有利，获益
- **quote** [kwəʊt] *vt. &vi* 引用
- **relevance** ['relɪvəns] *n.* 相关
- **scan** [skæn] *vt.* 扫描
- **selective** [sɪ'lektɪv] *a.* 有选择的
- **simulation exercise** 模拟练习
- **skim** [skɪm] *vt. &vi.* 浏览
- **source material** 原始资料
- **suitable** ['suːtəbl] *a.* 适合的
- **topic sentence** 主题句
- **venture** ['ventʃə] *n. /vt.&vi.* 历险，探险
- **voice** [vɔɪs] *vt.* 说出；*n.* 声音

Word List 17

- **answer the phone** 接电话
- **appeal** [ə'pi:l] *vi.* 呼吁；吸引
- **application form** 申请表
- **array** [ə'reɪ] *n.* 排列，编队；衣服；大批部署
- **aspect** ['æspekt] *n.* 方面
- **awkward** ['ɔːkwəd] *a.* 难使用的；笨拙的
- **beneath** [bɪ'nɪːθ] *ad.* 在……下
- **classify** ['klæsɪfaɪ] *vt.* 分类，分等
- **colonize** ['kɒlənaɪz] *vt.* 将……开拓为殖民地
- **confirmed** [kən'fɜ:md] *a.* 证实的；惯常的；慢性的
- **construction** [kən'strʌkʃən] *n.* 建筑，建筑物
- **controversy** ['kɒntrəvɜ:si] *n.* 辩论，论战
- **endurance** [ɪn'djʊərəns] *n.* 忍耐(力)，持久(力)
- **evolve into** 发展（进化）成
- **extinct** [ɪks'tɪŋkt] *a.* 熄灭的，灭绝的，耗尽的
- **fossil** ['fɒsl] *n.* 化石
- **cretaceous period** 白垩纪时期
- **lizard** ['lɪzəd] *n.* 蜥蜴
- **muscle** ['mʌsəl] *n.* 肌肉
- **predator** ['predətə] *n.* 食肉动物
- **prompt** [prɒmpt] *a.* 迅速的
- **remarkable** [rɪ'mɑːkəbl] *a.* 非凡的
- **reptile** ['reptaɪl] *n.* 爬行动物
- **specimen** ['spesɪmən] *n.* 标本
- **stand out** 站出来，突出，坚持抵抗

- **triassic period** 三叠纪时期
- **uncontested** [ˌʌnkən'testɪd] *ad.* 无人争夺的，无竞争的，无异议的

Word List 18

- **business studies** *n.* 商业学
- **calamity** [kə'læmɪti] *n.* 灾难，不幸事件
- **charity** ['tʃærɪti] *n.* 慈善
- **child care centre** 儿童看护中心
- **cleaner** ['klɪnə] *n.* 清洁工，保洁员
- **clerical assistant** 文员
- **comet** ['kɒmɪt] *n.* 彗星
- **degree** [dɪ'griː] *n.* 学位
- **delta** ['deltə] *n.* 三角洲
- **descended** [dɪ'sendɪd] *a.* 出身于……的
- **dwelling** ['dwelɪŋ] *n.* 住处
- **end with** 以……结束
- **flier** ['flaɪə] *n.* 飞行者
- **fossilization** [ˌfɒsɪlaɪ'zeɪʃən] *n.* 化石化的东西
- **glide** [glaɪd] *vt. &vi* 滑行
- **hollow** ['hɒləʊ] *a.* 空的
- **limb** [lɪm] *n.* 肢，翼
- **meanwhile** ['miːnwaɪl] *ad.* 其间
- **microscope** ['maɪkrəskəʊp] *n.* 显微镜
- **reign** [reɪn] *n.* 统治，统治时期
- **represent** [ˌreprɪ'zent] *vt.* 象征
- **routinely** [ruː'tiːnli] *ad.* 例行公事地
- **sailplane** ['seɪlpleɪn] *n.* 滑翔机

- **scale** [skeɪl] *n.* 刻度，衡量，比例
- **slender** ['slendə] *a.* 苗条的；微薄的，微弱的
- **species** ['spiːʃiːz] *n.* 种类
- **stare** [steə] *vt. &vi.* 凝视，盯着看
- **sun-baked** ['sʌnbeɪkt] *a.* 日晒的，晒干的
- **thermal** ['θɜːməl] *a.* 热的，由热造成的
- **transform** [træns'fɔːm] *vt. &vi.* 改变，转化
- **triumphant** [traɪ'ʌmfənt] *a.* 胜利的

Word List 19

- **acclimatize** [ə'klaɪmətaɪz] *vt. &vi.* （使）适应，（使）服水土
- **bedding** ['bedɪŋ] *n.* 卧具，寝具
- **blanket** ['blæŋkɪt] *n.* 毛毯
- **carpet** ['kɑːpɪt] *n.* 地毯
- **cigar** [sɪ'gɑː] *n.* 雪茄
- **culminate** ['kʌlmɪneɪt] *vt. &vi.* 达到最高点；达到高潮；告终
- **device** [dɪ'vaɪs] *n.* 装置，设备
- **disabled** [dɪs'eɪbld] *a.* 残疾的，伤残的
- **donate** [dəʊ'neɪt] *vt. &vi.* 捐赠
- **enquiry** [ɪn'kwaɪəri] *n.* 咨询
- **glorious** ['glɔːrɪəs] *a.* 光荣的，显赫的
- **goal** [gəʊl] *n.* 目标
- **guarantee** [ˌgærən'tiː] *vt.* 担保，保证
- **halls of residence** 学生公寓
- **international house** 国际学生公寓
- **interview** ['ɪntəvjuː] *n.* / *vt.* 面试
- **meteorite** ['miːtɪəraɪt] *n.* 陨星

- **office assistant** 办公室助理
- **overview** ['əvəvjuː] *n.* 综述，概述
- **part-time job** 兼职工作
- **promise** ['prɒmɪs] *n.* 承诺
- **reception desk** 接待处
- **registered** ['redʒɪstəd] *a.* 已注册的
- **sponsor** ['spɒnsə] *vt.* 赞助，发起
- **sports centre** 体育中心
- **trek** [trek] *n.* 徒步旅行
- **typing** ['taɪpɪŋ] *n.* 打字
- **vertebrate** ['vɜːtɪbreɪt] *n.* 脊椎动物
- **work out** 算出、得出、产生结果

Word List 20

- **automatically** [ˌɔːtə'mætɪkli] *ad.* 自动地
- **beam** [biːm] *vt.* 播送
- **contribution** [ˌkɒntrɪ'bjuːʃən] *n.* 捐款，贡献
- **current** ['kʌrənt] *n.* 潮流
- **depletion** [dɪ'pliːʃən] *n.* 损耗
- **float** [fləʊt] *n.* 漂浮物
- **foothill** ['fʊthɪl] *n.* 山麓小丘
- **global warming** 全球变暖
- **gorgeous** ['gɔːdʒəs] *a.* 极好的，华美的
- **health certificate** 健康证明
- **highlight** ['haɪlaɪt] *n.* 最精彩的部分
- **itinerary** [aɪ'tɪnərəri] *n.* 路线，线路

- **landscape** ['lændskeɪp] *n.* 风景，景色
- **leaflet** ['liːflɪt] *n.* 传单
- **marvellous** ['mɑːvɪləs] *a.* 不可思议的，奇妙的
- **minimize** ['mɪnɪmaɪz] *vt.* 使减到最少
- **ocean research** 海洋研究
- **peak** [piːk] *n.* 山峰，山顶
- **profile** ['prəʊfaɪl] *n.* 轮廓，外形，概况
- **pupil** ['pjuːpəl] *n.* 小学生
- **region** ['riːdʒən] *n.* 地区，区域
- **robotic** [rəʊ'bɒtɪk] *a.* 机器人的
- **rucksack** ['rʌksæk] *n.* 帆布背包
- **snow-covered** ['snəʊˌkʌvəd] *a.* 冰雪覆盖的
- **spectacular** [spek'tækjulə] *a.* 壮观的，雄伟的，引人入胜的
- **timetable** ['taɪmteɪbl] *n.* 时间表
- **trend** [trend] *n.* 趋势，流行
- **undertake** [ˌʌndə'teɪk] *vt.* 承担，着手，开始
- **waterfall** ['wɔtəfɔːl] *n.* 瀑布
- **wood carving** 木雕

Word List 21

- **activate** ['æktɪveɪt] *vt.* 使启动
- **basis** ['beɪsɪs] *n.* 基础，根据
- **boutique** [buː'tiːk] *n.* 流行女装商店
- **chains** ['tʃeɪns] *n.* 连锁店
- **chic** [ʃiːk] *a.* 时髦的
- **client** ['klaɪənt] *n.* 顾客
- **contemporary** [kən'tempərəri] *a.* 当代的

- **disorient** [dɪs'ɔːrɪent] *vt.* 使迷失方向
- **dispirit** [dɪ'spɪrɪt] *vt.* 使沮丧，使气馁
- **external** [eks'tɜːnl] *a.* 外部的
- **implication** [ˌɪmplɪ'keɪʃən] *n.* 含义，暗示
- **legislation** [ˌledʒɪs'leɪʃən] *n.* 法律，立法
- **mechanic** [mɪ'kænɪk] *n.* 技工
- **meteorology** [ˌmiːtɪə'rɒlədʒi] *n.* 气象学
- **mission** ['mɪʃən] *n.* 使命，任务
- **navy** ['neɪvi] *n.* 海军
- **ongoing** ['ɒnˌgəʊɪŋ] *a.* 继续进行的
- **onshore** ['ɒnʃɔː] *a.* 向陆地的，陆上的
- **ozone** ['əʊzəʊn] *n.* 臭氧
- **preserve** [prɪ'zɜːv] *vt.* 保护，维持
- **salinity** [sə'lɪnɪti] *n.* 盐分，盐度
- **satellite** ['sætəlaɪt] *n.* 卫星
- **science fiction** 科幻
- **surface** ['sɜːfɪs] *n.* 水面；表面
- **transfer** [træns'fɜː] *n.* /*vt.* & *vi.* 转移，中转
- **underlying** [ˌʌndə'laɪɪŋ] *a.* 根本的，基础的
- **variation** [ˌveərɪ'eɪʃən] *n.* 变化
- **weather forecasting** 天气预报

Word List 22

- **background** ['bækgraʊnd] *n.* 背景
- **bicentennial park** 二百周年纪念公园
- **campus** ['kæmpəs] *n.* （大学）校园
- **carnivore** ['kɑːnɪvɔː] *n.* 食肉动物

- ◆ **carnivorous** [kɑː'nɪvərəs] *a.* 肉食性的
- ◆ **chocolate** ['tʃɒkəlɪt] *n.* 巧克力
- ◆ **hotelier** [ˌhəʊtə'lɪə] *n.* 旅馆经营者
- ◆ **idyllic** [aɪ'dɪlɪk] *a.* 田园诗的
- ◆ **inviting** [ɪn'vaɪtɪŋ] *a.* 吸引人的，诱人的
- ◆ **jet lag** 时差
- ◆ **mansion** ['mænʃən] *n.* 大厦，公馆
- ◆ **maximise** ['mæksɪmaɪz] *vi.* 使最大化
- ◆ **module** ['mɒdjuːl] *n.* 单元
- ◆ **opulent** ['ɒpjulənt] *a.* 富裕的，豪华的
- ◆ **palm tree** 棕榈树
- ◆ **plush** [plʌʃ] *a.* 豪华的，舒适的
- ◆ **psychology** [saɪ'kɒlədʒi] *n.* 心理学
- ◆ **revelation** [ˌrevə'leɪʃən] *n.* 暴露，泄露
- ◆ **scenario** [sɪ'naːrɪəʊ] *n.* 剧情；方案；描述
- ◆ **sleek** [sliːk] *a.* 光滑的；时髦的
- ◆ **slogan** ['sləʊgən] *n.* 标语，广告语
- ◆ **stand still** 维持原状，一成不变
- ◆ **subjective** [səb'dʒektɪv] *a.* 主观的
- ◆ **surrounding** [sə'raʊndɪŋ] *n.* 环境
- ◆ **tourism** ['tʊərɪzəm] *n.* 旅游业
- ◆ **tropical** ['trɒpɪkəl] *a.* 热带的
- ◆ **underestimate** [ˌʌndər'estɪmeɪt] *vt.* 低估
- ◆ **underpin** [ˌʌndə'pɪn] *vt.* 打下基础，巩固
- ◆ **well-being** ['wel'biːɪŋ] *n.* 健康；福利

Word List 23

- **arena** [ə'riːnə] *n.* 角斗场；圆形舞台
- **car park** 停车场
- **circular** ['sɜːkjulə] *a.* 环形的
- **complex** ['kɒmpleks] *n.* 综合体，建筑群
- **demolish** [dɪ'mɒlɪʃ] *vt.* 推倒（建筑物），毁坏
- **demolition** [ˌdemə'lɪʃən] *n.* 破坏，毁坏
- **derelict** ['derɪlɪkt] *a.* 弃置的，被遗弃的
- **enrollment** [ɪn'rəulmənt] *n.* / *vt.* 注册，登记
- **escape** [ɪs'keɪp] *vt.* & *vi.* 逃跑
- **exploit** [ɪk'splɔɪt] *vt.* & *vi.* 开采，开发
- **fruitarian** [fruː'teərɪən] *n.* 水果主义者
- **handball** ['hændbɔːl] *n.* 手球运动
- **herbivore** ['hɜːbɪvɔː] *n.* 食草动物
- **herbivorous** ['hɜːbɪvərəs] *a.* 食草的
- **homestay** ['həumsteɪ] *n.* 住宿家庭
- **indulge** [ɪn'dʌldʒ] *vt.* & *vi.* 放纵，容许
- **insectivore** [ɪn'sektɪvɔː] *n.* 食虫动物
- **insectivorous** [ˌɪnsek'tɪvərəs] *a.* 食虫的
- **intermediate** [ˌɪntə'miːdjət] *a.* 中级的
- **keep up the pace** 跟上节奏
- **miniscule** [ˌmɪnɪskjuːl] *a.* (中古时期)小写草字体的
- **pamper** ['pæmpə] *vt.* 纵容，宠爱
- **passport** ['pɑːspɔːt] *n.* 护照
- **phenomenon** [fɪ'nɒmɪnən] *n.* 现象
- **plan on doing sth.** 打算做某事

- **predictability** [prɪˌdɪktəˈbɪlɪti] *n.* 可预见性
- **preference** ['prefərəns] *n.* 偏爱
- **shampoo** [ʃæm'puː] *n.* 香波
- **transport** ['trænspɔːt] *n.* 交通
- **vegetarian** [ˌvedʒɪ'teəriən] *n.* 素食主义者
- **veterinarian** [ˌvetərɪ'neərɪən] *n.* 兽医

Word List 24

- **accessible** [æk'sesəbl] *a.* 易接近的；可达到的
- **agricultural produce** 农产品生产
- **and so forth** 等等
- **assess** [ə'ses] *vt.* 评估
- **binoculars** [baɪ'nɒkjuləs] *n.* 双筒望远镜
- **boardwalk** ['bɔːdwɔːk] *n.* 木板路
- **boat shed** 船棚
- **book** [bʊk] *vt. & vi.* 预订
- **cover** ['kʌvə] *vt.* 涵盖，包括
- **diving** ['daɪvɪŋ] *n.* 跳水
- **gymnasium** [dʒɪm'neɪzɪəm] *n.* 体育馆，健身房
- **gymnastics** [dʒɪm'næstɪks] *n.* 体操
- **high-rise** ['haɪ'raɪz] *a.* 高层的
- **hire** ['haɪə] *vt.* 租，租用
- **indoor** ['ɪndɔː] *a.* 室内的
- **low-rise** ['ləʊ'raɪz] *a.* 低层的
- **nature reserve** 自然保护区
- **olympic site** 奥运会场所
- **ornamental** [ˌɔːnə'mentl] *a.* 装饰性的

- **outdoor** ['aʊtdɔː] *a.* 户外的
- **parking garage** （室内）停车场
- **parking lot** *n.* (露天)停车场
- **pond** [pɒnd] *n.* 池塘
- **property** ['prɒpəti] *n.* 财产；房地产
- **public transport** 公共交通(工具)
- **resident** ['rezɪdənt] *n.* 居民
- **rowing boat** （划）船
- **shopping complex** 购物中心
- **site** [saɪt] *n.* 地点，选址
- **stadium** ['steɪdɪəm] *n.* （室外）体育场
- **storehouse** ['stɔːhaʊs] *n.* 仓库，货栈
- **synchronized swimming** 花样游泳
- **track and field** 田径，田径赛
- **warehouse** ['weəhaʊs] *n.* 仓库，货栈

Word List 25

- **adaptable** [ə'dæptəbl] *a.* 可适应的
- **alert** [ə'lɜːt] *vt.* 警告，警示
- **amino acid** 氨基酸
- **be responsible for** 对……负责
- **carbohydrate** [ˌkɑːbəʊ'haɪdreɪt] *n.* 碳水化合物
- **commercially** [kə'mɜːʃəli] *ad.* 商业化
- **commonly** ['kɒmənli] *ad.* 通常地
- **estuary** ['estʃʊəri] *n.* 河口
- **geographical location** 地理位置
- **go into** （金钱，时间，精力等）投入某事

- **historical background** 历史背景
- **mangrove** ['mæŋgrəʊv] *n.* 红树
- **media room** 多媒体室
- **mineral** ['mɪnərəl] *n.* 矿物
- **multi-media** [ˌmʌltɪ'miːdɪə] *a.* 多媒体的
- **nope** [nəʊp] *ad.* 不，没有
- **overhead projector** 高射投影仪
- **presentation** [ˌprezen'teɪʃən] *n.* 个人演讲，自我陈述
- **refuge** ['refjuːdʒ] *n.* 藏匿处，避难
- **resources room** 资料室
- **role** [rəʊl] *n.* 作用
- **seminar** ['semɪnɑː] *n.* 研讨会
- **shelter** ['ʃeltə] *n.* 藏匿处，避难
- **sheltered** ['ʃeltəd] *a.* 掩蔽的
- **swan** [swɒn] *n.* 天鹅
- **take notes** 作笔记
- **upgrade** [ˌʌp'greɪd] *vt.* 升级，提高，改善
- **visual** ['vɪzjuəl] *a.* 视觉的
- **wetland** ['wetlænd] *n.* 湿地，沼泽地

Word List 26

- **arouse** [ə'raʊz] *vt.* 唤醒，激发
- **compare** [kəm'peə] *vt. &vi.* 比较，比作
- **cuisine** [kwɪ'ziːn] *n.* 烹饪
- **cultivate** ['kʌltɪveɪt] *vt.* 耕作，种植
- **detect** [dɪ'tekt] *vt.* 觉察
- **digest** [daɪ'dʒest] *vt. &vi.* 消化

- **diverse** [daɪ'vɜːs] *a.* 不同的，多种多样的
- **domesticate** [də'mestɪkeɪt] *vt.* 驯化
- **dramatically** [drə'mætɪkli] *ad.* 巨大地，大大地
- **embassy** ['embəsi] *n.* 使馆
- **encyclopaedia** [enˌsaɪkləʊ'piːdjə] *n.* 百科全书
- **enthusiastic** [ɪnˌθjuːzɪ'æstɪk] *a.* 热情的
- **extraction** [ɪks'trækʃən] *n.* 提取
- **flavor enhancer** 增味剂
- **glutamate** ['gluːtəˌmeɪt] *n.* 谷氨酸盐
- **identify** [aɪ'dentɪfaɪ] *vt.* 确认，识别
- **ingredient** [ɪn'griːdɪənt] *n.* 成分
- **monosodium glutamate** 谷氨酸钠
- **potato crisp** 油炸土豆片
- **process** ['prəʊses] *n.* 过程，进程
- **protein** ['prəʊtiːɪn] *n.* 蛋白质
- **rate** [reɪt] *n.* 比率
- **saltiness** ['sɔːltɪnɪs] *n.* 咸
- **seaweed** ['siːwiːd] *n.* 海草，海藻
- **sodium** ['səʊdiːəm] *n.* 钠
- **spoilage** ['spɔɪlɪdʒ] *n.* 掠夺，糟蹋
- **statistics** [stə'tɪstɪks] *n.* 统计数字，统计资料
- **tourist brochure** 旅游手册
- **toxin** ['tɒksɪn] *n.* 毒素
- **tutorial** [tjuː'tɔːrɪəl] *n.* 个别指导课
- **up-to-date** ['ʌptə'deɪt] *a.* 当今的，现代的

Word List 27

- **accomplish** [ə'kɒmplɪʃ] *vt.* 完成，实现，做成功
- **albeit** [ɔːl'biːɪt] *conj.* 尽管，即使
- **ancestor** ['ænsɪstə] *n.* 祖先
- **ancestral** [æn'sestrəl] *a.* 祖先的
- **anthropologist** [ˌænθrə'pɒlədʒɪst] *n.* 人类学者
- **archaeological** [ˌɑːkɪə'lɒdʒɪkəl] *a.* 考古学的
- **encode** [ɪn'kəʊd] *vt.* 编码
- **feed** [fiːd] *vt.* 喂养
- **overtake** [ˌəʊvə'teɪk] *vt.* 超过
- **prehistoric** [ˌpriːhɪs'tɒrɪk] *a.* 史前的
- **presence** ['prezəns] *n.* 存在
- **propagate** ['prɒpəgeɪt] *vt.* 传播，宣传
- **raise** [reɪz] *vt.* 饲养
- **reject** [rɪ'dʒekt] *vt.* 拒绝，反对
- **ruin** ['rʊɪn] *vt.* 破坏，毁掉
- **screen** [skriːn] *vt.* 审查，甄选
- **scrutiny** ['skruːtɪni] *n.* 细看
- **secrete** [sɪ'kriːt] *vt.* （生理）分泌
- **spray** [spreɪ] *n.* 喷雾
- **strain** [streɪn] *vt.* 过滤
- **survey** [sɜː'veɪ] *vt.* 眺望，纵览
- **swapping** ['swɒpɪŋ] *n.* 交换
- **transmission** [træns'mɪʃən] *n.* 传送，传动
- **urban** ['ɜːbən] *a.* 城市的

Word List 28

- **artificial** [ˌɑːtɪ'fɪʃəl] *a.* 人造的，人工的
- **bearing** ['beərɪŋ] *n.* 方向
- **biological** [ˌbaɪə'lɒdʒɪkəl] *a.* 生物学的
- **calibrate** ['kælɪˌbreɪt] *vt.* 校准
- **combat** ['kɒmbæt] *n.* 战斗，格斗，斗争
- **combine** [kəm'baɪn] *vt.* &*vi.* (使)联合
- **compass** ['kʌmpəs] *n.* 罗盘，指南针
- **component** [kəm'pəʊnənt] *n.* 成分，组成部分
- **compose** [kəm'pəʊz] *vt.* 组成，构成
- **conduct** [kən'dʌkt] *vt.* 管理，开展
- **confine** [kən'faɪn] *vt.* 限制，局限于
- **correspond** [ˌkɒrɪs'pɒnd] *vi.* 相符合，类似
- **credence** ['kriːdəns] *n.* 相信，信任
- **decline** [dɪ'klaɪn] *n.* 下降，减少，衰退
- **essay** ['eseɪ] *n.* 散文，随笔
- **footing** ['fʊtɪŋ] *n.* 基础，地位
- **forage** ['fɔːrɪdʒ] *vi.* 搜寻（食物）
- **framework** ['freɪmwɜːk] *n.* 构架
- **genetic** [dʒɪ'netɪk] *a.* 遗传（学）的
- **geneticist** [dʒɪ'netɪsɪst] *n.* 遗传学者
- **hail** [heɪl] *vt.* 致敬；向……欢呼
- **intricately** ['ɪntrəkɪtli] *ad.* 复杂地
- **landmark** ['lændmɑːk] *n.* 地标；明显的标志
- **megalopolis** [ˌmegə'lɒpəlɪs] *n.* 巨大都市

- **navigate** ['nævɪˌgeɪt] *vt. & vi.* 引航，导航
- **primitive** ['prɪmɪtɪv] *a.* 原始的，早期的

Word List 29

- **condemn** [kən'dem] *vt.* 判罪，处刑
- **discard** [dɪs'kɑːd] *vt.* 丢弃，抛弃
- **ecosystem** [iːkəʊsɪstəm] *n.* 生态系统
- **heritage** ['herɪtɪdʒ] *n.* 遗产，继承物
- **interbreed** [ˌɪntə'briːd] *vt.* (使)异种交配；(使)杂种繁殖
- **linguist** ['lɪŋgwɪst] *n.* 语言学家
- **locate** [ləʊ'keɪt] *vt.* 找出，指出(地点或位置)
- **majority** [mə'dʒɒrɪtɪ] *n.* 多数，大多数
- **migration** [maɪ'greɪʃən] *n.* 迁移，移居
- **minimally** ['mɪnɪməli] *adv.* 最低限度地，最低程度地
- **notion** ['nəʊʃən] *n.* 概念，观念
- **odour** ['əʊdə] *n.* 气味；臭气
- **origin** ['ɔːrɪdʒɪn] *n.* 起点；出身
- **perform** [pə'fɔːm] *vt.* 表演；履行
- **photosynthesis** [ˌfəʊtəʊ'sɪnθəsɪs] *n.* 光合作用
- **precaution** [prɪ'kɔːʃən] *n.* 预防措施
- **scout** [skaʊt] *n.* 侦察员
- **transmit** [trænz'mɪt] *vt.* 传播
- **triple** ['trɪpl] *a.* 三倍的；三部分的
- **territory** ['terɪtəri] *n.* 领土
- **undertake** [ˌʌndə'teɪk] *vt.* 担任，承担

Word List 30

- **accentuate** [æk'sentʃʊeɪt] *vt.* 使突出；强调
- **culprit** ['kʌlprɪt] *n.* 犯过错者，罪犯
- **dawn** [dɔːn] *n.* 开端，萌芽
- **ecologically** [ɪkə'lɒʒɪkəli] *ad.* 生态意义上
- **hence** [hens] *ad.* 因此，所以
- **preferential** [ˌprefə'renʃl] *a.* 优先的；优惠的
- **resolution** [ˌrezə'luːʃən] *n.* 正式决定，决议
- **surveillance** [sɜː'veɪləns] *n.* 监视
- **systematize** ['sɪstɪmətaɪz] *vt.* 使系统化；使成体系

第三章　雅思词汇分类拓展

一　动物类

amphibian *n.* 两栖类
arachnid *n.* 蛛形动物
ant *n.* 蚂蚁
ass *n.* 驴

birds of prey 猛禽
bird *n.* 鸟类
beaver *n.* 河狸，海狸
bee *n.* 蜜蜂
bioversity *n.* 生物多样性
budgie *n.* 虎皮鹦鹉
buffalo *n.* 水牛
bull *n.* 公牛

crustacean *n.* 甲壳类
calf *n.* 小牛
camel *n.* 骆驼
carnivorous *a.* 食肉的
chimpanzee *n.* 黑猩猩
cow *n.* 母牛
ox *n.* 牛
crab *n.* 螃蟹
crocodile *n.* 鳄鱼
cunning *a.* 狡猾的

deer *n.* 鹿
dingo *n.* 澳洲野犬
dolphin *n.* 海豚
doom to extinct 注定灭绝

eagle *n.* 鹰
endangered species
濒临灭绝的物种

feeding time 喂养时间
fierce *a.* 凶猛的
food chain 食物链
fox *n.* 狐狸
foal *n.* 小马驹

giraffe *n.* 长颈鹿
golden monkey 金丝猴
goldfish *n.* 金鱼
guinea pig 豚鼠

hound *n.* 猎犬
hare *n.* 野兔
hedgehog *n.* 刺猬

hippopotamus *n.* 河马

kangaroo *n.* 袋鼠
kitten *n.* 小猫
koala *n.* 考拉

lamb *n.* 羔羊
leopard *n.* 豹

mammal *n.* 哺乳类
marsupial *n.* 有袋类
mollusc *n.* 软体类
mole *n.* 鼹鼠
mouse *n.* 鼠
mule *n.* 骡

pachyderm *n.* 厚皮动物
poultry and game 家禽和野禽
primate *n.* 灵长目
puppy *n.* 小狗
panda *n.* 熊猫
parrot *n.* 鹦鹉
pet *n.* 宠物
pigeon *n.* 鸽子
pony *n.* 小马
preserve wildlife 保护野生动植物
prey *n.* / *vi.* 猎物 / 捕食，猎获

reptile *n.* 爬行类
rodent *n.* 啮齿类
rooster *n.* 公鸡
rabbit *n.* 兔子
rare animal / species
稀有动物 / 物种
rat *n.* (大)鼠
reindeer *n.* 驯鹿
rhinoceros *n.* 犀牛

seabird *n.* 海鸟
sea turtle *n.* 海龟
seagull *n.* 海鸥
seal *n.* 海豹
sea lion 海狮
shark *n.* 鲨鱼
Siberia Tiger *n.* 东北虎
snail *n.* 蜗牛
snake *n.* 蛇
squirrel *n.* 松鼠

tortoise *n.* 乌龟

walrus *n.* 海象
whale *n.* 鲸
wolf *n.* 狼
wombat *n.* 毛鼻袋熊

yak *n.* 牦牛

zebra *n.* 斑马
zoo *n.* 动物园

二 标识语类

24-Hours 24 小时便利店

Beware of Pickpockets
当心小偷

Do Not Leave Bags Unattended
请保管好自己的物品

Feeding the Animals Strictly Prohibited 禁止喂食

Fragile 易碎

Keep off the Grass 请勿践踏

Mind You Head 注意头顶
Mind Your Step 注意脚下

No Exit 无出口

No Parking 禁止泊车
No Queue Jumper 请排队
No Smoking 禁止抽烟
No Spitting 严禁吐痰
No Teasing 禁止嬉闹

Open / Closed 营业 / 打烊
Out of Order 暂无存货

Please Do Not Disturb
请勿打扰
Please Do Not Feed the Animals
禁止喂食
Please Do Not Lean out of the Window 请勿靠窗
Silence Examination in Progr-ess 考试请保持安静

三 财经类

accountant *n.* 会计

bank account 银行账号
bank loan 银行贷款
bank statement 银行结单
bill *n.* 账单；钞票

cash *n.* 现金
cheque / check *n.* 支票

credit card 信用卡
deposit *n.& vt.* 存款
discount *n.* 折扣

haggle *vi.* 讨价还价

income tax 个人所得税
inflation *n.* 通货膨胀

interest *n.* 利息

investment *n.* 投资
invoice *n.* 发票
mortgage *n.* 按揭

overdraft *n.* 透支额
overdrawn *vt.* 透支

profit *n.* 利润

purchase *vt.* 购买
receipt *n.* 收据
reduction *n.* 降低
refund *n.* 退款 / 偿还金额

salary *n.* 月薪

wage *n.* 周薪

四 身体类

ankle *n.* 关节
arm *n.* 手臂

back *n.* 背
blood *n.* 血液
brain *n.* 大脑
broad *a.* 宽的
bust *n.* 胸围

chest *n.* 胸
chubby *a.* 丰满的

ear *n.* 耳朵
eye *n.* 眼睛

finger *n.* 手指
foot / feet （复）*n.* 脚

hair *n.* 头发
hand *n.* 手

head *n.* 头
heart *n.* 心脏
hips *n.* 臀部

intestines *n.* 肠

kidney *n.* 肾脏
knee *n.* 膝盖

leg *n.* 腿
lip *n.* 嘴唇
liver *n.* 肝
lung *n.* 肺

mouth *n.* 嘴巴
muscular *a.* 肌肉形的

nail *n.* 指甲
neck *n.* 脖子
nose *n.* 鼻子

obesity *n.* 肥胖

palm *n.* 手掌

plump *a.* 微胖的

shoulder *n.* 肩膀

skin *n.* 皮肤

solid *a.* 结实的

stocky *a.* 矮壮的

stomach *n.* 肚子，胃

stout *a.* 肥胖的

tooth （复）/teeth *n.* 牙齿

thigh *n.* 大腿

thumb *n.* 大拇指

toe *n.* 脚趾

waist *n.* 腰部

五 个性行为类

a sinister smile 阴险的笑

a strong sense of lost 强烈的失落感

act on impulse 一时冲动做事

adapt oneself to 适应

aggressive *a.* 有进取心的

alert *a.* 机警的

aloof *a.* 疏远的，冷淡的

ambitious *a.* 有雄心壮志的

amicable *a.* 和蔼可亲的

analytic *a.* 善于分析的

aspiring *a.* 有抱负的

audacious *a.* 大胆的；有冒险精神的

bad-manner *a.* 没礼貌的

bad / ill-tempered *a.* 坏脾气的

baffle / perplex *vt.* 困惑，为难

be strict with oneself 对自己要求严格

bewilderment *n.* 困惑；为难

bold and uninhibited 胆大妄为的

bully *vt.* 欺压

calm *a.* 冷静的

changeable *a.* 可改变的

charming *a.* 有魅力的

comparison *n.* 攀比

compel *vt.* 强迫，迫使

competent *a.* 能胜任的

conscientious *a.* 尽责的

consultancy *n.* 顾问

creative *a.* 富有创造性的

cultured *a.* 有修养的

dashing *a.* 闯劲足的

dedicated *a.* 有奉献精神的
diffidence *n.* 缺乏自信
disparity / inequality *n.* 不平等
down-to-earth *a.* 实际的
drive off loneliness 驱赶孤独

earnest *a.* 认真的
egoist *n.* 自我主义者
emotional contact 感情交流
endowment *n.* 天资
easy to lose one's temper 容易发脾气
easy-going *a.* 随和的
expressive *a.* 善于表达的

gallant *a.* 英勇的

haughty / arrogant *a.* 傲慢的，自大的
hotheaded *a.* 性急的；鲁莽的

incompetent *a.* 不合格的；不胜任的
inexperience *n.* 缺乏经验，不熟练
introverted *a.* 内向的
isolated *a.* 孤立的

methodical *a.*有条理的
mischievous *a.* 恶作剧的

optimistic *a.* 乐观的
original *a.* 有独创性的
out of one's sense 失去理性

patriotic *a.* 爱国的
perseverance *n.* 毅力
pessimistic *a.* 悲观的

quick-minded / quick-witted *a.* 思维敏捷的

rash / imprudent *a.* 轻率的；匆忙的
self-centered *a.* 自我为中心的
self-esteem *n.* 自尊
sensitive *a.* 敏感的
sequacious *a.* 盲从的；缺乏创造性的
short-tempered *a.* 急性子的
shrewd-brained *a.* 头脑精明的
simple-minded *a.* 头脑简单的
spirited *a.* 精神饱满的
stingy *a.* 吝啬的
straightforward *a.* 诚实的；直截了当的
strong-willed *a.* 意志坚强的
stubborn *a.* 固执的

talent / gift *n.* 天才；才能
talkative *a.* 健谈的
thoughtless *a.* 欠考虑的
thrifty *a.* 节俭的
timid *a.* 胆小的
tireless *a.* 孜孜不倦的
tough *a.* 坚韧的

uncertainty and confusion 不稳定和慌乱
unsociable *a.* 不爱交际的
vanity *a.* 浮华的
versatile *a.* 多才多艺的
well-educated *a.* 受过良好教育的
willpower *n.* 意志力
with heroic spirit 有英雄气概的

六　影视类

accredited journalist 特派记者
act/action film / movie 动作片
actor *n.* 男演员
actress *n.* 女演员
admission ticket 入场券
advance *n.* 预发消息
advertising agency 广告公司
advertising *n.* 广告(业)
aerial *n.* 天线
American Beauty《美国丽人》
American Pie《美国派》
anecdote *n.* 轶闻趣事
animated cartoon 动画片
announcer *n.* 播音员

Berlin International Film Festival 柏林国际电影节
black-and-white film 黑白影片
Brave Heart《勇敢的心》
brief *n.* 简讯
bring reality to the public 把现实带到观众面前
broadcast *n.* / *vt.* & *vi.* 广播
broadcast alive 现场直播
broadcast news 播报新闻
broadcast speech 广播演讲
bulletin *n.* 新闻简报

camcorder *n.* 摄像机
Cannes International Film Festival 戛纳国际电影节
cast *n.* 演员表
censor *n.* 新闻审查
channel *n.* 频道
classical *a.* 古典的
classified advertisement 分类广告
close-up *n.* 特写镜头
colour film 彩色影片
comedy *n.* 喜剧

comic stuntman 特技演员
commercial advertisement 商业广告
commercials *n.* 商业片
copy *n.* / *vt.* & *vi.* 拷贝
covert coverage 秘密采访
credible *a.* 可信的
crime / detective film 犯罪 / 侦探片

detective film 侦探片
detective story 侦探故事
director *n.* 导演
documentary film 纪录片
domestic news 国内新闻
dub *vt.* 配音

edit *n.* / *vt.* 剪辑
education programme 教育节目
entertainment industry 演艺圈
episode *n.* 片段 / 插曲
ethical film 伦理片
exclusive *a.* 独家的

family enjoyment 家庭娱乐
family reunion 家庭团聚
feature film 故事片
film adapted from a play 根据剧本改编的电影
film festival 电影节
film fan 影迷
film star 电影明星
film studio 电影制片厂
Finding Nemo《海底总动员》
Forrest Gump《阿甘正传》
freedom of the press 新闻自由
frequency *n.* 频率
full page advertisement 整版广告

Gangs of New York 《纽约黑帮》
Ghost《人鬼情未了》
Gladiator《角斗士》
Gone with the Wind 《飘》

hearsay *n.* 小道消息
hero *n.* 男主角
heroine *n.*女主角
highlight *n* 要闻
holidays and festivals 节日及活动 / 节假日
horror film / movie 恐怖片 / 惊悚片
hot news 热点新闻

in-depth reporting 深度报道
international news 国际新闻
international perspective 国际视野
invasion of privacy 侵犯隐私(权)
irresponsible *a.* 不负责任的

kung fu film 功夫片

lightening *n.* 灯光
literary film 文艺片
live broadcast 实况转播
live report 现场报道
live television coverage 电视实况转播
Lord of the Rings《指环王》
love / romance story 爱情故事

mass media 大众信息 / 媒体
men of the year 年度风云人物
Mission Impossible《碟中谍》
music programme 音乐节目
musical *n.* 音乐剧

news agency 通讯社
news clue 新闻线索
news value 新闻价值
newscast *n.* 新闻广播
newsreel *n.* 新闻片

objectivity *n.* 客观性
on air 正在播放
Oscar / Academy Awards 奥斯卡金像奖 / 学院奖

photographer *n.* 摄影师
political event 政治事件
premiere *n.* 首映式
press conference 记者招待会
press release 新闻稿
producer *n.* 制片人
projector *n.* 投影机
provide people with all kinds of information 给人们提供各种各样的信息
pseudo-event *n.* 新闻
publicity *n.* 宣传

Rain Man《雨人》
recommend *vt.* 推荐，介绍
remote control 遥控器
round-up *n.* 综合消息

satellite dish 卫星天线
Saving Private Ryan《拯救大兵瑞恩》
scandal *n.* 丑闻
scenario *n.* 故事梗概
Schilder's List
《辛德勒的名单》
science fiction film 科幻片
sensational *a.* 具有轰动效应的
serial *n.* 电视连续剧
sex scandal 桃色新闻
shoot *vt.* 摄制
slant *n.* 主观报道
soap opera 肥皂剧
sound effect 声音效果

soundman *n.* 音效师
source of violence and pornography 暴力与色情的来源
special effect 特技
Speed《生死时速》
Spider Man《蜘蛛人》
sports programme 体育节目
spread computer viruses 传播计算机病毒
stage property 道具
stereo *n.* 立体声
studio *n.* 演播室
subhead *n.* 副标题
subjectivity *n.* 主观性
supporting role 配角
surf the net 上网
suspended interest 悬念

Tarzan《人猿泰山》
telecourse *n.* 电视课程
television advertisement 电视广告
television *n.*电视
The Bodyguard《保镖》
the charts 每周流行音乐排行榜
The Day After Tomorrow《后天》
The English Patient《英国病人》
The Graduate《毕业生》
the latest 最新的
The Matrix《骇客帝国》
The Matrix Reloaded《骇客帝国》
The Patriot《爱国者》
The Shawshank Redemption《肖申克的救赎》/《激情1999》
The Sound of Music《音乐之声》
ticket office 售票处
timbre *n.* 音质
timeliness *n.* 时效性
tragedy *n.* 悲剧
trailer *n.* 电影预告片
transform information 传递信息
transmitting station 发射台
TV serial 电视连续剧
TV play 电视剧
TV programme 电视节目
TV station 电视台

update fast 更新快
up-to-date *a.* 最新的

Venice Horse Prize Film Festival 威尼斯国际电影节
view *n.* 观点
villain *n.* 反面人物

walk on stilts 踩高跷
waveband *n.* 波段

wavelength *n.* 波长
weather forecast 天气预报
weatherman *n.* 气象员
Western *n.* 西部片
wide-screen film 宽银幕电影
www(world wide web) 万维网

七 气候类

a clear and crisp autumn day 一个秋高气爽的日子
average annual rainfall 年均降雨量

below zero 零下
blizzard *n.* 大风雪
blustery *a.* 大风的
breeze *n.* 微风

chilly *a.* 寒冷的
climate *n.* 气候
climate condition 气候条件
cloud *n.* / cloudy *a.* 云 / 有云的
continental climate 大陆性气候
continental weather 大陆性天气

damp *a.* 微湿的
degree *n.* 温度
downpour *n.* 倾盆大雨
drizzle *n.* 细雨
drought *n.* 旱灾
dry *a.* 干燥的

favour / agreeable / pleasant weather 气候宜人
fog *n.* 雾
foggy *a.* 有雾的
freeze *vt.* & *vi.* 结冰
fresh air 新鲜的空气
frost *n.* 霜

gale *n.* 大风
genial sunshine 和煦的阳光
gloomy *a.* (天气)阴沉的

hail *n.* 冰雹
heavy rain 大雨
high temperature 高温
hot *a.* 热的
humid *a.* 潮湿的
humidity *n.* 湿度
hurricane *n.* 飓风

icy / cold *a.* 冰冷的

lightning *n.* 闪电

maritime *a.* 海的，海上的，航海的

maritime climate 海洋性气候

maritime weather 海洋性气候

melt *vt. & vi.* 溶解

mild *a.* 温和的

mild weather 温和的天气

minus *n.* 零下

overcast *a.* 阴的，多云的

plateau weather 高原气候

rainy *a.* 有雨的

rainfall *n.* 降雨量

scorching *a.* 炎热的

severe weather 恶劣的天气

sleet *n.* 雨夹雪

slush *n.* 半溶化的雪

smog *n.* 烟雾

snowy *a.* 下雪的

snowflake *n.* 雪花

spring breeze 春风

stormy *a.* 暴风雨的

strong wind 大风

subtropical climate 亚热带气候

sultry *a.* 闷热的

sunny *a.* 阳光充足的

sunshine *n.* 阳光

temperate *a.* 温和的

temperature *n.* 气温

tempest *n.* 暴风雨

thaw *vt. & vi.* 溶化；解冻

thunderstorm *n.* 暴雨，雷雨交加

tornado *n.* 龙卷风

tropical *a.* 热带的

typhoon *n.* 台风

wet *a.* 湿的

whirlwind *n.* 旋风

windy *a.* 有风的

八 穿着类

belt *n.* 皮带

blouse *n.* 女衬衫

bootees *n.* 婴儿穿的软鞋

boot *n.* 靴子

brace *n.* 背带

button *n.* 扣子

cardigan *n.* 羊毛衫

checked *a.* 有格子花的

close-fitting *a.* 紧身的

coat *n.* 外套
collar *n.* 领子
corduroy *n.* 灯芯绒
cotton *n.* 棉
cuff *n.* 袖口

denim *n.* 劳动布，斜纹粗棉布
dress *n.* 晚穿礼服

flowery *a.* 有花的

glove *n.* 手套

hat *n.* 帽子

jacket *n.* 夹克衫
jeans *n.* 牛仔裤
leather *n.* 皮革
linen *n.* 亚麻布
lycra *n.* 莱卡（纤维织物运动服）

nylon *n.* 尼龙

pajama *n.* 睡衣
pin-striped *a.* 有条纹的
plain *n.* 平针
polka-dotted *n.* 圆点花纹

scarf *n.* 围巾
shoe *n.* 鞋子
shorts / underwear *n.* 短裤
sleeve *n.* 袖子
slipper *n.* 拖鞋
sock *n.* 短袜 / 鞋垫
spotted *a.* 斑点的
striped *a.* 有条纹的

suede *n.* 绒面革
suit *n.* 一套衣服
sweater / jumper *n.* 针织套衫

tartan *n.* 方格花纹
tie *n.* 领带
tights *n.* 紧身裤
trainers / sneakers *n.* 运动鞋
trousers *n.* 长裤
shirt *n.* 衬衫
velvet *n.* 天鹅绒
wellington *n.* 防水靴
woolen *a.* 毛织品的
zip *n.* 拉链

九 社会及犯罪类

a controversial issue 具有争议性的话题

a disciplined environment 守纪律的环境

a negative outlook on life 消极的人生观

a sense of belonging 归属感

a sense of respect and confidence 感到受人尊重和有自信心

a slot machine 老虎机

a teen court 少年法庭

a tooth for a tooth 报复

a vicious circle 恶性循环

abandon / abnegate *vt.* 放弃；放任

abstention *n.* 节制

adult business district 红灯区

alcohol prohibition 禁酒

anti-drug *n.* 禁毒

anti-drug campaign 禁毒活动

anti-drug parade 禁毒游行

armed robbery 持械抢劫

arrest warrant 逮捕证

arrest *vt.* 逮捕，拘留

arson *n.* 纵火

assassin *n.* 暗杀者

assault *n.* 袭击

at risk / at stake 处于危险之中

atone for their misconduct 将功赎罪

atrocity *n.* 残暴，暴行

attack *vt. & vi.* 进攻

attorney *n.* 律师

bail *n.* 保释金

ban *n.* 禁止

be acquitted 被无罪释放

be avid for 贪婪，渴望

be charged with 被指控犯罪

be convicted 被指控

be exposed to sexual material / stuff 接触到色情内容

be involved in 涉及

be surrounded with 被……环绕的

behead *vt.* 砍……的头

black market 黑市

blackmail *vt.* 敲诈 / 勒索

bomb squad 爆破小组

bootleg *a.* 违法的，贩卖的

break into 强行进入

breakdown of families 家庭破裂

break in 非法闯入

bribery *n.* 行贿；受贿
bug *n.* 窃听
bully *vt./ n.* 欺凌弱小者
bum rap 不公正的惩罚
burglary *n.* 入室盗窃

cannabis / hemp / marijuana *n.* 大麻
capital crime 死罪
car bangers 汽车窃贼
car theft 盗车
career criminal 职业罪犯
casino *n.* 赌场
cat thief / burglar 飞贼
cause of death 死因
censorship of the Internet 互联网审查制度
charge *vt. & vi.* 指控
chemical dependence 对化学药品的依赖
chemotherapy *n.* 化学疗法
child abuse / maltreatment 虐待儿童
chronically addicted 长期上瘾的
cocaine *n.* 可卡因
combine punitive and curative treatment 改造和惩处相结合
commit a crime / offence 犯罪
commit a heinous crime 犯下重罪
community service 社区服务
con game 骗局
continuous use 持续使用
correct their misconduct 改过自新
correction officer 惩教人员
corrupt the minds 腐蚀思想
counterfeit *n. / vt. & vi.* 伪造
crime against property / property crime 侵害财产罪
crime rate 犯罪率
criminal activity 犯罪活动
criminal behaviour 犯罪行为
criminologist *n.* 犯罪学者，刑事学家
criminal conduct 犯罪行为
cruel and barbaric practice 残忍和野蛮的做法
cyberspace *n.* 电脑空间

dancing outreach 摇头丸
deadly consequence 致命的后果
deadly weapon 致命武器
death penalty 死刑
debilitate *vt.* 减轻，使虚弱
decency *n.* 庄重
defendant *n.* 被告
degenerate *vi.* 堕落
deterrent *a.* 威慑的
deterrence *n.* 威慑（物）
dignity of life 生命的尊严
disorder *n.* 失调

domestic violence 家庭暴力
drug abuse 吸毒
drug addicts 瘾君子
drug king (czar) 毒枭
drug pushing/dealing 毒品交易
drug rehabilitation centre 戒毒中心
drug related crime/offence 涉毒犯罪
drug trafficker 毒枭 / 贩毒者
drugs and alcohol 毒品和酒精
drunken driving 酒后驾车
dupe *n.* 易受骗的人；易受愚弄的人
dysphoria *n.* 烦躁不安

ease the pain/lessen pain 减轻疼痛
eavesdrop *vi.* / *n.* 偷听
embezzlement *n.* 贪污，挪用，侵占
embody humanism 体现人道主义
emotional disturbance 情感上的困惑
enforce the laws 实施法律
enforce the rules 执行规定
engage in acts of crime 参与犯罪
environmental factor 环境因素
epidemic *a.* (风尚等)流行的
eradicate *vt.* 根除
espionage *n.* 间谍活动
execution *n.* 执行，实行
experiment with drugs 尝试吸毒
extinguish a person's life 结束生命
extreme violence 极端暴力

female violent crime 妇女暴力犯罪
forgery *n.* 伪造
fraud *n.* 欺诈；欺诈行为

gamble *vt.* & *vi.* 赌博
gambling enterprise 博彩行业
gangster *n.* 匪徒
gas chamber 毒气室
get away with 侥幸成功
go bankrupt 破产
go crazy / go mad 发疯
graffiti *n.* 涂鸦，乱涂，乱画
gun control 枪械管制
gun control advocate 主张禁枪者
gunshot *n.* 射击

hallucination *n.* 幻觉，幻想
hanging *n.* 绞刑，绞死
harass *vt.* 烦恼，骚扰
hardened criminal 死不悔改的罪犯

harsh law 苛刻和严厉的法律
harsh reality 残酷的现实
heartless *a.* 无情的
heroin *n.* 海洛因
hijack *vt.* 劫持
HIV disease / AIDS 艾滋病
holocaust *n.* 大毁灭，大屠杀
home-invasion robbery 入室抢劫
homicide *n.* 杀人罪
hooligan *n.* 小流氓
humanitarianism *n.* 人道主义

illegal operation 非法活动
illegal *a.* 非法的
immune system 免疫系统
impose the penalty 实施惩罚
improve our criminal justice system 改进刑事审判制度
impunity *n.* 不受惩罚，免于受罚
inappropriate for minors 未成年人不宜的
increase the punishment on the user and dealer 加强对毒品使用者和贩卖者的惩罚
incurable disease / terminal disease 绝症
insanity *n.* 精神错乱
instigate *vt.* 煽动，鼓动，诱发
insurance fraud 保险诈骗
intergenerational *a.* 两代间的
Internet community 互联网社区
Internet user 互联网用户
intravenous drug abuser 静脉注射的吸毒者
inviolable *a.* 神圣的，不可侵犯的，不可亵渎的
irresponsible behaviour 不负责任的行为

jealousy *n.* 嫉妒
job-seeking skill / technique 求职技能
juvenile delinquency 青少年犯罪

knavery *n.* 恶棍的行为
Ku Klux Klan 三K党

lack of communication 缺乏沟通
lack of life goal 缺乏生活目标
lack of parental care 缺乏父母关爱
larceny *n.* 偷盗
law enforcement officer 执法官员
law enforcement 执法部门
law-abiding citizen 守法公民
lead a productive / meaningful life 过积极有意义的生活
learning disorder / barrier / block 学习障碍
legal boundary 法律界限

legal guardian 法定监护人
legitimate *a.* 合法的
lengthy jail term 刑期长
lenient *a.* 仁慈的，宽大处理的
life imprisonment 无期徒刑
lower the crime rate
降低犯罪率

mafia *n.* 黑手党
manslaughter *n.*过失杀人
manhunt *n.* 追捕
massacre *vt.* & *vi.* 大屠杀，残杀
media violence 媒体暴力
menace / threaten *vt.* & *vi.* 恐吓，威胁
miscarriage of justice 误判，审判不公
misuse / abuse *vt.* / *n.* 滥用
mobster *n.* 歹徒
money laundering 洗钱
moral degradation 道德水准下降 / 道德退化
morphine *n.* 吗啡
mortal sin 不可饶恕的罪恶
mugging *n.* 行凶抢劫
murder *vt.* & *vi.* / *n.* 谋杀
muscle pain 肌肉疼痛

narcotic *n.* 麻醉药，吸毒者
not legally held 非法持有的

on parole 假释宣誓后获释(获准假释)
organised crime 集团犯罪
outlaw *n.* 逃犯，亡命之徒
outrageous *a.* 蛮横的，残暴的
overdose *n.* 用量过多，毒量过多
overreaction *n.* 反应过度

parental control 家长式的管理和控制
parental indulgence 父母的放纵
pathological feeling 病态的感觉
pathological gambler 病态赌徒
penalty *n.* 处罚
perjured testimony 伪证
physical abuse / punishment
体罚
pickpocket *n.* 小偷
porn shop 色情专售店
possession of firearms
拥有枪支
potential threat 潜在的威胁
powerful punishment 强有力的惩罚
premature death 非正常死亡
proliferation of drugs 毒品传播
prostitute / whore *n.* 妓女
psychoactive drug 神经性药物
public anger / public outrage 公愤 / 民愤
punished according to the law
依法处理

racketeer *n.* 敲诈者，获取不正当钱财的人
rampant *a.* 蔓延的，猖狂的
rape *vt.* 强奸
rapist *n.* 强奸犯
rascality *n.* 歹徒的作为；流氓集团
regulate *vt.* 监管；规范
rehabilitation *n.* 恢复，改过自新
rehabilitation centre 康复中心
relieve the strain on the limited budget 减轻政府财政负担
repeated exposure to violence 经常接触暴力
retaliate *vt. & vi.* 报复
robbery *n.* 盗窃

sabotage *vt. & vi.* 破坏
safeguard *vt.* 保护，捍卫
salvation *n.* 得救，拯救
scandalmonger *n.* 散步流言蜚语的人，到处传播丑闻的人
school shooting 校园枪击案
school violence 校园暴力
second-hand smoke 吸二手烟
self-defense *n.* 自卫
self-protection *n.* 自我保护
serial killer 连环杀手
set sb. free 释放某人
sexual material/stuff on the internet 网上色情内容
sexually explicit material 色情内容
shady dealing 肮脏的交易
shed blood 流血屠杀
shoplifter *n.* 在商店盗窃
slaughter *n.* 残杀，屠杀
source of crime 犯罪的源头
spiritual civilisation 精神文明

steal *vt. & vi.* 偷窃
street dealer 街头毒贩
street gang 街头黑帮
substance abuse 滥用毒品
swindler *n.* 骗子

terrorism *n.* 恐怖主义
thug *n.* 暴徒
turn a blind eye to 无视
turn to crime 付诸于犯罪
tyranny *n.* 暴政，专制

unauthorised *a.* 未经授权的，未经认可的
underdeveloped social skill 较差的社交技能
unstable family life 不稳定的家庭生活

vandal *n.* 故意破坏财产者
vigilante *n.* 义务警员，[美]治安维护会的成员
violence prevention 预防暴力

violent crime 暴力犯罪

white collar crime 白领犯罪

widen one's horizon 开阔视野

widespread *a.* 分布广泛的，普遍的

without permission 未经许可

wrongdoer *n.* 做坏事的人

十 人物描述类

a double chin 双下巴

about / around forty 大约40岁

beard *n.* 胡须

beautiful *a.* 美丽的

beer belly 啤酒肚

black / grey hair 黑 / 花白的头发

blonde *n.* 金发女子

broad face 宽脸

bushy eyebrows 浓密的眉毛

chubby *a.* 丰满的

clean-shaved *a.* 剃刮干净的

dimple *n.* 酒窝

double eyelid 双眼皮

dyed hair 染过的头发

fair hair 金发

fat *a.* 肥胖的

freckle *n.* 雀斑

fringe *n.* 刘海

handsome *a.* 帅气的

have got a ponytail 梳马尾辫

have got a straight / snub nose 有笔挺的鼻子 / 小而扁的鼻子

height *n.* 身高

high cheek bines 高高的颧骨

in one's late teens 在青年时期

long face 长脸

long / short plait 长 / 短辫子

make-up *n.* 化妆

medium height 中等个头

metrosexual *n.* 城市小资男，花样美男

middle-aged *a.* 中年的

mole *n.* 痣

moustache *n.* 小胡子

muscular *a.* 强健的

old *a.* 年老的

oval face 瓜子脸

overweight *a.* 超重的

pimple *n.* 暗疮
plump *a.* 丰满的
plump cheeks 胖乎乎的脸蛋
prominent forehead
突出的前额
quite tall 挺高
rather short 很矮
regular white / yellowish teeth
整齐洁白 / 发黄的牙齿
Roman nose 鹰钩鼻
slender *a.* 纤细的
slim *a.* 苗条的
smart *a.* 时髦的，聪明的
square face 方脸
stout *a.* 结实的
straight / curly / wavy hair 直发 / 卷发 / 波浪发
thick / thin hair 头发多/少
thin *a.* 瘦的
wear hair in a crew cut
理成平头
wear hair pushed back behind ears 将头发拢在耳后
weight *n.* 体重
well-built *a.* 体型好的
whisker *n.* 络腮胡子
with glasses 戴眼镜的
wrinkle *n.* 皱纹
young *a.* 年轻的

十一 教育类

academic atmosphere 学术气氛
academic performance
学习成绩
academic requirement 学术方面的要求
academic year 学年
accommodation *n.* 住所，住房
accounting *n.* 会计学
adapt to society 适应社会
adjunct professor 客座教授
adjust to 调整
admission *n.* 录取
adolescent attitude 年轻人的观点
advanced mathematics 高等数学
advanced research condition 先进的研究条件
adviser *n.* 导师
agriculture *n.* 农业
all-rounded *a.* 全面发展的
applying procedure 申请的程序
arouse one's interest 激发……的兴趣
art *n.* 艺术
assess *vt.* 评估，评定

associate professor 副教授
attend class 上课
Bachelor of Arts 文科学士
Bachelor of Science 理科学士
bachelor *n.* 本科
bilingual education 双语教育
biology *n.* 生物学
blackboard *n.* 黑板
budget one's time 安排好时间
build up one's confidence 树立信心
business study 商业课程

carve out a career 规划职业
cassette *n.* 磁带
cater to different needs 满足不同需求
challenge abroad 国外的挑战
challenge teacher's authority挑战教师的权威
chemistry *n.* 化学
classroom instruction 课堂教学
college *n.* 学院
college catalogue 学院目录
college of education 教育学院
college of engineering 工学院
comprehensive examination 综合考试
comprehensive school 综合学校
compulsory course 必修课
compulsory education 义务教育
computer *n.* 计算机
computer network 计算机网络
cramming / force-feeding *a.* 填鸭式的
creativity *n.* 创造力
credit *n.* 学分
criterion *n.* 标准
cultivate *vt.* 培养，培育
culture shock 文化冲击
curriculum *n.* 课程

degree *n.* 学位
demonstrate one's ability 展示某人的能力
desk *n.* 桌子
develop thinking ability 培养思考能力
development of personality 个性发展
different system of education and research 不同的教育和研究体制
diploma *n.* 文凭
distraction from study 学习分心
do part-time job in leisure time 在空闲时间做兼职
Doctor of Philosophy 哲学博士
Doctor's degree 博士学位
domestic testing system 国内考试体系

dormitory *n.* 宿舍
drop out from school 退学
dropout *n.* 退学

education industry 教育产业
educational innovation 教育革新
educational institution 教育部门
educational opportunity 受教育的机会
elite *n.* 精锐，精英
employment prospect 就业前景
emulate *vt.* 效仿
enrich one's experiences 增加阅历
enrich one's knowledge 丰富知识
enrich one's life experience 丰富人生阅历
enrollment *n.* 招生
eraser / rubber *n.* 橡皮
expensive course 昂贵的课程
experience a new culture 体验新的文化
extracurricular activity 课外活动
extracurricular training 课外补习

fail *vt. & vi.* 不合格
family background 家庭背景
feedback *n.* 反馈
financial burden 经济负担
fine art 美术
first-rate facility 一流的设施
form of assessment 评估方式
formal examination system 正规的考试体系
free education 免费教育
free way of life 无拘无束的生活方式
freshman *n.* 大学一年级学生
further one's study 深造

gain some social experience 获得一些社会经验
geography *n.* 地理
get a decent education 接受良好的教育
get used to 习惯于
government involvement 政府参与
government-funded *a.* 政府出资的
grade *n.* 分数，成绩
graduate school 研究生院
grammar school 语法学校
grasp an opportunity 抓住机会

hatred against learning 厌学
have an incomparable advantage over others 具有别人不可比拟的优势
have extracurricular course 补课

highly qualified teaching staff 高素质的师资队伍
high-quality education 高质量的教育
history *n.* 历史
homesickness *n.* 思乡

impose pressure on sb. 给某人造成压力
independent thinking and learning 独立思考和学习
infant school 幼稚园
information technology 信息技术
institute of physical education 体育学院
institution of higher education 高等教育机构
instructor *n.* (美)大学讲师
intellectual development 智力发展
international education background 国际教育背景
international finance trade 国际金融，贸易
international testing system 国际考试体系
investment in education 教育投资
junior college 大专
junior high school 初中
junior *n.* 大学三年级学生

keen competition 激烈的竞争
knowledge gained from textbooks 书本上获得的知识

lack of understanding 缺乏理解
language and cultural barrier语言和文化障碍
lead a different life 过一种不同的生活
learn how to be independent 学会如何独立
lecture *n.* 讲课，演讲
long academic tradition 悠久的学术传统

MA (Master of Arts) 文科硕士
main subject 主科
major *n.* 专业
make good preparations for 为……做好准备
master interpersonal skills 掌握人际交往的技巧
maths *n.* 数学
MBA (Master of Business Administration) 工商管理硕士
measure the quality of education 衡量教学质量
medical college 医学院

mental development 心智开发
mental frustration 心理障碍
misleading *a.* 误导的
miss out the fun of campus life 错过大学生活的乐趣
MPA (Master of Public Administration) 公共管理硕士
MSC (Master of Science) 理科硕士
multi-media technique 多媒体技术
multiple skills 多种技能
music *n.* 音乐

National College Entrance Examination 高考
non-profit *a.* 非盈利的
normal / teachers' university 师范大学
notebook *n.* 记事本

OHP *n.* 投影仪，投影片，透明胶片
open-book exam 开卷考试
opportunity of immigration 移民机会
optional course 选修课
outlook on life 人生观
overall development 全面发展
overall evaluation 总评
overseas student 留学生

pass *vt.* & *vi.* 通过考试
pencil *n.* 铅笔
philosophy *n.* 哲学
physical education / PE 体育教育
physics *n.* 物理
play truant 逃学
politics *n.* 政治
polytechnic 理工专科学校
Postgraduate Entrance Examination 研究生入学考试
postgraduate *n.* 研究生
practical capability 实际能力
primary school 小学
private school 私立学校
privileged school 重点学校
professor *n.* 教授
promote cross-cultural communication 促进跨文化交际
psychology *n.* 心理学
public school 公立学校
put knowledge into practice 将知识应用于实践

quality education 素质教育

radio and television university 广播电视大学
reform in testing system 考试体系的改革

require course / compulsory course 必修课
rudimentary knowledge 基础知识
ruler *n.* 尺

scholarship *n.* 奖学金
school ethos 校风
school pupil 在校学生
schooling expenditure 教育开支
scope of knowledge 知识面
secondary specialised school 中专
select course 选课
self-betterment *n.* 自我完善
self-funded *a.* 自己出资的
senior *n.* 大学四年级学生
senior high school 高中
sense of accomplishment / achievement 成就感
settle down 定居
skip classes 翘课
sociology *n.* 社会学
sophomore *n.* 大学二年级学生
speak a foreign language fluently 流利地说一门外语
specialised course 专业课
squeeze some time 挤出时间
stimulate interests 激发兴趣
stock investment 股票投资学
strong point 长处
student-oriented education 以学生为中心的教育
student's absence and their laziness 学生的缺课和懒惰
study and live abroad 在国外学习和生活
summer and winter vacations 寒暑假
supplementary course 补课
syllabus *n.* 教学大纲

take a course in 修一门学科
take a part-time job on-line 网上兼职
take up a part-time job 做兼职
tap potential 发掘潜力
teaching and learning environment 教学环境
teaching effectiveness 教学效果
teaching facility 教学设施
teaching faculty 教师队伍师资
teaching principle 教学原则
technical college 职业技术学校
temporary work 临时工作
tenure *n.* 终生教授
term / semester *n.* 学期
tertiary college 专科学校
test content 考试内容
test score 考试分数
testee *n.* 考生
tester / examiner *n.* 考官

testing method 考试方式
testing system 考试体系
testing technique 考试技巧
the latest academic achievement 最新的学术成果
tourism administration 旅游管理
training centre 培训中心
transcript *n.* 成绩单
tuition fee 学费
tuition *n.* 学费
tutorial *a.* 辅导的

undergraduate *n.* 本科生
universal access (美)普及教育
university *n.* 大学
university of aeronautics 航空大学
university / entrance exam 入学考试

video recorder 录像机

well-rounded individual 全面发展的个人
with high mark and poor ability 高分低能
work full-time job during summer vacation 暑假时做全职工作
work part-time job during the semester 学期中做兼职工作
a family of three 三口之家
Arranged Marriage 包办婚姻

十二　家庭类

at the age of 在……岁的时候
attend the elderly 照顾老人
aunt *n.* 阿姨

best man 伴郎
breadwinner *n.* 养家糊口的人
break up 破裂
bridegroom *n.* 新郎
bridesmaid *n.* 伴娘
bride *n.* 新娘
brother *n.* 哥哥
brother-in-law *n.* 小叔子；姐夫；姊妹的丈夫
change one's name 改名
child bride 童养媳
cousin *n.* 堂兄

daughter *n.* 女儿
daughter-in-law *n.* 儿媳妇
divorced *a.* 离婚的
divorce *v.* 离婚
domesticated *a.* 家养的，驯养的
do the laundry 洗衣服
do / wash the dishes 洗碗
engaged *a.* 订婚的

enjoy the happiness of family life 享受天伦之乐

extended family 大家庭

fall in love with sb. at the first sight 一见钟情

family name / surname / last name 姓

family tree 家谱

father-in-law *n.* 岳父，公公

fiance *n.* 未婚夫

fiancee *n.* 未婚妻

first name / given name 名

foster father 养父

full name 全名

generation gap 代沟

genial and devoted wife 温柔尽职的妻子

get married 结婚

grandfather *n.* 爷爷，姥爷

grandmother *n.* 奶奶，姥姥

have a special meaning / significance 有特殊含义

husband *n.* 丈夫

in one's twenties 在某人二十多岁时

independent *a.* 独立的

individuality *n.* 个性

kid *n.* 孩子

marriage status 婚姻状况

marriage *n.* 结婚

married *a.* 已婚的，婚姻的

menu *n.* 菜单

middle name 中间名

mother-in-law *n.* 岳母，婆婆

nephew *n.* 外甥，侄子

nickname *n.* 绰号

niece *n.* 外甥女，侄女

nuclear family 核心家庭

one-child policy 独生子女政策

page boy 小男傧相

pen name 笔名

personality *n.* 个性

pregnant *a.* 怀孕的

raise a child 养育孩子

remarry *vt.* & *vi.* 再婚

retire from 从……退休

sacrifice *v.* 牺牲，献出，舍弃

sibling *n.* 兄弟姐妹

single *n.* 单身

single-parent family 单亲家庭

sister- in-law *n.* 小姨子；嫂子；姑子；弟媳；妯娌

son-in-law *n.* 女婿

stage name 艺名

step mother 继母

the second of six brothers 在六兄弟中排行第二
the wedding 婚礼
traditional idea 传统观念
uncle *n.* 叔叔
widow *n.* 寡妇
widower *n.* 鳏夫

十三 饮食类

wife *n.* 妻子
a good place for socialising 聚会的好地方
abalone *n.* 鲍鱼
afternoon tea 下午茶
appetite *n.* 胃口
apple *n.* 苹果
apple juice 苹果汁
bake *n.* 烘烤食品
banana *n.* 香蕉
banquet *n.* 宴会盛宴
beer *n.* 啤酒
beverage *n.* 饮品
black tea 红茶
Blue Ribbon 蓝带（啤酒品牌）
boil *v.* 煮
braise *v.* 蒸，(用文火)炖（肉）等
brandy *n.* 白兰地
bread *n.* 面包
breakfast *n.* 早餐
Budweiser 百威（啤酒品牌）
butter *n.* 奶油，黄油
cabbage *n.* 卷心菜
cafeteria *n.* 自助餐厅
cantaloupe *n.* 甜瓜
canteen *n.* 食堂
captain *n.* 领班
carbohydrate *n.* 碳水化合物
carrot *n.* 胡萝卜
cauliflower *n.* 花椰菜，菜花
celery *n.* 芹菜
cereal *n.* 谷物
champagne *n.* 香槟
cheese *n.* 奶酪
cheeseburger *n.* 夹干酪和碎牛肉的三明治
cherry *n.* 樱桃
chicken *n.* 鸡肉
chili *n.* 辣椒
Chinese cabbage 白菜

chocolate *n.* 巧克力
cholesterol *n.* 胆固醇
clone *n.* 卡路里
Coca-Cola 可口可乐（饮料品牌）
cocktail *n.* 鸡尾酒
coconut *n.* 椰子
coffee *n.* 咖啡
cold drink 冷饮
condiment / seasoning *n.* 调味品
cooking *n.* 做饭
cucumber *n.* 黄瓜
cuisine *n.* 烹饪
cured meat 腊肉
cut / slice *vt. & vi.* 切片

delicacy *n.* 美味，佳肴
dessert *n.* 甜点
dice *vt.* 把（食物）切成丁
dining hall 餐厅
dinner *n.* 正餐
dinner party 晚宴
dumpling *n.* 饺子
durian *n.* 榴莲

eat out 外出吃饭
eel *n.* 鳝鱼
eggplant / aborigine *n.* 茄子
energy *n.* 能量
egg fried rice 蛋炒饭

Fanta 芬达（饮料品牌）
fast food (industry) 快餐（业）
feast *n.* 盛宴
fiber *n.* 纤维
find favour in people's eyes 受人们的喜爱
first-rate service 一流的服务
fish and chips 鱼和薯条
fish-flavoured *a.* 鱼香的
flavouring *n.* 调味品
freebie *n.* 免费赠品
French fries 炸薯条，炸土豆片
fried chicken 炸鸡
fry *vt. & vi.* 煎
fried squid roll 炝鱿鱼卷

garlic *n.* 大蒜
gateau *n.* 奶油水果蛋糕
genetically modified food 转基因食品
ginger *n.* 姜
grain *n.* 谷粒
grape *n.* 葡萄
greasy *a.* 油腻的
green / red tea 绿 / 红茶
grill *n.* 烤制食物，烤架

hamburger *n.* 汉堡包
healthy food 健康食品
herbal tea 草本茶叶
high / low fat 高 / 低脂肪
hot and spicy 麻辣的
hot dog / hamburger / salad

hot dog 热狗/汉堡/沙拉
hot drink 热饮
hotpot *n.* 火锅
hygienic *a.* 卫生的

ice tea 冰茶
icecream *n.* 冰激凌
ingredient *n.* 烹调的原料
insipid *a.* 淡而无味的

jellyfish *n.* 海蜇
juice *n.* 果汁
junk food 垃圾食品

Kentucky 肯塔基州，肯塔基河
kiwi fruit 猕猴桃

lean meat 瘦肉
lemon *n.* 柠檬
lemonade *n.* 柠檬汁
lettuce *n.* 生菜
lime *n.* 酸橙汁
lobster *n.* 龙虾
longan *n.* 龙眼
lunch *n.* 午餐

mango *n.* 芒果
mash *vt.* 捣碎
mayonnaise *n.* 蛋黄酱
McDonald 麦当劳
medium-rare *n.* 六分熟
milk *n.* 牛奶
milkshake *n.* 奶昔
mince *vt.* 用绞肉机绞
mineral *n.* 矿物质
mineral water *n.* 矿泉水
mix *vt.* & *vi.* 拌
mushroom *n.* 蘑菇
mushroom/spring up 如雨后春笋般出现
Muslim restaurant 清真饭店
mussel *n.* 河蚌
mutton *n.* 羊肉

noodle *n.* 面条
nourishment *n.* 营养

olive *n.* 橄榄
onion *n.* 洋葱
orange *n.* 柑橘
organic food 有机食品，绿色食品
oyster *n.* 牡蛎

peach *n.* 桃子
papaya *n.* 木瓜
pear *n.* 梨
pea *n.* 豆子
peel *vt.* 去皮
processed and fast food 加工过的食品
pepper *n.* 辣椒
Pepsi 百事可乐(饮料品牌)
pineapple *n.* 菠萝
pizza *n.* 比萨

plain-fry *vt.* 清炒
plum *n.* 李子
porridge *n.* 粥
potato *n.* 马铃薯
poultry *n.* 家禽
prawn *n.* 大虾
protein *n.* 蛋白质
public / serving chopsticks 公用筷子

quick-fry *vt.* 爆(炒)

radish *n.* 萝卜
rare *n.* 半熟
recipe *n.* 食谱
red wine 红酒
reserve seats 预订座位
restaurant *n.* 饭店，餐馆
rice *n.* 米饭，大米
rice noodle 米粉
roast *vt.* & *vi.* 烤
roast duck / goose 烤鸭 / 烤鹅
romantic atmosphere 浪漫的氛围

salad *n.* 沙拉
salmon *n.* 鲑鱼
salt *n.* 盐
salty *a.* 咸的
sandwich *n.* 三明治
sausage *n.* 香肠
savory dishes and famous delicacies 美味佳肴和驰名小吃
scallion *n.* 韭菜
sea slug *n.* 海参
seafood *n.* 海味，海鲜食品
Seven-up 七喜(饮料品牌)
shrimp *n.* 虾
simmer *vt.* 煨
smoke *vt.* 熏
snack *n.* 小吃
snake flesh 蛇肉
social interaction 社交活动
soda water 苏打水
soup *n.* 汤
sour *a.* 酸的
soy sauce 酱油
spaghetti *n.* 意大利面条
sparerib *n.* 小排骨
speciality *n.* 特产
spinach *n.* 菠菜
Sprite 雪碧(饮料品牌)
star fruit *n.* 杨桃
starchy food 淀粉类食物
steak / beefsteak *n.* 牛排
steam *vt.* & *vi.* 清蒸
steamed bread 馒头
stew *vt.* & *vi.* 炖，焖
stir-fry *vt.* 炒
strawberry *n.* 草莓
sugar-free *a.* 无糖的
sugar apple 番荔枝
supper *n.* 晚餐

sweet *a.* 甜的

take away food restaurant 外卖餐馆

takeout *n.* 外卖食品

tasty *a.* 美味的，可口的

tea *n.* 茶

the first course (西餐)第一道菜

time-saving and fast 省时快捷

tomato *n.* 番茄

undermine local cuisine and culture 破坏当地的饮食和文化

unique flavour 独特的风味

vegetarian restaurant 素菜馆

vinegar *n.* 醋

vitamin *n.* 维生素

waiter / waitress *n.* 男 / 女服务员

water *n.* 水

water-melon *n.* 西瓜

Western-style restaurant 西餐厅

wheat *n.* 小麦

whiskey *n.* 威士忌

wine list 酒水单

wine *n.* 红酒

wonton *n.* 馄饨

yogurt *n.* 酸奶

十四 全球问题类

a case of inevitable death 绝症

a forgotten group 被遗忘的群体

a male-dominated society 以男性为主导的社会

a sense of safcty 安全感

air pollution 空气污染

alleviate poverty 脱贫

an image recorded by the device CCTV CCTV摄像机拍摄的图像

anti-abortionist *n.* 反对堕胎者

anti-theft device 防盗报警系统

apartment for the old 老年公寓

artificial life 靠人工维持的生命

average lifespan 人均寿命

basic allowance 基本生活费

be laid off 被裁员

birth control 控制人口增长

birth rate 出生率

bring up 抚养培养

build up a better environment 创

造更好的环境

capacity to earn money 赚钱的能力

car crash 撞车

care more about appearances 更注重外表

casualty *n.* 伤亡人员

cater to the demands of the customers 迎合客户的要求

chat with friends 与朋友聊天

childless *a.* 无儿女的

condemned *a.* 受谴责的

competent *a.* 有能力的

competitiveness *n.* 竞争力

complication *n.* 并发症

contraception *n.* 避孕法

control one's feeling 控制感情

crack a criminal case / solve the cases 破案

create more job opportunities创造更多的就业机会

crime rate 犯罪率

cut the tax 减税

deal with pressure properly 正确对待压力

death rate 死亡率

deceitful words and cheats 欺骗性的言语

deformed *a.* 残废的，畸形的

deprive of 剥夺

deter would-be criminals 阻止可能的犯罪

different levels of salary 不同的工资水平

dilemma *n.* 进退维谷，进退两难的局面

discrimination *n.* 歧视

disparity *n.* 差异，不同，不等

do bussiness with 与……做生意

earthquake *n.* 地震

ease the patient's suffering 减轻病人的痛苦

economic advantage 经济优势

educational opportunity 教育机会

eligible children 适龄儿童

embryo *n.* 胚胎

emission *n.* 排放

employment *n.* 雇佣

emptiness *n.* 空虚

enact policies 制定政策

encourage graduates to live and work in the west 鼓励毕业生到西部工作和生活

equality *n.* 平等

establish one's enterprise 创业

euthanasia *n.* 安乐死

family planning 计划生育

family planning policy 计划生育政策

famine *n.* / famish *a.* 饥荒/饥荒的

felony *n.* 重罪
feminism *n.* 女权主义
filial piety 孝顺
flood *n.* 洪水
forest fire 森林大火
forge a social security network focusing on the elderly 建立以老年人为中心的社会保障体系
foster the younger generation培养年轻的一代

gap between the rich and the poor 贫富差距
gender *n.* 性别
genetics *n.* 遗传学
get a son as one's heir 传宗接代
good faith and honesty 诚信
guard against theft 防盗

healthcare *n.* 健康保健
heavy daily work 繁重的日常工作
high-paying *a.* 高工资的
home for the aged 敬老院
homeless *a.* 无家可归的
humanity *n.* 人性，仁慈

illiterate *a.* 文盲的
imbalance *n.* 不平等
impoverished *a.* 贫困的
incest *n.* 乱伦
increase efficiency by downsizing staff 减员增效
inequality *n.* 不平等
inferior *a.* 次于，劣于
infertile *a.* 不育的
interpersonal relationship 人际关系

jobless / out of job / unemployed 无工作的

keep a good balance between …and…保持好……和……的平衡
keep on good terms with others 与别人相处得好

lay off 解雇
life expectancy 预期寿命
life insurance 人寿保险
live under surveillance 在监视之下生活
loneliness *n.* 孤独
long-cherished virtue 长期所珍视的美德
longevity *n.* 长命寿命
lose one's job 失业

make life-and-death decision 做出生死抉择
maltreat *vt.* 虐待
meaningless existence 无意义的生存

medical insurance 医疗保险
monitor camera / video surveillance 监视器摄像头
moral values and standards 道德价值和标准

on strike 罢工
overdependence *n.* 过分依赖
overpopulation *n.* 人口过度

pace of life 生活节奏
painless *a.* 无痛的，不痛的
pass away 死亡
pension *n.* 养老金
perform euthanasia / mercy killing
实行安乐死
pollution / contamination *n.* 污染
poor region 贫穷地区
population aging 人口老化
population census 人口普查
population control 人口控制
population explosion 人口爆炸
pregnancy *n.* 怀孕
prejudice *n.* 偏见
pressure *n.* 压力
prevention of burglary 防盗
privacy *n.* 隐私
private enterprise 私人企业
professional skills 职业技能
prolong human life 延长人的生命
promotion *n.* 晋升
put an end to one's misery 结束一个人的苦难

raise the living standard of poor people 提高贫困人口的生活水平
raise the overall economic level 提高整体经济水平
reform *n.* 改革
refugee *n.* 难民
remedial *a.* 补救性的
remedial method 补救办法
reputation *n.* 名誉，声誉
requirement of customers 客户的要求
restart one's own business 二次创业
retirement home 退休之家
right to attend school 上学的权利

safety equipment 安全设施
sandstorm *n.* 沙尘暴
satisfy the requirements of society 满足社会的需求
self-deceiving *a.* 自欺欺人的
sexual discrimination 性别歧视
shelter *n.* 庇护所
shift one's focus on other things 转移注意力到别的事物上
sit in cafe 坐在咖啡厅里

social chaos 社会混乱
social security 社会保障
social stability 社会稳定
social status 社会地位
social welfare 社会福利
SOE(state-owned enterprise) 国有企业
sparsely-populated *a.* 人口稀少的
special skills and techniques 特殊技能
specialised institution 专门机构
spend one's reminding days happily 安度晚年
spiritually *ad.* 精神上地
strain *n.* 劳累，紧张
subsistence *n.* 生存
suffer lots of pressure 忍受许多压力
support oneself 养活自己
supportless *a.* 无助的
surveillance system 监控系统
survive in the severe competition 在激烈的竞争中生存
sustain *vt.* 支撑
symptom *n.* 症状

take it easy 放轻松，别紧张
terminally ill 绝症
the laid-off 失业者
the only child 独生子女
thickly-populated / denslypopulated *a.*人口稠密的
totally relaxed 完全放松
true-hearted / whole-hearted *a.* 真心的

unattended *a.* 没人照顾的
uneasy *a.* 不自在的
unemployment *n.* 失业
unemployment rate 失业率
unscrupulous *a.* 肆无忌惮的
upbringing *n.* 抚养，培养
upset *vt.* 使烦心，使不高兴

virtue *n.* 美德

war *n.* 战争
way of thinking 思维方式
well-being *n.* 福利
work overtime 加班

十五 兴趣爱好类

antique *n.* 古玩

be crazy about 对……着迷
be enthusiastic about 喜欢
be fond of 喜欢
be keen on 热衷于

card *n.* 牌
ceramic *n.* 木刻
cloisonne *n.* (嵌丝式)景泰蓝
commemorative stamp 纪念邮票
cooperative and competitive 合作和竞争的
cultivate cooperative spirit 培养合作精神

dart *n.* 飞镖游戏
digital camera 数码相机

embroidery *n.* 绣花
entertainment *n.* 娱乐

festive lantern 花灯
frisbee *n.* 飞盘

go to disco 蹦迪

handwork *n.* 手工

interesting and informative programme 有趣并使人增长知识的节目
ivory carving 象牙雕刻

jigsaw *n.* 拼图

karaoke *n.* 卡拉OK

leisure activity 休闲活动

mad with 对……满腔热情
make sb. energetic and vigorous 使人精力充沛、充满活力
make sb. stay fit and healthy 使某人保持身材和健康
marble *n.* 弹珠
mould one's temperament 陶冶性情

night life 夜生活

paper-cut *n.* 剪纸
pixel *n.* （相机）像素
play cards 打牌

recreational activity 娱乐活动
release sb. a bit 让人放松一点
resolution *n.* 分辨率

shadow play 皮影戏
skateboard *n.* 滑板
skipping rope / jump rope 跳绳
snapshot *n.* 快照
spare time / free time 业余时间
stamp collecting 集邮
stimulate appetite and exercise muscles
增强食欲和锻炼肌肉
stone carving 石雕
take photos 照相
time-consuming *a.* 耗费时间的
train sb. to have a quick response 训练某人的快速反应能力
video game 电子游戏
watch films / TV programmes看电影 / 电视节目
YoYo 溜溜球

十六 假日类

carnival *n.* 嘉年华
ceremony *n.* 宴会
Children's Day 儿童节
Christmas Day 圣诞节
Double Ninth Festival 重阳节
Dragon Boat Festival 端午节
Father's Day 父亲节
fiesta *n.* 宗教节日
Good Friday 耶稣受难节
greeting *n.* 问候
holiday and festival 假日
lantern *n.* 灯笼
Lantern Festival 元宵节
lucky money 压岁钱
lunar calendar 阴历
Mid-Autumn Festival 中秋节
moon cake 月饼
Mother's Day 母亲节
National Day 国庆节
pay a New Year visit 拜年
perform dragon dance and lion dancc 舞龙舞狮
Pure Brightness Festival
清明节
rice dumpling 粽子

Saint Valentine's Day 情人节
Spring Festival 春节
stick doublets on the door
贴春联
Thanksgiving Day 感恩节
the first day of the lunar year 大年初一
winter solstice 冬至
Women's Day 妇女节
Youth Day 青年节

十七 家乡住宅类

abound with/abundant 盛产
all-the-year-round tourist resort 四季旅游胜地
barley *n.* 大麦
basin *n.* 盆地
bathing beach 海滨浴场
be located / situated in 位于
be put down on the list of the important historical sites 被列入重点历史古迹的名单
be given special protection 被给予特殊的保护
be renovated in 翻新
be surrounded by 被……包围
be well-decorated 装修精美
be well-furnished 布置得体
block of flats 公寓楼
brick *n.* 砖
cathedral *n.* 大教堂
ceiling *n.* 天花板
coastal city 沿海城市
column *n.* 柱（子）
commercial centre 商业中心
cottage *n.* 农舍
cover *vt.* 覆盖
curtain *n.* 窗帘
desert scenery 沙漠风光
dining room 饭厅
display cabinet 陈列用的橱柜
famous mountains and great rivers 名山大川
fish tank 鱼缸
flat roof 平屋顶
freestanding *a.* 独立式的
French window 落地窗
fridge *n.* 冰箱
garage *n.* 车库

garden architecture 园林建筑
Gothic cathedral 哥特式教堂
grassland *n.* 草原
green belt 绿化带
grotesque stone 奇形怪状的石头
gulf *n.* 海湾
have a history of 有……年的历史
hectare *n.* 公顷
hi-fi *n.* 高保真音响设备
high-rise flat 高层公寓
hilly land 丘陵地

idyllic landscape 田园风光
in a fine / prime location 好位置
in the east / south / west / north of 位于……的东/南/西/北边
intact *a.* 完好无损的

landscape *n.* 风景
latitude *n.* 纬度
layout *n.* 布局
locate *vt.&vi.* 坐落于
longitude *n.* 经度
luxurious interior decoration 豪华的室内装修

manpower and material resources 人力和物力
mansion *n.* 大厦
medium-sized *a.* 中等的
microwave oven 微波炉
monument *n.* 纪念碑

natural cave 天然洞穴
natural environment 自然环境
natural resources 自然资源
natural spectacle 自然奇观

occupy an area of 占地面积达……
official residence 官邸
on both sides of the street 在街道的两边
on the conner 在拐角
on the eastern / southern / western / northern coast of 位于……的东 / 南 / 西 / 北海岸
ornament *n.* 装饰品，装饰
outer / inner wall 外 / 内墙

pendent lamp 吊灯
peninsula *n.* 半岛
plateau *n.* 高原
potted plant 盆栽植物
prairie *n.* 草原
quadrangle dwelling 四合院

real estate 房地产
rolling sea 波涛汹涌的大海

scenery *n.* 风景，风光，景色
scenic spot 景点
seaside city 海滨城市

shabby *a.* 简陋的
shutter *n.* 百叶窗
single-story house 平房
sink *n.* 水槽
sloping roof 斜屋顶
south-facing *a.* 朝南的
spacious *a.* 宽敞的
speciality *n.* 特产
spectacular *a.* 壮观的
square kilometre 平方公里
stair *n.* 楼梯
storeroom *n.* 储藏室
strait *n.* 海峡
stretch long and unbroken 延绵不绝
suburban / urban area 郊区 / 市区
summer resort 避暑胜地
symbol of Chinese history 中国历史的象征

toilet washroom *n.* 洗手间
tower block 塔楼
town planning 市政规划
traditional style 传统风格
two-story building 两层建筑

ventilation *n.* 通风
villa *n.* 别墅

wall lamp 壁灯
wardrobe *n.* 衣柜
well-known *a.* 著名的
well-preserved *a.* 保存完好的
with a good view/fine scenery 有美丽的景致
wooden floor 木地板

十八 工作类

accountant *n.* 会计
adviser *n.* 顾问
architect *n.* 建筑师

baker *n.* 面包师
barber / hairdresser *n.* 理发师
butcher *n.* 屠夫

carpenter *n.* 木匠
CEO 首席执行官
chef *n.* 厨师长
chemist *n.* 化学家
civil servant / governor 公务员

dentist *n.* 牙医

designer *n.* 设计师
doctor *n.* 医生；博士

economist *n.* 经济学家
electrician *n.* 电工
engineer *n.* 工程师
farmer *n.* 农民
firefighter *n.* 消防队员

gardener *n.* 园丁

human resource 人力资源

interviewee *n.* 面试者
interviewer *n.* 面试官

job responsibility 工作职责

lawyer *n.* 律师
library *n.* 图书馆

nurse *n.* 护士

pilot *n.* 飞行员
plumber *n.* 水管工
police office *n.* 警察办公室

receptionist *n.* 接待员

sales assistant 销售员
scientist *n.* 科学家
secretary *n.* 秘书
soldier *n.* 士兵
supermarket *n.* 超市
supervisor *n.* 监督者

tailor / dressmaker *n.* 裁缝
teacher *n.* 老师

vacant position 空缺职位

十九　厨房器具类

basin *n.* 脸盆
bowl *n.* 碗
bucket *n.* 桶

can *n.* 罐
carton *n.* 纸盒
chopsticks *n.* 筷子
cloth *n.* 布
coffee maker 咖啡机

cooker *n.* 电饭煲
corkscrew *n.* 开瓶器
cup *n.* 杯子

dishwasher *n.* 洗碗机
dustbin / wastebin *n.* 垃圾箱

food mixture 搅拌机
freezer *n.* 冰库

frying pan 煎锅

glass *n.* 杯子

jug *n.* 水壶

kettle *n.* 烧水茶壶

knife *n.* 刀

mop *n.* 墩布

mug *n.* 有柄杯子

plate *n.* 碟子

refrigerator / fridge *n.* 冰箱

sack *n.* 麻布袋

saucer *n.* 茶碟

shelf *n.* 架子

spoon *n.* 汤勺

tap *n.* 水龙头

tea towel 擦拭茶巾

teapot *n.* 茶壶

tissue *n.* 餐巾纸

washing machine 洗衣机

二十 文化及旅游类

A Dream of Red Mansion《红楼梦》

a fascinating book 精彩的书

a novel about the war time 关于战争年代的书

adapt a novel to the stage 将小说搬上舞台

an exciting and absorbing book 引人入胜的书

an illustrated book 带插图的书

an informative and instructive book 使人增长知识并有教育意义的书

an inspiring book 励志书

best-seller *n.* 畅销书

biography *n.* 自传

broaden one's horizon 开阔眼界

camping *n.* 露营

character *n.* 角色

detective novel 侦探小说

expand one's knowledge 拓展知识面

Forbidden City 紫禁城

get one's peak 达到某人的鼎盛时期

help understand the culture 帮助了解文化
historical novel 历史小说

increase investment on infrastructure 增加基础设施的投资
itinerary *n.* 路线，旅行计划

Journey to the West 《西游记》
journey / trip *n.* 旅行

make a novel into a movie 将小说改编成电影
mausoleum *n.* 陵墓

Outlaws of the Marsh 《水浒传》

plot *n.* 情节
popular novel 通俗小说
Potala Palace 布达拉宫
protect old buildings and historical relics 保护古老建筑和历史遗迹
publicity *n.* 公众的注意；宣传

remote area 偏远地区
remove one's bad mood 让坏心情一扫而光

romance novel 爱情小说
Romance of the Three Kingdoms 《三国演义》

seascape *n.* 海景
smooth one's nerves after a whole day's hard work 舒缓经过工作一天后的劳累神经
splendid scenery 壮丽景观
statue *n.* 雕像
Strange Tales from Make-Do Studio 《聊斋志异》
Summer Palace 颐和园
swordsman fiction / martial arts novel 武侠小说

temple *n.* 寺庙
Terracotta Warrior 兵马俑
Three Gorges on the Yangtze River 长江三峡
tour guide 导游
tourist attraction 旅游胜地
travel book 游记
travelling *n.* 旅游

universal language 通用语言

West Chamber 《西厢记》

二十一 数学、物体及颜色类

10 cm long 10厘米长
10 cm tall 10厘米高
10 cm thick 10厘米厚
10 cm wide/broad/across 10厘米宽
1/2：a/one half
1/3：a/one third
1/4：a/one fourth/a quarter
3/4：three fourths/three quarters
18/55：eighteen over fifty-five
100 millimetres 毫米(mm)=centimetre 厘米(cm)
100metres=1 kilometre千米(kin)
1 inch 英寸=25. Millimetres 毫米
12 inches 英寸=1 foot 英尺=30. 48 centimetres 厘米

addition *n.* 增加
amber *a.* 琥珀色的
azure *a.* 天蓝色的

baked clay 陶土
ball *n.* 球状物
beige *a.* 米色的
blue *a.* 蓝的
blunt *a.* 钝的
bottle-green *a.* 深绿色的
brown *a.* 棕的

chocolate *a.* 红褐色的，巧克力的
circle *n.* 圆圈
circular *a.* 圆形的
coffee *a.* 咖啡色的
conical *a.* 圆锥形的
copper *n.* 铜
cube *n.* 立方体
curved *a.* 卷曲的
cylindrical *a.* 圆柱形的

dainty in design 样式别致的
delicate *a.* 精巧的
diamond-shaped *a.* 钻石型的
division *n.* 除
durable *a.* 耐用的

exquisite *a.* 精美的，高尚的

flat *a.* 扁平的

gold *a.* 金的
green *a.* 绿的
grey *a.* 灰的

height *n.* 高度

hollow *a.* 空心的

inlay *vi.* 镶嵌
iron *n.* 铁

jade green 翡翠绿

khaki *a.* 土黄色的

labour-saving *a.* 省力的
length *n.* 长度
light / dark / bright colour 浅色 / 深色 / 亮色

multiplication *n.* 乘

narrow *a.* 狭窄的
navy/sky blue 海军蓝的/天蓝的

octagon *n.* 八角形
olive green 橄榄绿
opaque *a.* 不透明的
orange *a.* 橙色的
oval *a.* 椭圆的

pentagon *n.* 五边形 / 五角大楼
perimeter *n.* 周长
pink *a.* 粉红的
purple *a.* 紫色的
pyramid *n.* 金字塔

rectangle *n.* 长方形，矩形
red *a.* 红的
ring *n.* 环形物
rose *a.* 玫瑰色的
rough *a.* 粗糙的
round *a.* 圆的

scarlet *a.* 鲜红的
semi-circular *a.* 半圆形的
sharp *a.* 尖锐的，锋利的
silver *n.* 银
smooth *a.* 平滑的
solid *a.* 结实的
sphere *n.* 球体，球面
spiral *n.* 螺旋体
square *a.* 正方形的
straight *a.* 直的
subtraction *n.* 减

thick *a.* 厚的
thin *a.* 薄的
tin *n.* 锡
transparent *a.* 透明的
triangle *n.* 三角形
triangular *a.* 三角形的

violet *a.* 紫罗兰色的

waved *a.* 波浪形的
white *a.* 白色的
width *n.* 宽度
wool *n.* 羊毛

yellow *a.* 黄的

zinc-plating *a.* 镀锡的

二十二 音乐类

abstract painting 抽象画
accordion *n.* 手风琴

blues *n.* 布鲁斯（风格）

campus song 校园歌曲
cartoon *n.* 卡通
channel *n.* 海峡
classical music 古典音乐
composer *n.* 作曲家
computer *n.* 电脑
concert *n.*音乐会
correspondent *n.* 通信者，通信员
country music 乡村音乐

discovery *n.* 发现
documentary *n.* 记录本
drum *n.* 鼓

erhu *n.* 二胡

fiddle *n.* 提琴
film *n.* 电影
flautist *n.* 长笛演奏者
flute *n.* 长笛
folk music 民间音乐

graceful rhythm 优美的韵律
guitar *n.* 吉他
guitarist *n.* 吉他弹奏手

improvise *vt.&vi.* 即兴创作

jazz，*n.* 爵士乐
journalist *n.*记者

light / gentle music 轻音乐
lyrics *n.* 歌词

magazine *n.* 杂志
mass media 大众媒体
melodious *a.* 悠扬的
melody *n.* 旋律
music hall 音乐厅

nature program me 自然类节目
newspaper *n.* 报纸

opera *n.* 歌剧

painter *n.* 画家
pianist *n.* 钢琴家
piano *n.* 钢琴
pipa *n.* 琵琶
pop music 流行音乐

quick rhythm 快节奏的

radio *n.* 收音机

remind sb. of the past 勾起某人对过去的回忆
reporter *n.* 记者，通讯员
rock and roll 摇滚乐

satellite TV 卫星电视
saxophonist *n.* 萨克斯演奏家
sentimental *a.* 感伤的，多愁善感的
soap opera 肥皂剧
soul *n.* 灵魂
soulful *a.* 充满热情的，深情的
strong beat 节奏强劲的

talk show 脱口秀
traditional music 传统音乐
tuneful *a.* 悦耳的
violin *n.* 小提琴
waist drum 腰鼓

二十三　性格类

ambitious *a.* 雄心勃勃的，有抱负的

conservative *a.* 保守的
considerate *a.* 体贴的

dynamic *a.* 有活力的

frank *a.* 坦率的
friendly *a.* 友好的

good-natured *a.* 脾气好的

handy *a.* 手巧的
hardworking *a.* 工作勤奋的
honest *a.* 诚实的
hospitable *a.* 好客的
humorous *a.* 风趣的

intelligent *a.* 聪明的

noisy *a.* 吵闹的

open-minded *a.* 开明的

polite *a.* 有礼貌的

romantic *a.* 浪漫的

sluggish *a.* 怠慢的
sociable *a.* 好交际的
stylish *a.* 时髦的
sympathetic *a.* 有同情心的

tolerant *a.* 宽容的

versatile *a.* 多才多艺的

worldly person 世故的人

二十四 污染类

a thick layer of dust 厚厚一层灰土
achieve high efficiency 取得高效率
air pollution 空气污染
air quality 空气质量
arouse people's awareness of environmental protection 唤起公众的环保意识
carbon dioxide 二氧化碳
carbon monoxide 一氧化碳
chemical *n.* 化学物质
classify *vt.* 分类
clean-up *n.* 清除
coal *n.* 煤
conscious preserver 自觉的环保者
conservation *n.* 保护
conservation area 保护区
conservation law 保护法
construction *n.* 建设
contaminate *vt.* 污染
cut down 砍下

declining *a.* 衰退的，减少的
decomposition *n.* 分解，腐烂
deforestation *n.* 森林砍伐
densely-populated *a.* 人口密集的
destroyer *n.* 破坏者
develop a modern waste disposal technology 开发现代垃圾处理技术
dirty air 污浊的空气
disaster *n.* 灾难
disposable packaging and item 一次性的包装和用品
dispose of 处理
drainage *n.* 排水

ecology *n.* 生态学
EL Nino “厄尔尼诺”现象
enforce *vt.* 执行
enforce penalty 实施处罚
environmental deterioration 环境恶化
environmental standard 环境标准
environmentalist *n.* 环保人士
environmental-friendly material 环保材料
equipment to purify the waste water 废水净化设备
erosion *n.* 腐蚀
exhaust *n.* 排气管
exhaust *vt.* 用尽，耗尽

fatal disease 致命的疾病
fertiliser *n.* 化肥
financial incentive 经济激励

fine *vt.* 罚款
forbid construction during the night 禁止晚间施工
forbid the blowing of car horn禁止鸣笛

global warming 全球气候变暖
greenhouse effect 温室效应

high decibel 高分贝

ignorance *n.* 无知
illegal dumpling 非法倾倒垃圾
incinerate *vt.* 焚化
increase energy efficiency 提高能源利用率
industrialisation *n.* 工业化
intensify environmental management 加强环境管理

lack resources and manpower 缺乏资源和人力
land subsidence 地陷
limit the bussiness time of entertainment enterprises 限制娱乐行业的营业时间
limlt the numbcr of cars running in the street 限制路上的汽车数量
litter
vt.&vi. （在公共场合）乱扔（废弃物）

modernisation *n.* 现代化

nature reserve 自然保护区
nitrogen *n.* 氮
non-renewable *a.* 不可再生的

overdevelopment *n.* 过度开发
ozone layer 臭氧层

pass regulation 通过立法
perish *vt.&vi.* 腐烂
pesticide *n.* 杀虫剂
plant tree 植树
play music loudly 大声地放音乐
poisonous material 有毒物质
pollution *n.* 污染
preventive *a.* 预防的
purify the air 净化空气
purify water in rivers and lakes 净化河流和湖泊里的水

reconstruct *vt.* 重建
recycle *vt.* 再循环
reforestation *n.* 重新造林
restriction *n.* 限制
reuse *vt.* 再利用

sandstorm *n.* 沙暴
sanitary *a.* 卫生的，清洁的
severity *n.* 严重
sewage purification 污水净化
sewage treatment 污水处理
short-sighted *a.* 目光短浅的
soil *n.* 土壤

sound pollution 噪音污染
sulphur dioxide 二氧化硫
supervision and management of enterprise environment 企业环境监管
sustainable development 可持续发展

take stronger and harsher measure 采取更强有力的措施

take measures 采取措施
toxic *a.* 有毒的

unbearable noise 难以忍受的噪音
waste management law 垃圾管理条例
work out better ways to purify the air 找出更好的方法净化空气

二十五 购物和服饰类

a big sale 大甩卖
apron *n.* 围裙
arts and crafts shop 工艺美术品商店
attire *n.* 服装

bargain *n.* 便宜货
bathing suit 浴衣
blouse *n.* 女衬衫
boutique *n.* 时装店
bowtie *n.* 蝶形领结

cafeteria *n.* 自助餐厅
casual *a.* 休闲的
catwalk show 时装表演
cellphone / telephone *n.* 手机
clingy *a.* 依附的，易于粘住的
consumer *n.* 消费者
consumer goods 生活品
consumption *n.* 消费
convenient store 便利店
cosmetics *n.* 化妆品
cotton *n.* 棉花
credit card 信用卡

daily necessity 日常必需品
decent *a.* 得体的
department store 购物中心
dress in a self-expressive way 穿着有个性
dress properly 穿着得体
drugstore / pharmacy *n.* 药店

elegant *a.* 雅致的
elevator *n.* 电梯
embroider *vt.&vi.* 刺绣

escalator *n.* 自动扶梯
evening suit / dress 晚礼服

flea market 跳蚤市场
food supermarket 食品超市
for sale 待售
fur *n.* 毛皮
furniture *n.* 家具

garish *a.* 俗丽的，穿着花哨的
glamour *n.* 魅力
go with 与……相配
grocery store 杂货店

hardware store 五金店
high-heeled *a.* 高跟的
household electrical appliance 家用电器
in good taste 有品位的
in vogue / fashion 正在流行的

jacket *n.* 夹克
jeans *n.* 牛仔裤
jewellery *n.* 珠宝
jump into one's clothes 匆忙地穿上衣服
jumper / wollen sweater 羊毛衫

leather *n.* 皮革
lighting shop 照明器具商店
linen *n.* 亚麻布
lingerie *n.* 女士贴身内衣
loose *a.* 宽松的
low-heeled *a.* 低跟的

marketing *n.* 市场营销
men's/women's wear 男式 / 女士服装
merchandise / goods *n.* 商品
miniskirt *n.* 超短裙
musical instrument shop 乐器店

neckline *n.* 领口
nylon *n.* 尼龙

old-fashioned *a.* 过时的
on sale / discount 减价 / 打折
optician's 眼镜店
out of season 过季的，不合时宜的
out of stock 断货
overcoat *n.* 外套大衣

packaging *n.* 包装
password *n.* 密码
payment by check 支票支付
plain clothes 便服
product *n.* 产品
promotional campaign 促销活动
pullover *n.* 针织紧身套头衫

pyjamas *n.* 睡衣裤

raincoat *n.* 雨衣
ready-made *a.* （衣服）现成的
record bar 唱片店
refund *n.* / *vt.* 退款

scarf *n.* 围巾
shipment *n.* 运载的货物
shirt *n.* （男式）衬衣
shop online 网上购物
short / long-sleeved *a.* 短 / 长袖的
sports sweater 运动服
silk *n.* 丝绸
skirt *n.* 裙子
sleeveless *a.* 无袖的
snack bar 小吃店
sock *n.* 短袜
stage costume 戏服
stationery *n.* 文具店
stereo equipment 立体声音响设备
stocking *n.* 长筒袜
street vendor 街头小贩
sweater *n.* 毛衣
swim suit 泳装

temperament *n.* 气质
thin and light 又轻又薄的
tights *n.* 紧身衣
time-consuming *a.* 耗时的
traditional Chinese handicraft 中国传统手工艺品
trend / tendency *n.* 潮流，趋势
trousers *n.* 长裤
Tari-shirt *n.* T恤衫
turnover *n.* 流通

under-dressed *a.* 穿着不正式的
underpants *n.* 内裤
uniform *n.* 制服

v-necked *a.* V型领的
vogue area 潮流区

waistcoat *n.* 背心
watchmaker's shop 钟表店
waterproof *a.* 防水的
well-fitting *a.* 合身的

二十六　疾病与健康类

allergic to 对……过敏
allergy *n.* 过敏症
anti-anxiety drug 抗焦虑的药物
anti-stress technique 减压技巧
asthma *n.* 哮喘

biological makeup 生理结构
bruise *n.* 瘀伤

caffeine *n.* 咖啡因
cancer stick *n.* （香烟）癌棍
cardiovascular disease 心血管病
carnivore *n.* 食肉动物
cholera *n.* 霍乱
cold *a.* 冷的

eat a well-balanced diet 均衡饮食
emotional turmoil / mood swing 情绪波动
emphysema *n.* 肺气肿
excessive caffeine 过量的咖啡因
excessive workload 工作负荷大

fast-paced *a.* 节奏快的
fatigue *n.* 疲乏，疲劳
fever *n.* 发烧
flu *n.* 流感

handle / manage stress 处理压力
hangover *n.* 宿醉（酒醒后的头痛和不舒服）
headache *n.*头痛
heart disease 心脏病
hectic life 快节奏的生活
hepatitis *n.*肝炎

in hospital 住院
in the hospital 在医院工作，去医院
induce stress 诱发压力

kidney disease 肾病
kidney stone formation 肾结石

lump *n.* 肿块

maintain the necessary physiological balance 维持必要的生理平衡
malaria *n.* 疟疾
massage *n.* 按摩
measles *n.* 麻疹
migraine *n.* 偏头疼
mumps *n.* 流行性腮腺炎

natural instinct 天性

nonsmoker *n.* 不抽烟的人

on diet 节食
omnivorous *a.* 杂食的，什么都吃的

passive smoking 被动吸烟
perfectionism *n.* 完美主义
perfectionist *n.* 完美主义者
physiological dependence 生理依赖
pneumonia *n.* 肺炎
poor digestion 消化不良
pose serious risks to health 对健康造成严重威胁
pulmonary disease 肺病

rash *n.* 皮疹，疹子
rejuvenate *vt.* 恢复精神，恢复活力
relieve stress 减压
resist its temptation 抵挡住它的诱惑
respiratory failure 呼吸衰竭
rheumatism *n.* 风湿病

SARS 非典型肺炎
sick *a.* 生病的
sleep disturbance 睡眠问题
No Tobacco Day 戒烟日
smoking room 吸烟室
sneeze *vi.* 喷嚏
soothing music 轻松的音乐
staple food 主食的
stomachache *n.* 胃病
symptom *n.* 症状，征兆

take deep breath 深呼吸
take out the feeling on 把情绪发泄到
tedious *a.* 单调乏味的
tension between coworkers 同事间的紧张关系
therapy *n.* 治疗
toothache *n.* 牙痛
top killer 头号杀手

ulcer *n.* 溃疡

vegetable *n.* 蔬菜
vegetarianism *n.* 素食主义者
vomit *vt.&vi.* 呕吐

water impunlty 水质不洁
weariness *n.* 疲倦,厌烦
well-being *n.* 安康,安宁,福利

二十七　体育与健康类

withdraw symptom 戒烟后的症状
a balanced diet 均衡饮食
a diet moderate in sugar 含糖适中的饮食
a pro-active constructive lifestyle 积极的生活方式
an abuse of performance-enhancing drugs 滥用有助于提高成绩的药物
adhere to 坚持不懈
aerobic exercise 有氧运动
alcoholic drink 含酒精的饮料
animal flesh 动物的肉
anorexia *n.* 食欲减退，厌食
artery *n.* 动脉
arthritis *n.* 关节炎

badminton *n.* 羽毛球
balanced food intake and food variety 均衡的食物摄入和均衡的食品种类
baseball *n.* 棒球
basketball court 篮球场
be good for one's health 对健康有益
bicycle commuter 骑单车上班的人
boxing *n.* 拳击
build up one's physique 锻炼身体
burn up / consume 消耗，烧掉
blood circulation 血液循环

calisthenics *n.* 健美体操，健身操
calorie *n.* 卡路里
championship *n.* 冠军身份，冠军称号
cheerleader *n.* 拉拉队长
cholesterol *n.* 胆固醇
cholesterol intake 胆固醇的投入量

calorie intake 热量的摄入量
collaboration *n.* 协作
collectivism *n.* 集体主义
commercialisation of sports 体育商业化
competitive spirit 竞赛精神
constitution *n.* 体质
consumption of meat 肉的消费量
convenience food 方便食品
coronary heart disease 冠心病
corporate sponsor 赞助公司
cricket *n.* 板球
cycling *n.* 骑自行车

dart *n.* 飞镖
decrease your travel time 减少路途时间

deplete *vt.* 耗尽，使衰竭
develop intellectual resources 开发智力
diabetes *n.* 糖尿病
digestion *n.* 消化吸收
discus *n.* 铁饼
disorder *n.* 失调，紊乱
diving *n.* 潜水，跳水
do sports 锻炼

ease the strain 减轻压力
excessive fat 过量的脂肪
elite and community-based sports 精英运动和社区运动
elite athlete 运动员精英
elite performer 表演精英
embark on a healthy lifestyle 开始健康的生活方式
energetic / vigorous *a.* 精力充沛的，积极的
energy consumption / expenditure 能量消耗
energy intake 能量摄入
excessive protein 过量的蛋白质
extracurricular activity 课外活动

fast food outlet 快餐店
faster, higher, stronger 更快，更高，更强
fatty and fried food 肥腻和油炸的食物
fitness craze 健身热
food intake 食物的摄入量
food selection 食物的选择
food variety 食物种类丰富
foods low in fat and high in fibre 低脂肪高纤维食品
football field 足球场
football / soccer *n.* 足球
fruitarian *n.* 常吃水果的人

genetic factor 基因方面的因素
go hiking/expedition 徒步旅行
go in for 参加，从事
go to health club 去健身俱乐部
go walking 去散步
golf *n.* 高尔夫
gorge *n.* / *vt.* & *vi.* 暴食
growth-hormone abuse 滥用生长素
gymnasium / gym *n.* 健身房

have a picnic 去野餐
high-calorie snack 高热量零食
highly processed food 经过高度处理的食品
home team / host team 主队，东道主队
hormone *n.* 荷尔蒙，激素
horse racing / jockey club 赛马 / 马术俱乐部
hypertension *n.* 高血压

immune system 免疫系统
indolent *a.* 懒惰的
indoor stadium 室内运动场
instinct *n.* 本能
intercollegiate game 校际间比赛
International Olympic Committee Delegate 国际奥委会代表团

jogging *n.* 慢跑
joyful *a.* 快乐的
junk food 垃圾食品

karate / judo *n.* 柔道

lack of exercise 缺乏运动
lean meat 瘦肉
live a sustainable and active lifestyle 采取积极的生活方式
living habit 生活习惯
low-energy expenditure 低能量消耗
lower the risk of diabetes 降低患糖尿的危险

maintain a good health 保持健康
maintain sensible eating and exercise habits 保持合理的饮食和运动习惯
martial arts / kung fu *n.* 武术
mass sports activity 群众体育运动
medicare *n.* 医疗保险
meet special nutrient needs 满足特殊的营养需要
metabolise *vt.* 产生代谢变化
mineral *n.* 矿物质
moderate exercise 适当的运动
mortality *n.* 死亡率
motor / car racing 赛车
muscular *a.* 肌肉的，强健的

national pride 民族自豪感
national team 国家队
nimble *a.* 敏捷的
non-competitive Physical recreation 非竞赛性的体育娱乐活动

Olympic Games 奥林匹克运动会
opening ceremony 开幕式
osteoporosis *n.* 骨质疏松症
outscore *vt.* 得分超过
overeat *vt.&vi.* 吃得过多

pedal *n.* 脚踏板
physical a nd mental health 身心健康
physical development 生理发展
physical fitness 体格健康
physical-fitness programme 健身计划
physical / manual labor 体力活
physique *n.* 体格，体型
play bowling 打保龄球

play even 打成平局
poor dietary habit 不良饮食习惯
poor dietary 不良饮食
public arena 公共体育馆
put on / lose weight 增 / 减重

radiant *a.* 容光焕发的
referee *n.* 裁判
refresh *vt.* 使精神振作，使精力恢复
regular exercise 经常性运动
relaxation *n.* 松弛，缓和
relieve *vt.* 减轻，解除
relieve tension and pressure 消除紧张和压力
renew *vt.&vi.* 使恢复
reveal the countries' cultural elements 展示国家文化
roller skating 溜旱冰
rope skipping 跳绳
rowing *n.* 划船
rugby *n.* 橄榄球
running *n.* 跑步

sailing *n.* 航海
skiing *n.* 滑雪
slimness *n.* 苗条
spirit of fair play 公平竞争精神
sponsorship *n.* 赞助
sports event 体育赛事
sports facility 体育设施
sports field 运动场
sports talent 体育天才
sportsmanship *n.* 运动家精神
stamina *n.* 毅力，持久力，精力
strenuous sports 激烈的体育运动
surplus fat 多余的脂肪
swimming *n.* 游泳
swimming pool 游泳池

table tennis 乒乓球
taijiquan / shadow boxing 太极拳
team work 团队协作
tennis *n.* 网球
tension *n.* 紧张，状态不安
the average life expectancy 平均寿命
tie game 平局
tournament *n.* 锦标赛

universal participation 全球参与

vim / vigor *n.* 活力，精力
visiting team 客队
vitality *n.* 活力生命力
volleyball *n.* 排球

weight gain 体重增加
weight lifting 举重
weight loss 体重减轻
withdraw participation 退出比赛

yoga *n.* 瑜伽

二十八 学生与学习类

a college orientation session 新生介绍会
abandon oneself 放任
affect school achievement 影响学校成绩
after school activity 课后活动
an immense asset 极大的财富
anti-social behaviour 反社会的行为
aspirant *n.* 有抱负的人

be acquainted with 与……熟悉
be addicted to 上瘾的
be immersed in 全心投入
brain drain 人才外流
bring into full play 充分发挥

cocky *a.* 骄傲的，自大的
core competency 核心能力
couch potato 终日懒散在家的人
cultural assimilation 文化同化
cultural penetration 文化渗透

degenerate *vi.* 退化
distinguish between fantasy and reality 辨明虚幻与现实
distinguish right from wrong 辨明是非
distracting *a.* 分心的

eccentric *n.* 行为古怪的人
emotionally damaging 伤感情的
extroverted *a.* 外向的

forget food and sleep 废寝忘食
fruitful *a.* 有成效的

global awareness 全球意识
go astray 误入歧途

impracticable / unpractical / unrealistic *a.* 不切实际的
indigenous *a.* 本土的
instill *vt.* 逐步地灌输
integrate with 与人交往
intellectual *n.* 知识分子
juvenile delinquency 青少年犯罪

lag behind 落在后面
lifelong memories 毕生的记忆
living allowance 生活费

moral decline 道德水准下降
moral value 道德观
multimedia device 多媒体设备

naive *a.* 幼稚的

outlandish *a.* 奇装异服的
overindulge in / wallow in 沉迷于

passive *a.* 被动的
peer influence 同伴的影响
preserve cultural identity 保护文化特性
pornography *n.* 色情文学
prejudice / bias *n.* 偏见，成见
promote friendship 增进友谊
put you a step ahead of the rest 优于他人

remove loneliness and disorientation 消除孤独感和不适应感
returned student 归国留学生
revel in 酷爱，沉迷于
run into trouble 遇到麻烦
school authority 校方
schoolfellow *n.* 同学，校友
self-control *n.* 自控能力
shortage of talent 人才短缺
shortsighted *a.* 近视的，目光短浅的
stereotype *n.* 老套
stimulate one's interest 激发兴趣
strong will 坚强的意志

video arcade / hall 游戏机室
violent episode 暴力情节
virgin mind 纯洁无瑕的思想
virtue *n.* 美德，优点，功效

worldly wise 见多识广的

二十九 科学技术类

accumulated knowledge and experience 经验和知识的积累
accurate *a.* 精确的
advanced *a.* 先进的
anti-biotic *n.* 抗生素
astrophysics *n.* 天体物理法
attachment / enclosure *n.* 附件

BBS(bulletin board system) 网上论坛
become addictive上瘾
biological technology 生物技术
break in 入侵；非法进入
caller display 来电显示
car culture 汽车文化
change the way of life 改变生活方式
chat online 网上聊天
computer programming 计算机编程
computer virus 电脑病毒
computer-aided research project 计算机辅助研究项目
computer-assisted instruction 计算机辅助教学
computer's role in industry 计算机在工业中的作用

congested road 拥挤的道路
congestion *n.* 拥堵
computer game 电脑游戏
creative *a.* 创造性的
curiosity about new technology 对新技术的好奇心
cybercrime *n.* 网络犯罪

different functions 不同的功能
digital age 数码时代
digital camera 数码相机
distance learning 远程教育
DIY(do it yourself) 自己动手
download information下载信息

easier and more comfortable travel 更便利和更舒适的旅行
easy commuting 便利的通行
e-commerce *n.* 电子商务
experiment *n.* 试验

genetic engineering 基因工程
GPS(Global Positioning System) 全球卫星定位系统
great mobility 更强的机动性

hacker *n.* 电脑黑客
handy and convenient 方便的
highly intelligent computer 高智能电脑

imagination *n.* 想象力
impact *vt.* & *vi.* / *n.* 影响
improve efficiency 提高效率
in a noticeable way 以明显的方式
in case of emergency 以防紧急情况
in common use / widely used 广泛应用
industrial revolution 工业革命
infant mortality 婴儿死亡率
influence *n.* / *vt.* 影响
information *n.* 信息
information explosion 信息爆炸

innovative *a.* 革新的
Internet account 网上账户

keyboard *n.* 键盘
knowledge-based *a.* 以知识为基础的

laser technology 激光技术
look at things from a new point of view 从新的角度看待事物

machine translation 计算机翻译
machinery 机器
medical advancement 医学进步
medical breakthrough 医学突破
microchip *n.* 芯片
modern invention 现代发明
mouse *n.* 鼠标
movie website 电影网站

nanotechnology *n.* 纳米技术
novelty *n.* 新奇事物

online advertising 网上广告
online anonymity 网上匿名
online shopping 网上购物
organise files 整理文档

password *n.* 密码
penicillin *n.* 青霉素
phone bill 电话单
portable *a.* 可携带的
printer *n.* 打印机
process documents 处理文件

research a topic 研究一个课题
robot *n.* 机器人

save time and money 节省金钱和时间
scientific research and discovery 科学研究和发现
security flaw 安全漏洞
send e-mail 发邮件
simultaneous interpretation 同声传译
sophisticated *a.* 尖端的
surf the Internet 上网

the newer…the better……越新，……越好
the newer, the best… 最新的是最好的
think and do things in another way 用不同的方式思考和办事情

upgrade *vt.* 升级

vedio recorder 录像机
virtual office 虚拟办公室

web page 网页
wonder drug 灵丹妙药
a chain collision 连环撞车

三十 交通类

airplane / aeroplane *n.* 飞机
ambulance *n.* 救护车

bike / bicycle *n.* 自行车
boat *n.* 船
brake *n.* 刹车
bridge toll *n.* 过桥费
bus *n.* 公共汽车

car insurance 汽车保险
car theft 汽车盗窃
careless driving 粗心驾驶
car-pool *n.* 合伙用车的一伙人
casualty *n.* 伤亡者

commit traffic offence 交通违规
crowded condition / congestion 人山人海

drunk driving 酒后驾驶

emit *vt.* 排放
excessive speed 超速

fatigue driving 疲劳驾驶
ferry *n.* 渡轮
financial pressure 财政压力
fire engine 消防车

give way 让路

headlight *n.* 车前灯
head-on collision 两车相撞
helicopter *n.* 直升飞机
high-speed transportation network 高速运输网络
highway / expressway *n.* 高速公路
horn *n.* 喇叭
horsepower *n.* 马力

land transportation 陆地运输
maglev *n.* 磁悬浮

marine transportation 海上运输
metro / subway / tube/underground *n.* 地铁
motorbike / motorcycle *n.* 摩托车

one-way road 单行线
overpass *n.* 天桥
overweight vehicle 超载车辆

parking *n.* 停车场
pedestrian *n.* 行人
public transportation 公共交通
rear-view light / mirror 后视镜
red / green / amber light 红 / 绿 /黄灯
roadside *a.* 路旁的
run the red light 闯红灯
rush / peak hour 交通高峰期

safety first 安全第一
ship *n.* 船
sidewalk *n.* 人行道
sleeper *n.* 火车的卧铺车厢
speed limit 车速限制
steering wheel 方向盘

taillight *n.* 车尾灯
taxi *n.* 出租汽车
traffic accident 交通事故
traffic flow 交通流量
traffic lane 车道
traffic light 交通信号灯
traffic regulation 交通规则
trailer *n.* 拖车
train *n.* 火车
trams / trolley bus *n.* 电车
tunnel *n.* 隧道

第四章 雅思重点词汇辨析

abnormal, disordered, uncommon

abnormal　　*a.* 不正常的，不规则的。指现象或行为，比如气候的异常。

disordered　　*a.* 杂乱的，混乱的，失调的；精神或身体有病的。

uncommon　　*a.* 不平常的，罕见的，非凡的，杰出的。指很少经历、很少见到的情况。

absurd, silly, ridiculous, stupid, dumb

absurd　　*a.* 荒谬的，可笑的，不合理的。指不符合常识/逻辑或者违反真理。

silly　　*a.* 愚蠢的，糊涂的。指由于头脑简单而显得愚笨。

ridiculous　　*a.* 可笑的，荒唐的，滑稽的。指愚昧无知，含有蔑视成分。

stupid　　*a.* 呆头呆脑的，愚蠢的，迟钝的。表示天生呆头呆脑，反应迟钝的。

dumb　　*a.* 美国俚语，表示理解力差。

adhere, abide, conform, comply

adhere　　*vi.* 粘附，紧粘，遵守，坚持。adhere to

abide　　*vi.* 遵守，同意。abide by

conform　　*vi.* 遵照，遵守，符合。conform to

comply　　*vi.* 遵守，服从。用于正式的场合。comply with

agree with, agree to, agree on

agree with　　与sb. 搭配，意为同意某人。
agree to sth.　　常与sth. 搭配使用，表示同意某事。
agree on　　在……上达成一致意见。

aggravate, increase, strengthen, reinforce, intensify

aggravate　　*vt.* 加重(负担、罪行、病情等)，使之恶化。
increase　　*vt.* & *vi.* 增加(指数量上的增加)。
strengthen　　*vt.* & *vi.* 加强，巩固，增强。相当于to become stronger。
reinforce　　*vt.* 增援(军队或警察的行动)，加强。
intensify　　*vt.* & *vi.* 使变得更强烈，加强，相当于to become more intense。

alone, lonely, exclusively, solely

alone　　*ad.* 表示只有一个人，独自，单独。
lonely　　*ad.* 带有感情色彩，表示孤独、孤单的状态。
exclusively　　*ad.* 强调对象的专一性/专有性。
solely　　*ad.* 表示单独的、唯一的。

ambiguous, obscure

ambiguous　　*a.* 指文章或讲话中，意思可能有多种理解，令人捉摸不定，会引起歧义的。
obscure　　*a.* 语气最强，指晦涩难懂，模糊的；含糊不清的。obscure to

append, complement, supplement

append　　*n.* 附加，特别指文字添加、附加。append to
complement　　*n.* 补充物/补足。complement to / of
supplement　　*n.* 增补，补充；增刊。supplement to

● as, though, although

as　　conj. 引出让步状语从句时只用于倒装语序结构中，语气强于另外两个连词。

though　　conj. 与although在意义上几乎毫无区别，在习惯用法上有以下差异：

1. though可引出倒装语序的让步状语从句，although则不能。
2. though可与even连用，although则不能；在as though结构中用though，不能用although。
3. though可以置于从句末，而although则不能。
4. 引出省略句时，通常用though。

although　　conj. 较正式，语气比though强。

● assign, allocate, allot

assign　　vt. 表示一种权威性的分派，派定，指定。assign to

allocate　　vt. 拨出，拨给，分配。指为了特定的需要而从整体中拿出一部分，比如钱和物。

allot　　vt. 表示裁决性质的分配。allot to

● premise, presumption

premise　　n. 假定，假设，前提。论述的前提/基础，指某个命题。

presumption　　n. 推测；假定，设想。指任意的接受未经证实的事物在未被证伪前是正确的；presumption that。

● basic, fundamental, elementary, essential, vital

basic　　a. 基本的，基础的。表示具体事物/抽象事物。basic to

fundamental　　a. 根本性的，基础的。fundamental to

elementary　*a.* 初步的，初级的。primary / elementary school 小学
essential　*a.* 必要的，不可缺少的。essential to / for
vital　*a.* 极其重要的，必不可少的。vital to / for

- **before long, long before**

before long　不久以后=soon
long before　很久以前=a long time ago

- **be going to, be about to, be to do**

be going to　侧重打算和计划要做的事。be going to do sth.
be about to　表示事情动作马上、很快就要发生。be about to do sth.
be to do　侧重意志，计划，安排。

- **because, because of**

because　*conj.* 连接两句话。
because of　后接词或短语。

- **choose, pick, elect, select**

choose　*vt. & vi.* 以理由为基础作出选择，强调明智地挑选。
pick　*vt.* 挑选，强调主观性强。
elect　*vt.* 选举，特别指大会的选举。
select　*vt.* 挑选，指经过权衡之后进行的挑选 / 选择。

- **conception, thought, idea, notion**

conception　*n.* 概念，指具有理性的概括。
thought　*n.* 指具体的思想活动。具有一定的系统性的思想 / 思维。
idea　*n.* 表示观念，观点，思想。
notion　*n.* 指代念头或者想法。

• condemn, reproach, scold, blame

condemn　*vt.* 谴责，多用于政府/政治的谴责。用于比较正式的、严肃的场合。

reproach　*vt.* (书面语)责备，斥责，表示不满。reproach for / with

scold　*vt. & vi.* 责骂，唠唠叨叨地责备。

blame　*vt.* 把……归咎于，责怪，责备，指责。blame on / for

• controversy, argument, debate, dispute, quarrel

controversy　*n.* 争论，辩论，争议。指团体之间在某一重大事件上的争议。

argument　*n.* 争执，争吵；辩论，通过陈述理由、提出论证以阐明自己观点。argument about / over / with; argument for / against

debate　*n.* 辩论，讨论，争论。常指分组/个人的争论，为了辨清真理。debate with

dispute　*n.* 争论；争执。指激烈的长时间争论。dispute about / on / over / with / against

quarrel　*n.* 争吵；不和；吵闹。既可表示温和的争论，也可表示激烈的争吵，多指吵架。quarrel with / between / about

• considerate, considerable

considerate　*a.* 体贴的；体谅的；考虑周到的。considerate of / to / toward

considerable　*a.* 相当大的，相当多的；值得考虑的；重要的。

• contradictory, opposite, conflicting, contrary

contradictory　*a.* 矛盾的，对立的。比如一方真实，另外一方

	虚假。contradictory to
opposite	*a*. 相反的，对立的。多用于方向、位置的相反。opposite to
conflicting	*a*. 相矛盾的，冲突的。指兴趣，感情，利益等，强调事物的冲突。
contrary	*a*. 相反的，对立的。指观点、态度、主张等，表示存在本质区别。contrary to

• continuous, constant, incessant, continual

continuous	*a*. 连续的，不断的。强调中间不停顿。
constant	*a*. 不停的，接连不断的，持续的。强调始终如一地经常出现。
incessant	*a*. 不停的，连续的，持续不断的。强调令人厌烦地重复出现。
continual	*a*. 多次重复的，频繁的。表示时断时续的发生。

• denote, suggest, imply, indicate, hint

denote	*vt*. 表示，预示，代表。特指一个词的字面意义，比较正式，多用于论文中。
suggest	*vt*. 建议，提议。表示通过词语或符号暗示内容。suggest that
imply	*vt*. 暗指，暗示，意味着。imply that
indicate	*vt*. 指示，指出。表示同语或符号可以清楚明白地表示内容。indicate that
hint	*vt*. 暗示，示意。hint that

• decrease, diminish, decline, reduce

decrease	*vt*. & *vi*. 减；减少，减小。强调逐渐地下降或减少的过程。 decrease in / to
diminish	*vt*. & *vi*. (力量、势力)减少，减小，缩减。强调

	由于某种原因而减少，这种减少可以造成能够为人们所察觉的后果或损失。
decline	*vt.* & *vi.* (数量、数字、价格、比率)下降，下跌，减少，衰退。
deduce	*vt.* 减少，缩小，降低。指通过人为的方法在数量、规模、范围等方面减少，也可以指在地位、重要性方面降低等级。

● discrepancy, variation, unlikeness, distinction, divergence, dissimilarity

discrepancy	*n.* 不一致，不符，差异，不一致之处。是指本应一致或匹配的事物，因意外条件而不一致，造成了事物间的差异。discrepancy between / in
variation	*n.* 变化，变动。指相同事物等级或种类的差别。
unlikeness	*n.* 不同，不像，相异。经常暗含着较大和较明显的差别。
distinction	*n.* 区别，分清。通常的意思为相似的事物间的细节差异，只能通过仔细的检查才能知道。distinction between
divergence	*n.* 分歧，分离，相异。指差异性逐渐地改变。
dissimilarity	*n.* 不同。是指在其他方面很相似或非常类似的事物间的差异。

● element, factor, ingredient, component, constituent

element	*n.* 元素，组成部分，要素。
factor	*n.* 因素，要素，侧重指原因。
ingredient	*n.* (混合物的)组成部分；(烹涮的)原料；(构成)要素，因素。
component	*n.* 零部件；(某事物的)组成部分；成分。

constituent n. 成分，要素，组成部分。

● embark, commence, initiate, originate

embark vi. 上船(或飞机等)。embark on a ship上船；embark on / upon从事，着手，多指开始一项困难的重大工作。

commence vt. & vi. 表示“开始”。commence doing；commence with；commence to

initiate vt. 开始，创始，开始实施。initiate in / into

originate vt. 发源，来自，产生。originate in / with / from

● evident, plain, distinct, obvious, apparent

evident a. 明显的；明白的。常指包含一定的迹象。evident to / that

plain a. 清楚的，明白的，平易的。指因为浅显而清楚。

distinct a. 与其他不同的，有区别的。指轮廓或意义清晰。distinct from

obvious a. 明显的；显著的。obvious to；obvious that

apparent a. 明显的，显而易见的，明白无误的。表示根据某事进行推理，从而得出明显的结论。apparent that

● expect, hope, anticipate

expect vt. 预计……可能发生(或来到)；预料；预期。强调一种期待的心情。expect that

hope vt. & vi. 希望，盼望。强调一种积极向上的心态，表示一种憧憬和希望。hope to

anticipate vt. 预期，期望，预料。不仅指一种等待的心情，还表示为预防不好的结果而采取预防行为。anticipate doing；anticipate that

● excite, motivate, stimulate, encourage, inspire

excite vt. 刺激；使兴奋；使激动

motivate　　*vt.* 给……动机，刺激，激发。强调激发动力去做某事。

stimulate　　*vt.* 刺激，激励，使兴奋，促使。强调刺激反应的结果。stimulate to；stimulate into

encourage　　*vt.* 鼓励，促进。含有"使增强勇气或给予希望"的意味。

inspire　　*vt.* 鼓舞，激励，驱使。常常带有"启迪，启发"的意思。inspire to

• feeble, fragile, faint, weak

feeble　　*a.* 虚弱的，无力的。常用来形容人的行为等虚弱。

fragile　　*a.* 脆弱的，易碎的，脆的，易损坏的。

faint　　*a.* 虚弱的，眩晕的。通常指不是天生体质上的虚弱而是由于某种原因造成的暂时情况。faint for / from / with

weak　　*a.* 弱的，虚弱的，衰弱的。既可以指身体虚弱的、无力的，也可引申为在力量、权力、技能、影响等方面有欠缺或软弱。

• feeling, passion, sensation, emotion

feeling　　*n.* 感觉，触觉。指一般的情绪、感觉。

passion　　*n.* 热情，激情，欲望，盛怒。passion for

sensation　　*n.* 感觉，知觉。指人体感官受到外部刺激时产生的感觉、知觉。

emotion　　*n.* 情感，感情。指喜怒哀乐等较激动。

• found, set up, construct, build, establish

found　　*vt.* 建立；建造

set up　　*vt.* & *vi.* 建立，创立

construct　　*vt.* 建造，构成。指用各种材料建成一个整体，着重构筑。

build　　vt. & vi. 一般指建立、修建(桥梁、房子)。

establish　　vt. 建立，设立，创办。有稳固建成的意思(建立学校、政府等)。

- **prohibit, forbid, ban**

prohibit　　vt. 禁止，不许。指通过颁布法令来绝对禁止某事物。prohibit doing sth.

forbid　　vt. (以法令、规定等)禁止。指绝对禁止，要求人们能遵守政府的意愿。

ban　　vt. 禁止，禁令。指具有权威性的禁止。ban on / against

- **former, preceding, prior, foregoing, previous**

former　　a. 从前的，早前的，旧时的；在前的；(两者中)前者的。通常与latter所指事物构成对比。

preceding　　a. 在前的，在先的；前面的。指在时间或地点上占先。

prior　　a. 在先的，在前的，居先的。有“更为重要”的意思。

foregoing　　a. 前面的；前述的，上述的。指之前讲话的内容。

previous　　a. 先的，前的，以前的。指已经存在或发生过的。

- **genius, talent, gift, aptitude, knack**

genius　　n. 天资，天赋，才华。表示与生俱来的非凡才能。genius for

talent　　n. 天才，天资。指先天具备、后天培养的才能。talent for

gift　　n. 天赋，才能。gift for

aptitude　　n. 天资，才能，颖悟。强调获得某种知识和技能的速度快，或掌握熟练。aptitude for

knack　　n. 本领，熟练技巧。knack of / for

● inquiry, examination, probe, research, investigation

inquiry	*n.* 询问，打听，质询。inquiry about / into
examination	*n.* 检查，调查。指细致的调查。examination to / of
probe	*n.* / *vt.* & *vi.* 刺探；探索，彻底调查。probe into
research	*n.* (学术)研究，调查，探究。research in / into / on
investigation	*n.* 正式研究，调查。指为了弄清事实真相而展开的调查。investigation on / of / into

● inorder that, inorder to

inorder that	后接句子，表示目的。
inorder to	后接动词原形，表示目的。

● in place of, in the place of

in place of	代替
in the place of	在……地方

● in secret, in the secret

in secret	秘密地，暗自地，偷偷地。一般用作状语。
in the secret	知道内情，知道秘密。一般用作表语。

● instead, instead of

instead	副词，放在句首或句末，代替的意思。
in stead of	介词短语，放在句中，升替的意思。

● interrupt, interfere, disturb, intervene

interrupt	*vt.* & *vi.* 打断(讲话或讲话人)，中断，插嘴，阻碍。
interfere	*vi.* 妨碍，冲突，抵触，介入，干涉，干预。interfere with / in
disturb	*vt.* 妨碍，打扰。表示有困难产生。
intervene	*vi.* 干涉，干预，调停。较为正式。intervene in / between

• involved, complex, complicated, intricate

involved　*a.* 复杂的，纠缠的，混乱的。强调若是把各部分混在一起将是难以区分的。

complex　*a.* 复杂的，错综复杂的，难懂的。

complicated　*a.* 复杂的，难懂的，结构复杂的。强调各部分之间的细微关系。

intricate　*a.* 难理解的，难分析的。强调各部分交织在一起很难区分或分析。

• join, associate, unite, relate, combine, connect

join　*vt. & vi.* 连结，使结合。暗指使本无关联的事物有接触或联系。join to / together / up

associate　*vt. & vi.* 联想，把……联想在一起。表示空间或逻辑上共同发生或存在。associate with

unite　*vt. & vi.* 使联合，统一，使团结。强调多个个体结合。

relate　*vt. & vi.* 使有联系。指一种真实的连接，客观存在。relate to / with

combine　*vt. & vi.* 使结合，使联合。强调整体性。combine with

connect　*vt. & vi.* 连接，连结。指一种松散的联合。connect with / to

• judge, deduce, conclude, infer

judge　*vt. & vi.* 判断，断定，认为。强调对前提进行判断及衡量。judge that

deduce　*vt.* 演绎，推论。指有依据地进行逻辑推理而得出结论。deduce from; deduce that

conclude　*vt.* 推断出，断定。指由已知事实总结出一定的命题、结论、意见、概念。conclude that

infer　　*vt.* 推断，推论；猜想。强调由已知事实推出结论。infer from; infer that

● kind, kindly, benevolent, benign

kind　　*a.* 亲切的；和蔼的。强调心地善良，仁慈，乐于助人。kind to sb.

kindly　　*a.* 亲切的，和蔼的，温和的，爽快的。强调善良，有同情心，仁慈。

benevolent　　*a.* 仁慈的，厚道的，有爱心的。强调宽容，仁慈，有同情心。

benign　　*a.* 仁慈的，亲切的。强调上级的仁慈和长者的慈爱、温柔。

● landscape, scenery, scene, view, sight

landscape　　*n.* (陆上的)风景，景色。

scenery　　*n.* 风景，景色。指一个国家或某一地区的自然风景。

scene　　*n.* 景色，景象，(舞台)布景。指自然形成的或者人工造成的。

view　　*n.* 景色，风景画、风景照片。多指从远处或高处所见的景色。

sight　　*n.* 名胜，观光地。侧重指旅游观光的风光，包括城市景色、自然景色或者人造景物。

● legitimate, lawful, legal, legislation

legitimate　　*a.* 合法的，合法婚姻所生的。表示法律承认或习惯已认可的。

lawful　　*a.* 合法的，法律上正当的。指一定的控制、强制行为具有法律依据。

legal　　*a.* 法律的，法定的，合法的。

legislation　　*n.* 立法，法律的制定(或通过)。

more than a year, more than one year

more than a year 一年多。

more than one year 超过一年(两年或三年等)。

natural, normal, regular, typical

natural *a.* 自然的，有关自然界的，天然的，自然状态的，蒙昧的，未开垦的。

normal *a.* 正常的，正规的，标准的，(人的精神，身体)正常发育的。

regular *a.* 规则的，有规律的；固定的；正常的；定期的，定时的。

typical *a.* 典型的，有代表性的。特有的，独特的；表现特征的。typical of

obtain, get, gain, acquire, attain

obtain *vt.* 得到，获得。强调挑选某物。

get *vt.* 获得，得到，赢得。

gain *vt. & vi.* 得到，获得，赢得(战争、诉讼等)。

acquire *v.* 取得，获得，学到，养成。强调是一种逐渐习得的过程。

attain *vt. & vi.* 达到，获得。attain to

of the day, of a day

of the day 每一天的，当时的，当代的。

of a day 暂时的，不长久的。

pay, salary, wage, income

pay *n.* 付，支付，付款给，付款，偿还债务。pay for / to

salary *n.* 薪资，薪水。指月薪，其来源于salt，是古罗马支付文官的方式之一。

wage　　n. 薪水，报酬。指周薪。

income　　n. 收入，收益，所得。常指定期的收入。

- **preference, choice, option, selection, election**

preference　　n.更加喜爱，偏爱；偏爱的事物(或人)。

choice　　n. 选择机会；选择权；选择能力。表示从一系列的人或物中进行挑选。choice of / between

option　　n. 选择；选择权；可选择的东西；选修科目。

selection　　n. 被挑选出的人(或物)；精选品；选手。

election　　n. 选举；当选。

- **peculiar, strange, odd, queer, eccentric**

peculiar　　a. 奇怪的；乖癖的；罕见的。(个人或团体)特有的，独有的；独特的。peculiar to

strange　　a. 奇怪的，陌生的。强调不常见的，生疏的。

odd　　a. 奇特的，古怪的。强调"违反正常情况"。

queer　　a. 奇怪的，古怪的。口语体，指神经不正常的，不舒服的。

eccentric　　a. (人、行为等)古怪的，反常的。

- **practicable, practical, feasible, pragmatic**

practicable　　a. 能实施的，可行的。表示一种可能性，但是结果不一定可行。

practical　　a. 实践的，实际的，有实用价值的，注重实效的，有实际经验的。

feasible　　a. 可行的，可实行的。feasible to / for

pragmatic　　a. 实际的；实干的；(依据前因后果)系统论述史实的；实用主义的。

- **proper, fit, suitable, appropriate**

proper　　a. 适合的，恰当的，合乎体统的，循规蹈矩的，正派的，高尚的，严格意义上的。proper to

fit　　a. 适合于。fit for

suitable　　a. 适当的，合适的，适宜的。意味着适合某种情况。suitable to / for

appropriate　　a. 适当的，恰当的，相称的。指适合于特殊的人及场合 / 地位等。appropriate to / for

- **profit, advantage, benefit, interest**

profit　　n. 利润，盈利，收益，红利。

advantage　　n. 有利条件，优点，优势。take advantage of

benefit　　n. 利益，好处，优势。兼指物质及精神的好处。

interest　　n. 利息，股份，股权。

- **produce, make, compose, design, invent, create, manufacture**

produce　　vt. & vi. 生产，制造，创作。指通过劳动加工而生产产品。

make　　vt. 做；制造，建造；形成，组成。

compose　　vt. 作(诗，曲等)；构(图)；组成，构成。compose of

design　　vt. & vi. 设计，构思，绘制，计划，谋划。指制作某物之前深思熟虑地构思。

invent　　vt. 发明，创造。多用于科技上的发明创造。

create　　vt. 创造，创作，设计。指有目的地把原材料制成新产品。

manufacture　　vt. (大量)制造，加工。manufacture from / into

- **puzzle, embarrass, perplex, confuse, bewilder**

puzzle　　vt. 使迷惑，使为难，使窘困。强调不理解。

embarrass　　vt. & vi. 使窘迫，使不好意思，使局促不安。embarrass with / by

perplex　　vt. 使杂乱，指疑虑，使困惑，使费解。

confuse　　vt. 把……弄糊涂，使困惑，把……混同，混

	淆。confuse with
bewilder	*vt.* 语气最重，指使迷惑，使糊涂，难住。强调非常困惑，通常表现为心智紊乱。

● quotation, citation, reference

quotation	*n.* 引用，引证，引文，语录。指不改动原文，照搬引用。
citation	*n.* 引用，引证，列举。指引用某人的话语。
reference	*n.* 提及，涉及，参考，参照，参考文献，出处。指参考，经过改写，不是原样照抄。

● region, district, zone, area, vicinity

region	*n.* 地区，地带，行政区域。指行政区划上较大的地区，如自治区。
district	*n.* 区，辖区，行政区，地区，区域，地带。指行政区划上的小范围地区，如县级区。
zone	*n.* 带；气候带，动植物分布带。指特定的地方、地带，如经济特区。
area	*n.* 地区，区域。面积较大，但不指行政单位。
vicinity	*n.* 附近地区，近处，近邻。vicinity of

● respectable, respectful, respective

respectable	*a.* 值得尊敬的，有好名声的。
respectful	*a.* 尊重他人的，恭敬的。
respective	*a.* 单个的，分别的。

● restrain, refrain, constrain

restrain	*vt.* 抑制，遏制。指通过管束阻止某事发生，是及物动词，习惯用法是restrain sb. (sth.) from doing。
refrain	*vi.* 忍住，抑制，节制，戒除。refrain from
constrain	*vt.* 强迫，限制，束缚，拘禁。

• resolution, resolve, decision, determination

resolution　　*n.* 决心，决定，(会议等的)正式决定，决议。含极强的主观能动性。resolution to

resolve　　*n.* 解决，解答，消除(疑惑等)。语气较强，强调下决心干一件具体的事。

decision　　*n.* 决定，决心，判断，结论。既可指重大的/一般的决定或决心，又可指在某种情况下作出果断的抉择。

determination　　*n.* 坚定，果断，决断力。常指坚决肯定地决断，强调顽强的意志力。determination to

• roam, ramble, stroll, wander, linger

roam　　*vt.* & *vi.* 漫步，漫游，流浪。常指自得其乐的无固定目标的漫游。roam about / through / around

ramble　　*vi.* 闲逛，漫步。一般指走走停停，心情愉快。ramble about/over/through

stroll　　*vi.* 散步，溜达，缓步走，流浪，(为谋生)辗转各地。指无目的地悠闲而缓慢地漫游。

wander　　*vt.* & *vi.* 漫游，闲逛，流浪，徘徊。指无目的地到处徘徊或闲荡。wander about / off / over / through

linger　　*vi.* 继续逗留，徘徊，磨蹭，拖延。linger over; linger on

• robber, burglar, bandit, thief, gangster, arson

robber　　*n.* 抢劫者，强盗。指以暴力、威胁等行为强行夺取他人财物。

burglar　　*n.* 夜贼，破门盗窃者。指夜间破门撬窗行窃。

bandit　　*n.* 强盗，土匪。指在乡间/小地区的帮派势力，使用恐吓或暴力行窃的人。

thief　　*n.* 贼，小偷。

gangster　　*n.* (结成团伙的)歹徒，匪盗，流氓。指结伙进行各种非法活动的武装歹徒。

arson　　*n.* 纵火(罪)，放火(罪)。

● serious, important, vital, significant

serious　　*a.* 严重的，危急的，令人担心的。

important　　*a.* 重要的，重大的。强调值得重视。important to / for

vital　　*a.* 生命的，维持生命所必需的。表示极其重要的，生死攸关的。vital to / for

significant　　*a.* 有意义的，意义(或意味)深长的，重要的，重大的，值得注意的。

● secure, assure, insure, ensure

secure　　*vt.* 使安全，握紧。指确保不会发生意外或不幸。secure from / against

assure　　*vt.* 向……保证，担保，使确信，使放心。assure of

insure　　*vt.* 为……投保，接受保险。强调为确保某一结果而预先采取某一措施。

ensure　　*vt.* 保证，担保。强调事实上的保证。

● sensitive, sentimental, sensible, sensational

sensitive　　*a.* 敏感的，易受伤害的；灵敏的，灵敏度高的。sensitive to

sentimental　　*a.* 多愁善感的，感伤的。

sensible　　*a.* 明智的，合情理的；意识到的，察觉到的。sensible of

sensational　　*a.* 引起轰动的，轰动社会的；感觉的，知觉的。

● specially, especially, particularly

specially　*ad.* 特别地，专门地。强调为做某事而“专门地、特意地”。

especially　*ad.* 特别，尤其，格外。多用于正式文体。

particularly　*ad.* 特别，尤其，具体地，明确地。

- **spread, propagate, circulate, distribute**

spread　*vt.* & *vi.* 使伸展，使延伸。指传播疾病、思想、文化、习惯等。

propagate　*vt.* 传播，使普及。指自觉地努力推广、宣传。

circulate　*vt.* & *vi.* 使传播，传递，传阅。指在一定范围内传播物品、刊物或思想、语言等。

distribute　*vt.* 分发，分配。指把具有一定数量的东西分成若干等份进行分发。distribute to / among

- **strain, stress, tension, pressure**

strain　*n.* 拉紧，拖紧，伸张，尽力，使劲。指某人为克服外界压力而造成的身心和情绪等方面的压抑。

stress　*n.* 压力，紧张，压迫。着重指承受外来的压力，也指由于某种原因而引起的心理、生理或情绪上的紧张。stress on

tension　*n.* (精神上的)紧张；紧张局势，紧张状况。

pressure　*n.* 困扰，艰难；[物]压力，压强。

- **the number of, a number of**

the number of　后接谓语动词单数，表示数量。

a number of　后接谓语动词复数，表示许多。

- **transition, transaction, transformation, transfer, transform, transmission**

transition　*n.* 过渡，过渡时期；转变，变迁，变革。transition from / to

transaction	*n.* 办理，处置，执行，交易，业务，买卖。
transformation	*n.* (外观或性质的)变化，转变，变形，变质。
transfer	*n.* 转移，转让；(工作的)调动；(旅途中的)换乘，改变路线。transfer from / to
transform	*v.* 使改变；使改观，将……改成，改造，改革，改善。transform into
transmission	*n.* 传送，传达。(广播、电视等的)发射，播送，传输。

• take, clasp, clutch, grasp, grab, grip, snatch, seize

take	*vt.* 拿，取，握，抱。指用手抓、取某东西或控制某物。
clasp	*vt.* & *vi.* 紧抱，紧握，扣住，扣紧，钩住。指用手紧握或用臂紧抱。
clutch	*vt.* 抓住，攫取，强调匆忙、紧急地抓。clutch at
grasp	*vt.* 抓牢，握紧，抱住。指紧紧抓住、抓牢。
grab	*vt.* 攫取，抓取，夺取，霸占。指粗暴而急迫地抓住。
grip	*vt.* & *vi.* 紧握，紧咬，夹住。指用手的最大力量紧紧抓住。
snatch	*vt.* & *vi.* 夺走，夺得。指突然抢走，强调动作更快，具有暴力性质。
seize	*vt.* & *vi.* 抓住，捉住。指突然抓住某物，强调突然的猛烈动作。

• too much, much too

too much	后接不可数名词。
much too	后接形容词。

• trip, travel, voyage, journey

trip	*n.* 指短期的旅途。
travel	*n.* 是最常用的，指一般的旅行。

voyage　　n. 指海上航行。
journey　　n.指稍长的旅途。

turbulent, fierce, wild, violent

turbulent　　a. 骚动的，骚乱的，动荡的，混乱的。可以形容天气和心情的动荡。
fierce　　a. 凶猛的，残酷的，好斗的。普通用词，指人或兽的凶猛残酷。
wild　　a. 野的，野生的，未被人驯养的。既可指自然界的荒芜、未被驯化的状态，又指人的无法无天、不文明的野蛮行为。
violent　　a. 激烈的，猛烈的，强烈的，由暴力引起的，暴力的。指人时侧重极为不安，也指破坏性的或不可控制的自然力量。

twilight, dusk, dawn

twilight　　n. 黄昏，黎明。指日落后或日出前的微明。
dusk　　n. 薄暮，黄昏。指接近夜晚的黄昏时刻。
dawn　　n. 黎明，拂晓。指天刚亮时的黎明。

upset, perturb, agitate, disturb

upset　　vt. 使心烦意乱，使不舒服。侧重指失去精神上的平静。upset about / at / over
perturb　　vt. 使心绪不宁，使不安，烦扰。指使人焦急烦恼，扰得心情不安。
agitate　　vt. 使激动，使焦虑。侧重指内心的焦虑。
disturb　　vt. 妨碍，打扰。指因某人的行动、扰乱等而使人不得安宁。